Political Corruption in Africa

Political Corruption in Africa

Extraction and Power Preservation

Edited by

Inge Amundsen

Senior Researcher, Chr. Michelsen Institute (CMI), Bergen, Norway

Cheltenham, UK • Northampton, MA, USA

Published by
Edward Elgar Publishing Limited
The Lypiatts
15 Lansdown Road
Cheltenham
Glos GL50 2JA
UK

Edward Elgar Publishing, Inc.
William Pratt House
9 Dewey Court
Northampton
Massachusetts 01060
USA

A catalogue record for this book
is available from the British Library

Library of Congress Control Number: 2019950541

This book is available electronically in the **Elgar**online
Social and Political Science subject collection
DOI 10.4337/9781788972529

ISBN 978 1 78897 251 2 (cased)
ISBN 978 1 78897 252 9 (eBook)

Typeset by Columns Design XML Ltd, Reading
Printed and bound by CPI Group (UK) Ltd, Croydon, CR0 4YY

Contents

Contributors

EDITOR

Inge Amundsen is a political scientist and senior researcher at the Chr. Michelsen Institute (CMI) in Bergen, Norway. Amundsen is focusing on democratic institutionalisation, political corruption, political economy, parliaments, political parties and natural resources (petroleum resources management and revenue management). His main study areas are Malawi, Palestine, Bangladesh, Nigeria, Angola and Ghana. Amundsen completed his PhD in comparative African studies at the University of Tromsø in 1997. He was Research Director at CMI from 2000 to 2003, Director of the U4 Anti-Corruption Resource Centre from 2002 to 2006, and he has coordinated three CMI institutional cooperation programmes.

AUTHORS

Kofi Takyi Asante is a research fellow at the Institute of Statistical, Social and Economic Research, University of Ghana. He obtained his PhD in sociology from Northwestern University, USA, in 2016. His research interests include economic and political sociology, colonialism, state formation and sociology of citizenship. His publications have appeared in *Ghana Studies*, *African Economic History* and *International Journal of Politics, Culture, and Society*, among others. Until 2017 he was a research fellow at the Institute for Advanced Study in Toulouse. He is currently undertaking a long-term research project on citizenship and local government in Ghana.

Trevor Budhram is an assistant professor at the Department of Police Practice, University of South Africa (Unisa). He holds a PhD in police science and an MSc in forensic investigation from Unisa. His main interest is in addressing white-collar crime, corruption and intelligence-led policing. He was a member of the South African Police Service for 11 years, of which the majority of this was spent investigating white-collar crime. He has also held portfolios in various public and private sector organisations in which he was responsible for combating white-collar crime, corruption, maladministration and irregularities. Budhram has published on white-collar crime, corruption and intelligence-led policing, and he has contributed to book chapters on forensic investigation. He serves as the chairperson of the Policing Association of Southern Africa (POLSA) and sits on various committees at Unisa.

Michelle D'Arcy is an assistant professor in political science at Trinity College Dublin, in Ireland. She holds a PhD in political science from University College Dublin, and an MSc from the London School of Economics. D'Arcy looks at the effect of institutions on development, and especially at the relationship between democratisation and state building, and she has conducted research on both contemporary developing countries and European states in historical context. Her current work includes a project on the impact of institutional sequencing, asking the question if democratisation in weak states leads to the same outcomes as democratisation in strong ones. She has previously worked as a researcher at the Quality of Government Institute at the University of Gothenburg.

Boniface Dulani is a senior lecturer at the Department of Political and Administrative Studies, University of Malawi. He holds a PhD in comparative politics with a minor in international relations from Michigan State University, USA. Dulani is a senior member of the Afrobarometer network where he serves as Fieldwork Operations Manager for Southern and Francophone Africa. He also holds the position of a visiting researcher at the Centre for Social Science Research, University of Cape Town, South Africa. His primary research work focuses on public opinion and attitudes on governance, democracy, tolerance and related issues. He has done work on executive succession, democracy, elections, social movements, presidential term limits, legislature and executive relations.

Moses Khisa is an assistant professor of political science at North Carolina State University, Raleigh NC, USA. He got his PhD in political science from Northwestern University, USA, in 2016. His research and teaching interests include the political economy of development and the politics of institutional change, focusing on contemporary Africa. He is a weekly columnist for *Daily Monitor* newspaper, a research associate with the Centre for Basic Research and co-founder of a political think tank, Society for Justice and National Unity (SoJNU), all based in Kampala.

Adriano Nuvunga is a professor of political science at the Department of Political Science and Public Administration at Eduardo Mondlane University, Mozambique. He holds a PhD in development studies from the International Institute of Social Studies at Erasmus University Rotterdam, the Netherlands. Nuvunga is also the executive director of CDD, the Centre for Democracy and Development. Formerly he was the executive director of the Maputo-based anti-corruption organisation Centre for Public Integrity (Centro de Integridade Pública, CIP). Its work focuses on anti-corruption, good governance and transparency.

Emmanuel Oladipo Ojo is an associate professor of historical sciences in the Department of History and International Studies, Ekiti State University, Nigeria. His research interests are particularly in Nigerian/African (political) history, democracy and development studies. He has published several scholarly articles in reputable onshore and offshore journals and attended several local and international academic conferences. He is an academic member of the Athens Institute of Education and Research, Athens, Greece, and a visiting scholar in the Department of General History, Institute of Humanities, Siberian Federal University, Krasnoyarsk, Russia, where he teaches African and Asian history.

Aslak Orre is educated in political science and social anthropology, and his key competence areas include local government reform and the politics of decentralisation, corruption and anti-corruption, as well as political parties and opposition in Africa. Orre's research focus is on Angola and Mozambique, and over the last 15 years he has closely followed political development in Venezuela. His current research interests include the political economy of oil in Africa; the role of China in Africa; media, public space and press freedom; taxation and public sector reform; and the telecom sector. Orre has lived and worked in Mozambique and Portugal.

Vaclav Prusa has an MA in political economy of development from the University of Birmingham, UK. He has previously worked for the German development agency GIZ in Rwanda as senior adviser on good governance and anti-corruption, and for UNDP in Vietnam and Mongolia as monitoring and evaluation officer. Prusa has since 2017 been adviser and programme manager (anti-corruption) at the Civil Society Legislative Advocacy Centre (CISLAC) in Abuja, Nigeria as seconded personnel from GIZ. CISLAC is a non-governmental advocacy, information-sharing, research and capacity-building organisation.

Preface

It took some time from when I started studying the corruption problem and teaching on anti-corruption until I came to the conviction that *political* corruption is much more of an impediment to development in the developing world than is bureaucratic corruption.

First, I worked for the U4 Anti-Corruption Resource Centre, as its first director and later in different roles as topic expert and training facilitator and presenter. Second, I have been able to include the issue of corruption in several research and commissioned studies on Palestine, Uganda, Angola, Bangladesh, Ghana and Nigeria. Slowly, the conviction took root and evolved.

This book has therefore been in the making for a long time. Some of the ideas on political corruption were 'aired' in a very early working paper, entitled 'Political corruption, an introduction to the issues', and published as a CMI Working Paper in 1999. This little introduction became widely downloaded, read and cited (downloaded 65,000 times and cited 375 times), and this huge interest in the topic of political corruption inspired and compelled me to take it further.

Some recent reports argue that the anti-corruption efforts of national and international civil society activists, international organisations and donor agencies – as well as well-meaning governments and politicians in the developing world – have had very little success in curbing corruption. The amount of academic work, activism and professional advocacy on anti-corruption has exploded over the last two decades, awareness is high, and the international legal anti-corruption framework is in place. Still, the aggregate indexes and country evidence tell us that the success stories are few, so obviously there is something fundamentally wrong with the prevailing analysis and approach.

This book is a modest attempt at getting the analysis back on the track I believe it should be. This 'track' is based on the following four main arguments.

One, political corruption is very different from bureaucratic or administrative corruption. The problem with political corruption is that it serves a function beyond greed and personal enrichment; it may keep the regime together and afloat. Furthermore, political corruption not only gives the incentives for controlling the state, it is also a means to maintain control of the state. The rulers will have no political will to eradicate political corruption as it gives them wealth and power, whereas bureaucratic corruption can be eradicated if the rulers so desire.

Two, political corruption has two core elements: it is about getting the money in and it is about reinvesting in safeguarding the hold on power. The first, extractive political corruption, is mainly for the purpose of wealth and status. It is extractive when political power-holders are enriching themselves, their family and relatives, their political friends and allies, and their ruling parties and governments. The second, power-preserving political corruption, is when power-holders are using the proceeds and other funds, state or private, to maintain and/or strengthen their hold on power in illicit or immoral ways. Power-preserving corruption is one of several mechanisms of power abuse that incumbent leaders employ to safeguard their vital interests: wealth, status and power.

Three, political corruption is serving the interests of the ruling elite, and therefore it cannot be solved by technical–administrative measures alone. The rulers will have no interest in curbing their powers.

Four, consequently, political corruption should be seen as power abuse, as a democratic problem, and it should be addressed as a political problem. Technical and administrative anti-corruption measures can solve some of the bureaucratic corruption problems, if there is a political will to do so. Even authoritarian governments may want to do this when it gives them legitimacy and when it serves the purpose of getting rid of rivals to power. Power abuse can only be countered by political action.

The first chapter of this book outlines these arguments in more detail, and the following seven chapters take the arguments further by giving some flesh and bones to the different forms of political corruption as experienced in the seven countries.[1] Unfortunately,

---

[1] All mention in this volume of individuals, institutions, businesses and regimes stated to be corrupt and power-abusive have been named previously in the news, in academic reports, CSO and official reports, and these are duly referred to.

the overall picture is rather bleak – the corrupt power-preserving methods are often quite effective, even though they sometimes backfire.

Acknowledgements

The first and foremost people to thank are the authors of the individual chapters of this volume, for sharing their insights and analysis, for spending a lot of their time to dig up the facts and to distil the plausible from the sensational, and for analysing the intricate corruption stories in an understandable and readable manner. They should also be thanked for patiently enduring my pushing and pulling to get the final result in time and shape. They have, for instance, had to endure my incessant insistence in getting the references right. Without their effort, hard work, and conviction that this was a worthwhile undertaking, this book would never have materialised. I really hope my expressed gratitude, and our readers' prospective appreciation and the 'fame and reputation' they will get from it, will compensate for doing it all for free.

The time granted by my institute, the Chr. Michelsen Institute (CMI) in Bergen, Norway, and the encouragement and constructive criticism I have received from colleagues at the institute have also been helpful. I would guess the academic and research institutions where the chapter authors are working on a daily basis have also had to release some time for them to do this job. This has been invaluable and laudable.

Thanks also to the U4 Anti-Corruption Resource Centre, which is hosted at CMI, and the fine people working there. I served as its first director (2002–6) and have been involved on and off ever since, which has given me the opportunity to follow research on corruption and anti-corruption practice for a number of years, and it has exposed me to the work of a number of bilateral donor agencies and their partners in anti-corruption.

A number of anonymous reviewers and some of the chapter authors did a fine job on reality checks and strengthening the arguments of the various (other) chapters. Their helpful collaboration is much appreciated. Finally, gratitude is extended to the publisher, Edward Elgar, for their professional encouragements and follow-up in the process from ideas to this fine end result.

1. Extractive and power-preserving political corruption

Inge Amundsen

POLITICAL CORRUPTION AND POLITICAL WILL

Political corruption is different from administrative/bureaucratic corruption. A corrupt president, government minister or ruling party is a different sort of problem than is, for example, a teacher or nurse taking bribes to offer services. The problem with political corruption is that it serves a function beyond greed and personal enrichment – it may keep the regime together and afloat. Political corruption not only gives the incentives for controlling the state, it is a means to maintain control of the state. The rulers will have no political will to eradicate political corruption as it gives them wealth and power, whereas bureaucratic corruption can be eradicated if the rulers so desire.

The distinction between political and bureaucratic corruption is important for the analysis and measurement of corruption, and the distinction is essential in order to make meaningful anti-corruption interventions. Nevertheless, even the most respected scholarly literature on corruption frequently undercommunicates, misunderstands or ignores the distinction, to the detriment of a sound understanding and analysis of the problem, and to the impairment of anti-corruption efforts.

Some of the classic and authoritative scholarly work on corruption, such as Heidenheimer and Johnston (2002) and Heywood (2015), make no clear distinction between the two forms of corruption. For instance, in their book *Political Corruption: Concepts and Contexts*, Heidenheimer and Johnston (2002) are using the term 'political corruption' synonymously to the term 'corruption', although with a political context in mind and with the 'aim of bringing the term into the political realm', but without explicitly ruling out the non-political forms of corruption. In the introduction, for instance, the editors discuss corruption as 'political and bureaucratic behaviour' (ibid.: 12), which makes it clear they subsume bureaucratic corruption under the term 'political corruption'.

Likewise, Heywood in his *Routledge Handbook of Political Corruption* (2015) fails to make the distinction. He states that political corruption 'is now as likely to take the form of conflicts of interests, abuse of office, lobbying [...] and inappropriate use of public information as it is to take more traditional forms such as bribery and embezzlement' (ibid.: 4). This is largely but not exclusively mechanisms found on the 'political' side, but Heywood offers no specific definition of political corruption, and throughout the book political corruption is understood as corruption anywhere in the public sector.

Some researchers use the term 'political corruption' very narrowly, for instance as corruption in elections (only) or as political donations (only), and others use it to attract attention. An example of a dubious and sensationalist use of the concept of 'political corruption' is Hjellum (2007). In his book *Political Corruption as a Democratic Problem* he makes no analytical distinction between political and bureaucratic/administrative corruption, and he mixes the terms throughout even when his text is almost exclusively on administrative corruption. At the same time, the book cover depicts senior politicians in Norway.

The biggest and most influential of the world's anti-corruption non-government organisations (NGOs), Transparency International (TI), makes the distinction in theory, but not in practice. TI's *Global Corruption Report*, special issue 2004 on political corruption, defines political corruption as 'the abuse of entrusted power *by political leaders* for private gain' (TI 2004: 1).[1] It specifies political corruption as corruption in political finance, vote-buying, sale of appointments, abuse of state resources, trading in influence and the

---

[1] See also TI's definition of political corruption in their online glossary: 'manipulation of policies, institutions and rules of procedure in the allocation of resources and financing by *political decision makers*, who abuse their position to sustain their power, status and wealth' (www.transparency.org/glossary/term/political_corruption, accessed 17 August 2018, my emphasis).

granting of favours. Furthermore, it separates political from bureaucratic corruption by stating that political corruption is 'distinct from petty or bureaucratic corruption in so far as it is perpetrated by political leaders or elected officials who have been vested with public authority and who bear the responsibility of representing the public interest' (ibid.: 11).

This clarification has, however, had few consequences for TI's further work on corruption. Most glaring is TI's annually updated Corruption Perceptions Index (CPI), which lacks the distinction entirely and is lumping together very different social phenomena under the one heading. The index is measuring 'public sector corruption', explicitly understood as political *and* bureaucratic corruption combined. A TI background paper on the CPI methodology states: 'As has been emphasized in the background documents of previous years, the sources do not distinguish between administrative and political corruption' (Lambsdorff 2007: 5).

Many researchers use 'corruption' and 'political corruption' almost interchangeably (Heywood 2015: 7), applying the term 'political' to denote both political *and* bureaucratic corruption. One example is Hessami (2014: 373), who talks about political corruption as involving 'the political and bureaucratic decision makers'. Others are using the term 'public sector corruption' (Johnston 2011) to refer to both political and bureaucratic corruption. Yet other researchers use concepts like 'government' (Frederickson 2015), 'executive' (V-Dem Institute 2016) or 'elite' corruption (Tangri and Mwenda 2013) to denote high-level political corruption.

A few researchers have, however, made the distinction explicit, and even applied the distinction in their research. Among the few are Loftis, who uses a measure that 'differentiates political corruption from corruption at lower levels of government' (2014: 728) in a dataset on policy-making in ten former communist European Union member states. Another example is Villoria et al., who argue that (most) studies 'have not examined administrative corruption separately from political corruption'. They highlight their understanding of the two forms of corruption in stating that 'grand or political corruption refers to corrupt actions by elected politicians, and petty or administrative corruption as involving public sector employees or bureaucrats' (2013: 85–6), and they are applying this distinction in their survey on popular perceptions of corruption and politics in Spain.

There is a need to make the distinction clear and explicit. This is what we present in the following: a conceptual and theoretic distinction between political corruption and bureaucratic corruption. Despite the blurred boundaries and many overlaps between politics and administration (in theory as well as in practice), we offer a relatively clear-cut distinction.

After this exercise, we are outlining two basic and often interrelated forms of political corruption, namely 'extractive' and 'power-preserving' political corruption. The short version is that both forms of corruption are for the purpose of gains in wealth, status and power, but extractive political corruption is mainly for the purpose of wealth and status. It is extractive when political power-holders are enriching themselves, their family and relatives, their political friends and allies, and their ruling parties and governments. It is a form of abuse of power 'to get the money in'. It includes practices such as embezzlement, economic crime, 'privatisations' and crony capitalism (favouring their own businesses), and, most importantly, bribe taking in public procurement.

Power-preserving political corruption, on the other hand, is mainly for maintaining and/or strengthening political power-holders' hold on power. It is when they are using (reinvesting) their corruptly acquired means and other resources in corrupt ways to safeguard and perpetuate their power position. It is one of many forms of power abuse utilised to maintain the grip on power, and it often comes in addition to (or prior to) the use of violence, intimidation, threats and manipulation of elections. Power-preserving political corruption includes practices such as buying friends (favouritism, co-optations, clientelism and nepotism), buying support from businesses (by favouring the businesses of political supporters), buying institutions of oversight and control (through appointments and inducements), the use of state resources to win elections, and buying judicial impunity. We are giving a number of examples to illustrate these mechanisms.

Finally, we are looking at the implications of specifying and distinguishing between political corruption and bureaucratic/administrative corruption. The distinction has wide-ranging consequences for research on corruption, because these qualitatively distinct social phenomena require different analytical frameworks, conceptual models, and investigation and data collection methods.

More importantly, they require different approaches to anti-corruption. Bureaucratic corruption can fruitfully be understood within the principal-agent framework, and measures to stem bureaucratic corruption can be implemented in terms of monitoring, oversight, sanctions and punishment. These can be very effective in curbing corruption if the principals, the government, have the political will to do so. Political corruption cannot, however, as political corruption destroys the political will of politicians to curb corruption. Corrupt leaders will not restrict their enrichment and risk their hold on power. To stem political corruption, we need a better understanding of the political economy and political incentives in a given situation, and politically informed action.

POLITICAL CORRUPTION DEFINED

'Corruption' is a concept much used and misused in social sciences as well as in the general parlance; it usually encompasses a large number of illegal and/or deplorable social activities and a number of human actions that someone might consider detrimental or unacceptable. Without a proper definition, the concept is too broad for analytical purposes.

According to the World Bank's thumb-rule definition, corruption is 'abuse of public power for private benefit' (World Bank 1997: 8). There are also a number of other and more elaborate definitions of corruption, such as the classic definitions that 'corruption is behaviour of public officials which deviates from accepted norms in order to serve private ends' (Huntington 1968: 59), and that it is 'behaviour that deviates from the formal duties of a public role (elective or appointive) because of private-regarding (personal, close family, private clique) wealth or status gains; or violates rules against the exercise of certain types of private regarding influence' (Nye 1967: 419).

The common denominator is that there is always a public servant or politician involved – those holding public power. They are making a 'private benefit' of that; they are pocketing something, big or small.[2]

---

[2] That is, some, like TI, will insist there is also private-to-private corruption, not involving public officials or politicians. This is reflected in their definition of

On the other side of the corrupt act is the non-public actor, either a private business (a company, contractor), a private citizen (as user of public services, taxpayer and so on), a civil society organisation, or any other non-public entity. These are the 'corruptors' seeking some return or benefit from corrupting a public official. Thus, corruption is a relationship between at least two actors, from which both parties will gain something.[3]

Who will gain more, at the end of the day, the corrupter or the corrupted, is an empirical question. It is not given a priori who will be the winner, but information on who took the initiative to establish the corrupt deal in the first place is usually an indicator as to who believes he or she will benefit more.

Political corruption takes place at the highest levels of the political system, and involves political decision makers: politicians, government ministers, senior civil servants, and other elected, nominated and (self-) appointed senior public-office holders. Political corruption is when these officials, who make the laws (the 'rules of the game'), are abusing their public power for private benefit.

By political decision makers we mean presidents and heads of state (including vice-presidents and core personnel of the president's office and inner cabinet), heads of government (prime ministers) and government/cabinet ministers (including vice-ministers, their advisors and the like). We also include ruling party officials (party presidents and general secretaries, for instance), top

---

corruption as 'abuse of *entrusted* power for private gain' (TI website, https://www.transparency.org/whoweare/organisation/faqs_on_corruption#defineCorruption, accessed 17 August 2018, my emphasis), as for instance involving a private company employee and a customer. In my opinion, this relationship should be excluded from the debate on corruption. Firstly, because 'private-to-private' corruption is largely self-regulatory (the employee will be punished swiftly and harshly when detected). Secondly, 'private-to-private' corruption is less damaging. It can harm the profits and reputation of a firm and increase the overall acceptance of corruption in society, but it will not directly affect public services or the quality of politics. Besides, for our purpose (analysing political corruption), a definition that necessarily includes the corrupted public side is preferable.

[3] The exception is embezzlement, where the public officials steal from public coffers, alone with no corrupters. It is still 'abuse of public power for private benefit'.

military, police and security officers, and high-level bureaucrats.[4] We also include parliamentarians of the ruling party or party coalition, and a number of people nominated by the president: supreme and military court judges, heads of government special institutions (such as auditors, public prosecutors, ombudsmen, tax commissioners, election commissioners, national bank directors) and heads of public companies.[5] Other researchers have been using related terms such as 'the ruling elite' and 'the powerful few'.

Some researchers regard political corruption to be the same as 'grand corruption', for example Moody-Stuart (1997) when he says that grand corruption 'occurs at the highest levels of government and involves major government projects and programs'. However, even when political corruption can be grand in scale, it is not necessarily so. To buy a vote in Kenya, for instance, will cost no more than one US dollar. It is a question of level, not of scale.

In contrast to political corruption, bureaucratic or administrative corruption takes place at the implementation end of politics, and mainly in public service delivery such as education, health, water and utilities. Bureaucratic corruption is sometimes called 'petty', 'everyday', 'routine' and 'street-level' corruption,[6] but these concepts give some incorrect connotations as bureaucratic corruption can be huge in economic terms and widespread in social terms, and it can form the basis of an upward spiral of extraction.

---

4 The British comedy series *Yes, Minister* should illustrate why the top-level bureaucrats are included.

5 In many presidential systems, in particular in the developing world, the president of the Republic has wide authorities to nominate (and sack) people. As an illustration, the president of Angola is Head of State, Head of Government, Commander-in-Chief of the Armed Forces, and president of the ruling party, and he appoints (and can remove) the vice-president and the Council of Ministers (cabinet), the prime minister, line ministers and vice-ministers, the Attorney General, the Governor of the Central Bank, generals and other commanders of the armed forces, police, and security services, members of the judiciary including the Supreme and Military Court, and all provincial governors (according to Constituição da República de Angola, January 2010; articles 119, 120, 122, 123 and 128).

6 The TI Glossary (ibid.) defines 'petty corruption' as the 'everyday abuse of entrusted power by low- and mid-level public officials in their interaction with ordinary citizens, who often are trying to access basic goods or services in places like hospitals, schools, police departments and other agencies'. Likewise, 'facilitating payments' have been defined as 'small sums that are paid with the intention of motivating low-level officials to expedite routine procedures' (Argandoña 2017: 71).

Bureaucratic corruption can be distinguished from political corruption in the same way as politics can be distinguished from public administration. In the textbook understanding, politics or policy-making is the 'distribution of favours and burdens in society' or 'the authoritative allocation of values for a society' (Easton 1965: 50), whereas public administration is concerned with the 'implementation of government policy' (Encyclopædia Britannica). This distinction seems intuitive and uncomplicated, until one takes a closer look.

As politicians lack absolute control, leaving quite a lot of discretionary decision-making to the bureaucrats, and the perennial principal-agent problem, policy-making and implementation cannot always be separated. Often, politicians will interfere in the implementation of policies and service delivery, and bureaucrats will interfere in policy-making. Likewise, politicians can instruct their bureaucrats to do the dirty jobs for them (to extract and protect), sometimes they will do it out of loyalty or fear. A permanent secretary can 'find' money for the minister's wife's shopping spree.

Besides, the two levels are dependent upon each other. The politicians 'define the essential lines of the public administration' and they influence 'both the risks and opportunities of bureaucratic corruption' (della Porta and Vannucci 1999: 131). At the same time, politicians are dependent on public administrations for the implementation of policies, including the corrupt ones. It has even been argued that bureaucrats can 'denounce the illegitimate actions of politicians, or they can refuse to carry out the measures' (ibid.). (This opens up a possible inroad to anti-corruption: bureaucrats can to some extent restrict the corrupt behaviour of politicians, if they want to – the same was as politicians can restrict the corrupt behaviour of bureaucrats, if they want to).

Political and bureaucratic corruption also tend to be mutually reinforcing. Andvig et al. (2001) assume that 'political corruption is usually supported by widespread bureaucratic or petty corruption, in a pyramid of upward extraction. And corruption in high places is contagious to lower level officials, as these will follow the predatory examples of, or even take instruction from, their principals' (2001: 11).

Thus, it seems obvious that political and bureaucratic corruption can go together, in a mutually reinforcing evil circle. But it is not necessarily so. Political corruption can take place in a polity with little or no bureaucratic corruption. France can serve as an example, with its Napoleonic civil code, bureaucratic *ésprit de corps* and stiff penalties and social stigma on bureaucratic misbehaviour; and with its *Ile de France* (see below) and *ELF Aquitaine* corruption scandals that reached the top of French politics.[7]

Likewise, bureaucratic corruption can take place in systems with little or no political corruption. Examples are few, however, and tend to disappear after a while as new clean governments (typically elected on an anti-corruption ticket) tend to be caught up quickly (some say 100 days) by the corruption opportunities and pressures.[8]

Despite these mutual dependencies that create ambiguities in the distinction between political and bureaucratic corruption, we still believe it is meaningful and fruitful to argue for a separation. We base this on the argument that political corruption involves those entrusted with the power to formulate the rules and the regulations, whereas bureaucratic corruption involves those with the delegated authority to implement political decisions and provide public services. In other words, political corruption is when the power holders and politicians who make the laws (the 'rules of the game') are abusing their public power for private benefit.

Furthermore, political and bureaucratic behaviour (and the appurtenant corruption) is regulated differently. Whereas political behaviour is regulated by the separation of powers, institutional checks and balances, constitutions, established practice and – last but not least – by elections and democratic procedures, bureaucratic behaviour is regulated by political guidance, civil service laws and regulations, codes of ethics, and so on. The legal sanctions on political and bureaucratic corruption are also often defined differently; civil servants are punished less hard for misbehaviour than are elected politicians.

---

[7] According to the journalist Nick Cohen, the Elf scandal in 1994 in France was 'the biggest fraud inquiry in Europe since the Second World War [...] Elf became a private bank for executives who spent £200 million on political favours, mistresses, jewellery, fine art, villas and apartments' (Cohen 2007).

[8] The 'rainbow coalition' government in Kenya (2002–5) is one example of a 'zero-tolerance government' that quickly ran into problems with government procurement including the new police telecommunications and new passport system (dubbed the Anglo-Leasing scandal).

Although the distinction between political and administrative corruption is not cut in stone – there are grey areas of bureaucratic discretionary decision-making, unclear areas of responsibility, and the perennial principal-agent problem – the distinction is very productive in analytic and practical terms, as we will see later.

EXTRACTION AND POWER PRESERVATION

Going from who (politicians, government ministers, senior civil servants and other elected, nominated and (self-) appointed senior public office holders) to why and how, we can also identify the functions of political corruption. We will argue that political corruption can and should be divided into two basic, critical and related processes.

The first process we name *extractive* political corruption. This is when political power holders are enriching themselves by abusing their hold on power to extract from public and private resources. The second we name *power-preserving* political corruption, which is when political power holders are using the corruptly acquired means, as well as other resources, in corrupt ways to maintain and/or strengthen their hold on power.

The consequences of these two forms of political corruption are serious. In economic terms, the consequences are devastating for investments: it impedes normal economic activities, it exacerbates economic inequalities and inefficiencies, and when systemic it jeopardises countries' economic development potential. In political terms, political corruption annihilates the political will of politicians to address the corruption problem, it erodes trust and legitimacy in government and politics in general, it makes political decisions non-transparent, it undermines political accountability mechanisms and it often leads to authoritarianism.

Alas, political corruption is often the main incentive for holding on to political power at the same time as political corruption provides the means to hold on to power. An evil circle of extraction and reinvestment in power occurs when these two forms of political corruption feed into each other. When political corruption produces the incentives for controlling the state, at the same time as it produces the means to retain control of the state, we have a situation that has been called a kleptocratic form of government,[9] which is particularly hard to democratise.

EXTRACTIVE POLITICAL CORRUPTION

Extractive political corruption is when political leaders use their political power (formal and informal position, information and influence) to extract resources from the public and from the private sector (as in from the nation's wealth), for individual and/or group enrichment, in an illegal and/or immoral way.

Extractive political corruption is sometimes called 'graft', and takes many forms. Andvig et al. (2001: 8–10) made a typology of the forms of corruption one can expect to find in a given administration. Below, we list the commonly used forms of corrupt extraction: bribery, embezzlement, fraud and extortion.

Bribery

Bribery is the classic form of corruption: it is any amount of money or favours in kind paid to a political power holder (in person, or to their family members, organisation or the ruling party). It is offered and paid by national and international companies to obtain rent-seeking opportunities: access to natural resources, concessions, state contracts in civil engineering projects, construction works, defence supplies, and so on. It is high-level bribery when politicians, against 'a fee', alter the rules and regulations and mediate the market to create market protection, provide state loans and guarantees, make tax 'havens' and 'honeymoons', reduce environmental and worker standards, and so on, for the benefit of private firms.

However, with more international and national attention to and knowledge of the problem of bribery, and with strengthened national and international legislation, the classic forms of bribe taking have shifted to some less visible and more 'legal' forms of

---

9 *Kleptocracy* is, literally, rule by thieves, and focuses on the corrupt state officials as the main culprits. In contrast, *state capture* is a type of systemic political corruption in which private interests significantly influence a state's decision-making processes to their own advantage, with a focus on the corrupting private side as the main culprits.

corruption, fraud in particular. It has also shifted to military procurement, businesses owned and run by military and security forces, and large infrastructure projects, which are increasingly exposed to this form of corruption, and particularly hard to control because of the involvement of senior politicians, national interests, and secrecy.[10]

One example of top-level bribery is the 'arms deal' scandal in South Africa, where millions of rand were channelled from arms dealers through local companies and brokers to politically connected figures (Nattrass 2014: 72). Sweetheart deals proliferated in the arms procurement programme, allegedly giving friends of senior politicians (including President Thabo Mbeki's brother) a share of the defence pie under the rubric of 'black empowerment' (TI 2004: 62, see also Chapter 8 on South Africa in this volume).

Another example is the scandal that erupted in October 2004 when the former president of Costa Rica, Miguel Angel Rodríguez, was forced to resign as Secretary-General of the Organization of American States. According to TI, 'he stepped down after allegations implicated him in a bribery scheme involving the French telecommunications company, Alcatel. In mid-2004, details emerged that Alcatel had been awarded a contract to improve the country's cellular phone system allegedly after its officials successfully bribed José Antonio Lobo, Rodríguez's protégé and a former director of the state electrical company, with a USD 2.4 million "prize". Lobo said he had been "advised" to accept the sum by Rodríguez, who is reported to have demanded 60 per cent of it. Digging deeper into Alcatel's dealings, allegations emerged that it had attempted to influence previous and current Costa Rican politicians as well' (TI 2006: 146–7).

---

[10] In Turkey, for instance, despite losing much of its political power recently, the military is a substantial economic actor with a stake in 60 companies in sectors ranging from cars to chocolate bars. There are two unique channels through which the military is directly involved in market activities: two state investment funds (the Armed Forces Trust and the Pension Fund (OYAK)), and the Foundation for Strengthening the Turkish Armed Forces (TSKGV) (Demir 2010: 4). In Angola, the ruling party MPLA owns a company called GEFI (Sociedade de Gestão e Participações Financeiras), which has a business portfolio that includes participation in 64 companies operating in the sectors that include hotels, industry, banking, fisheries, aviation, media, construction and real estate (Amundsen 2014: 176). In Rwanda, the situation is the same with party-owned enterprises that get preferential treatment by the government, as analysed by Booth and Golooba-Mutebi (2012).

A third example is the Ile de France trials of 2005, in which an extensive system of corruption in procurement contracts for the renovation of high schools was revealed. The case involved 47 defendants, charged with collusion, concealing corruption and influence peddling. The accusations centred on allegations that companies paid major political parties to win contracts to renovate schools around Paris. The defendants include a former cooperation minister, an ex-president of the Ile de France regional council and a former labour minister, as well as the former treasurers of three political parties (TI 2006: 158–9).

Embezzlement

Embezzlement is the theft or misappropriation of state assets (funds, property and services) from the public institution where someone has a position of authority and trust; it is theft of resources they are supposed to administer on behalf of the public. Embezzlement can occur regardless of whether the offender keeps the personal property or transfers it to a third party. Often the trusted individual is embezzling only a small proportion of the total of the funds or resources they receive or control, in an attempt to minimise the risk of the detection of the misallocation.

In embezzlement, there is often an element of fraud (see below). While legally not considered as corruption in most legal systems (but as a separate crime, along with fraud), embezzlement is nevertheless covered in the definition of corruption as abuse of public power for private benefit.

One recent, well-known high-level embezzlement case is Malaysia's former prime minister Najib Razak who was accused in 2015 of channelling to his personal bank accounts over 2.67 billion ringgit (nearly 700 million US dollars) from the 1Malaysia Development Berhad (1MDB), a government-run strategic development company. This led to the prime minister being ousted in the May 2018 election, and for his party to lose power for the first time since 1957 (Fraud Magazine 2018, The Guardian 2015).

Another prominent example is the Baikonur scandal in Kazakhstan. This was embezzlement of funds paid by Russia for renting the Baikonur space facility in the Kazakh steppes. It involved the head of the presidential administration, Tasmagambetov, who was prime minister when the deal was struck, and had signed the agreement and nominated the preferred operator. Moreover, Ermegiyaev, son of the vice-president of the ruling party, had supervised the tender commission, and Alexander Pavlov, the deputy prime minister, had monitored the execution of the deal (TI 2006:185–6).

Fraud

Fraud is the use of false representations, manipulation or distortion of information, facts and expertise to secure an unfair or unlawful gain. Fraud is a method of extractive political corruption when power holders take a share for 'closing their eyes' on economic crimes and, more seriously, when they have an active role in it.

Fraud has an element of cheating and intentional deception (thus including 'imposter scams' and 'money-making scams'), and in most jurisdictions the requisite element of fraud is the intentional misrepresentation or concealment of an important fact. Self-interest is often one of these hidden facts, leading to situations of concealed conflicts of interest.

One example of high-level political fraud is when politicians enter businesses themselves and create companies that get politically mediated preferential treatment, contracts, subventions, tax exemptions and monopolies. The self-interest is concealed. It is fraud when politicians render favours to the companies of their family, political supporters, the ruling party and the military, concealing the self-interest and interests of their political supporters and backers. It is high-level fraud also when 'privatisation' processes create politically connected billionaires, in line with what happened in Russia after the fall of the Soviet Union.

Another example of high-level fraud, as it falls under the definition of 'abuse of public power for private benefit' (although it is perfectly legal in the countries concerned), is the establishment of anonymous companies by regime insiders. These so-called 'dead meat' companies (oil companies in particular) are shell companies owned by people such as previous and current ministers and state oil company directors, that the major foreign oil companies are 'invited' to take into consortiums as a part of the government's 'nationalisation' and 'local content' policies. These companies contribute very little in terms of investments, personnel, technology or other inputs, but they appear on the scene when profits are distributed (Amundsen 2014: 176).[11]

In Kenya, according to John Githongo (the former head of the Kenya Anti-Corruption Commission), senior officials in the Kibaki regime were linked to graft and fraud. He found strong evidence that several senior members of the government were involved in a series of fraudulent contracts with the non-existent Anglo Leasing Company, and they also actively attempted to cover up this and other fraudulent transactions once it became clear that they were the subject of investigations (Bachelard 2010: 191).

Extortion

Extortion is the use of force, threats, harassment or persisting demands by the state or its security services to extract money or other resources from individuals, groups and businesses.

One of the most glaring examples of high-level and violent extortion is the 'nationalisation' (outright seizure) of white farms in Zimbabwe and their redistribution to the members of the ruling elite. In one account, 'this extractive institution had devastating effects on the population and economy. Many white farmers fled the country, taking their agricultural expertise with them. With no plan in place to keep the planting and harvesting cycles turning, approximately 400,000 farm workers were left unemployed, and the government failed to manage the farms, leading to shortages of food such as corn and export crops such as tobacco' (Cain 2015: 2).

An example from Angola was the importer and salesman of Honda cars, whose quite profitable business was outright confiscated by a regime insider. The Honda company in Japan simply got a notification from the Ministry of Trade that another person had taken over the import licence. Although the latter was 'politically exposed', Honda accepted, and the original salesman's protests and court case led to nothing.[12]

---

11 The Norwegian state-owned oil company Statoil was involved in a case criticised by the Norwegian Auditor General and reported by Global Witness (2008): 'In Angola, StatoilHydro is in partnership with a local private oil company despite suspicions that the company's undisclosed owners may include government officials, in a country perceived to be one of the most corrupt in the world.'

12 Personal interviews, Luanda, October 2013.

Less known and less serious is extortion in the form of ruling political parties (or coalition partners or prospective ruling parties) putting pressure on businesspeople and private companies to finance their party organisations and political campaigns. Political 'donations' can be extortion when the private businesses have reason to fear future losses of government contracts.

One example is from the Côte d'Ivoire, where the ruling party PDCI held a party congress in Abidjan in 1996, asking local private businesses to host the congress, house and feed the delegates and so on – a request that no company dared refuse.[13]

POWER-PRESERVING POLITICAL CORRUPTION

Power-preserving political corruption is the corrupt use of fraudulently acquired resources (but also other privately owned means and various state resources) for political support and protection purposes.

Corruption is, however, not the only power-preserving tool. There is a long list of methods of power abuse, power enhancement and preservation that are not necessarily corrupt. It should suffice to mention guns and tanks (violence), manipulation of elections (or not holding elections), harassment and intimidation of the opposition, amendments to the constitution (for instance to remove the ban on more than two presidential terms), stifling of the free press and freedom of speech, and the two methods that have become increasingly popular: (1) to target and jail opposition leaders, activists and rivals in anti-corruption drives and (2) ferocious tax collection.[14] It is the corrupt use of the funds that distinguishes power-preserving political corruption from the other forms of misuse of state power.

---

[13] Personal interviews, Abidjan, September 1996.

[14] In September 2017, *The Economist* published the article entitled 'Beware the Taxman. Tax Authorities are the Latest Tools of Repression in Africa', describing among other cases the story of Diane Rwigara, who announced her candidacy for the presidential elections in Rwanda, and days after was disqualified for alleged tax evasion and charged with 'offences against state security', and the story from Zambia, where most of the media favoured Edgar Lungu, the president, in the election in 2016, except for a 'punchy tabloid called the Post', which the Zambia Revenue Authority shut down, saying it owed some US$6 million in unpaid taxes.

Corrupt power-preserving methods serve the purpose of creating a favoured group of allies and impunity through a selected allocation of tangible resources. The methods include some well-known tactics such as favouritism (the buying of friends, allies and supporters through government favours to hand-picked individuals and groups – also called nepotism, clientelism, patronage and cronyism, depending on techniques used and the characteristics of the favoured), and co-optations (the buying off of rivals and opponents, by for instance providing them with rewarding positions in state and government).

Corrupt power-preserving methods also include the fraudulent manipulation and weakening of institutions for the purpose of creating impunity for the power holders. The 'buying off' of officials of various institutions of oversight and control such as courts, auditor generals, anti-corruption agency commissioners and so on, is a widely used political corruption tool.

This selected or purpose-fit allocation of resources make the political power-holders into active bribers. The initiative is taken by the power holders, and it is clearly in their personal interest (individual and group benefit) to preserve their power positions. Furthermore, in the same way as the corrupt use of funds distinguishes power-preserving political corruption from other forms of misuse of state power, the corrupt methods of power preservation distinguish it from a democratic distribution of favours (and burdens), as the decisions are made by the few and for the benefit of the few.

Favouritism and Co-Optations

Favouritism is, crudely put, the unfair favouring of one person or group at the expense of others, for political purposes. Favouritism is partiality in the allocation of public resources, and it can be used as a tool for power enhancement and preservation. Rival politicians, military and business elites of strategic importance, influential 'families', clans and social groups sometimes 'need' to be 'bought' through favours.

Political loyalty can be bought in many ways, through a strategic distribution of government projects, infrastructures, public jobs and appointments, and public and political positions with perks. Political loyalty can also be bought with direct bribes, and advantages channelled to private businesses owned by friends and supporters (for example state contracts, loans, guarantees, protection, monopolies).

Favouritism and patronage are in many cases the 'glue' that holds regimes together when state institutions are weak, and in cases of violent conflict it can be central to a political settlement – formal or informal – to secure the government. Clientelist favouritism (also called patronage and cronyism) is to favour your own kin (clan, tribe, ethnic, religious or regional group) and your political supporters (friends, followers, allies and loyalists). Often, favouritism will contribute to the durability of authoritarian regimes (Zaum 2013: 1).

In Kenya, the *harambees* ('voluntary' contributions to community development projects) have reportedly become a tool for patronage used by politicians to garner votes, maintain loyalty of their electorate, and solidify and shape political leadership at the local level (Baskin and Mezey 2014: 57). In Angola, the so-called 'Christmas bonuses' were another form of favouritism, where 'worthy' members of the political establishment, including ruling and 'opposition' party MPs, received an annual 'bonus', paid in cash at the presidency (Amundsen 2014: 180–81).

Nepotism is a particular form of favouritism in which the office holder gives preference to his or her kinfolk and family members (wife, brothers and sisters, children, nephews, cousins, in-laws and the extended family). The preferences are basically jobs in the state apparatus or political positions in government and the ruling party, regardless of professional merit, but can also involve advancement and favours rendered to their businesses.

Nepotism is hard to detect, as decision making regarding hiring and promotions involves complex and sometimes unwritten rules and procedures, and the subjective elements that come into play when choosing among candidates can mask the abuse of power. In order to see it, one has to know the legitimate requirements for a particular position and compare this with the characteristics of candidates selected for the position.

One example is from Indonesia, where Olken (2007) found that family members of government and project officials were more likely to have found work than others, in over 600 Indonesian village road projects. He also found that family members of village officials were more likely than people without family ties to be employed in a higher-wage category on the project.

Co-optation is another example of favouritist treatments that can be used for political purposes. Co-optation refers to the 'intentional extension of benefits to potential challengers to the regime in exchange for their loyalty' (Corntassel 2007: 139). In other words, co-optation is the buying off of political rivals. Co-optations are used to build political loyalty and support from certain 'opposition' parties and politicians, and to build coalitions (Amundsen 2006: 4).

Manipulation of Institutions

By corrupt means, power holders can secure their hold by buying and manipulating public institutions of accountability and control. They can buy parliamentary majorities and favourable legislative decisions, and they can buy favourable decisions and lenient controls by various control agencies (ombudsmen, comptrollers, auditors, prosecutors). Even loyal decisions from electoral commissions and high courts have been bought.

The latter point is clear from the example of the questionable impartiality of the election commission in Bangladesh. The problem is that appointments to various positions in the commission have allegedly been made based on political considerations, bringing into question the impartiality of the commission (Amundsen 2006: 7).

Vote-buying ranges from the bribing of election officials to the bribing of voters by offering pecuniary benefits, local development projects, money, gifts and jobs. It has been defined by Brusco et al. as 'the payment by political parties of minor benefits (food, clothing, cash) to citizens in exchange for their votes' (2004: 66), and in their study on Argentina they found that in two elections these handouts significantly boosted the probability of a vote.

Vote-buying also includes the buying of parliamentary votes and majorities. One example is vote-buying in congress in Brazil. In 2005, the minority ruling Labour Party was accused of paying a monthly allowance of 30,000 Brazilian reals (12,500 US dollars) to congressmen from two allied parties in return for their votes (Amundsen 2006: 7).

The buying of legal impunity is another method of power-preserving political corruption. Glaesera et al. (2002: 199, 213–14) argue that in many countries the operation of legal, political and regulatory institutions is subverted by the wealthy and the politically powerful for their own benefit, and tell the story about how the subversion of political and legal institutions brought crony capitalism to Yeltsin's Russia.

The example of the Nicaraguan pact demonstrates how an informal agreement between the leaders of the two biggest parties has secured them both a seat in the National Assembly, and thus immunity, and this has blocked investigations of corruption (Amundsen 2006: 7).

One example of the use of state resources for party campaigning and electioneering is the 'Dashain allowance' in Nepal. In 2005, the Royal Commission for Corruption Control began the prosecution of six former ministers for misusing the prime minister's relief fund to distribute some 4 million Nepalese rupees (57,000 US dollars) to political supporters (ibid.).

IMPLICATIONS FOR RESEARCH AND ACTION

The distinction between political and bureaucratic corruption has consequences for analysis and methodology as well as for anti-corruption work. We believe that by employing the distinction we can better understand some of the reasons why the record of anti-corruption interventions has been so poor. As argued by Marquette and Peiffer, anti-corruption interventions are based on a theoretical misunderstanding of the nature of corruption. In their words, 'principal-agent theory has fallen short in providing viable solutions to the [corruption] problem' (Marquette and Peiffer 2015: 2).

Measurement and Research

The main implication of the political-bureaucratic distinction of corruption is that it makes research and analysis more precise. Instead of lumping the two together – which is done in too many studies that contribute to more confusion than clarification – the distinction opens up for more precise measures, data, and diagnostic tools.

Bureaucratic corruption takes place at the implementation end of politics, where civil servants meet the public. Thus, opinion surveys, score cards and other direct reporting procedures can give relatively precise data of the magnitude and mechanisms of bureaucratic corruption. Good survey data outstrips all other data sources if you want to understand with accuracy and measure bureaucratic corruption, as one can directly measure people's experiences in having to pay a bribe.

However, these data collection methods cannot be used to measure political corruption. The public cannot directly observe it. And, due to the nature of the crime, there is severe underreporting; the data that police and other law enforcement agencies, NGOs and the media collect and report on are very patchy. This 'anecdotal evidence' does not come close to the true number of cases. In fact, there are no methodological tools that can directly and precisely measure political corruption.

We will therefore have to break down political corruption into its constituent components, first into extractive political corruption and power-preserving political corruption, and second into the two forms' manifestations as described above, and then measure these, directly if possible and indirectly if necessary.

We will argue that extractive political corruption cannot be assessed using the generic and indirect methods often used to assess corruption in general, like the World Bank Institute's Control of Corruption indicator and TI's Corruption Perceptions Index,[15] because these are (indirectly) measuring political *and* bureaucratic corruption combined (or rather, the sum of opinions of those who, when asked to rank corruption in their country, have political corruption in mind and those who have bureaucratic corruption in mind).[16] This is not good enough – as we have seen, there are

[15] The 'control of corruption' indicator is one of six indicators of the Worldwide Governance Indicators (WGI) (http://info.worldbank.org/governance/wgi/#home), which covers over 200 countries, and TI's Corruption Perceptions Index (https://www.transparency.org/news/feature/corruption_perceptions_index_2017) covers 176 countries.

[16] The WGI 'control of corruption' indicator captures 'perceptions of the extent to which public power is exercised for private gain, including both petty and grand forms of corruption, as well as 'capture' of the state by elites and private interests' (Kaufmann et al. 2010: 4).

countries in which political corruption by far overshadows bureaucratic corruption, and vice versa.

There are some other, possibly useful, proxy indicators – for example indexes such as the World Bank Groups' Ease of Doing Business (EDB) index and the Global Financial Integrity's Illicit Financial Flows (IFF) reports.[17]

The EDB ranks the national regulatory environment; a higher score means it is more conducive to the starting and operation of a local firm; it indicates better, usually simpler, regulations for businesses and a stronger protection of property. If it takes a very long time to register a business this can indicate that other ('politically exposed') businesses are already 'in', being given preferential treatment and perhaps an informal monopoly. If there is a low level of legal protection of private property, this can indicate that someone is rather interested in appropriations and 'land grabs'.

The IFF measures money or capital movement from one country to another, and classifies it as illegal when the funds are illegally earned, transferred and/or utilised. This includes drug and terrorist money, money from human trafficking, trade mis-invoicing, transfer pricing and tax evasion, as well as corrupt public officials' money transfers and deposits. The problem with this index is that data on the latter (corrupt public officials' money) are combined in the index with drug and terrorist money and other 'hot money outflows', and there is no distinction made between private businesses, state bureaucrats and politicians.

Another possible proxy is to use the 'red flags' method on public procurement. The red flags are warning signals identified in the literature as associated with institutionalised corruption. Many of these are measurable, such as an extremely short submission period, single bids (which signals lack of competition and closed access), and contract performance at a price considerably higher than originally contracted. Combining these elementary risk indicators into a composite index can give a risk score that is robust over time and across countries (Tóth and Fazekas 2014: 2).

Two more possible proxies are the Political Influence Indicator, which gauges the degree of political influence on companies'

---

[17] See: www.doingbusiness.org/rankings and www.gfintegrity.org/issue/illicit-financial-flows.

market success (assuming that, in a systematically corrupt environment where political favouritism drives procurement markets, a government change will make some companies 'unexpectedly' much more successful than their peers while others 'unexpectedly' lose ground), and the Political Control Indicator, which measures if the supplier or bidder has or has had political office holders among its owners and managers (assuming that political connections may be exploited to gain undue advantage in competing for government contracts) (ibid.: 2–3).

The problem with these and other indexes is that they cover only some aspects of extractive political corruption. Combined, however, and combined with other methods, they can shed much light on the issue.

Power-preserving political corruption can to some extent be assessed with the many democracy and integrity indexes. These include the Economist Intelligence Unit's (EIU's) State of Democracy Index, the World Bank Institute's Worldwide Governance Indicators (WGI), the Index of Public Integrity (IPI) and the Ibrahim Index of African Governance (IIAG).[18] Again, the problem is that even when these indexes give an overall picture of the level of governance, democracy and integrity, the issue of power abuse encompasses much more than corruption for power-preservation purposes.

More useful yet are the indexes on specific government institutions such as the parliament and the judiciary, and the efficiency of 'checks and balances' (restricted government). Regarding parliaments, good, comparable, updated and publicly available statistics on parliamentary performance and levels of accountability do not exist. To our knowledge, there is only the outdated Fish and Kroenig (2009) Parliamentary Powers Index (PPI). This provides a snapshot of the state of legislative power in the world as of 2007, and it uses a panel of experts to gauge the legislature's sway over the executive, its institutional autonomy, its authority in specific areas and its institutional capacity, but the background data are not available.

[18] See: https://infographics.economist.com/2017/DemocracyIndex, http://info.worldbank.org/governance/wgi/#home, http://integrity-index.org, and http://mo.ibrahim.foundation/iiag/.

There is, however, a useful proxy on transparency in the budget process. Since the parliament is the main institution responsible for raising and using public funds, and the main authority for checking on the government's spending of public money, this is a good indicator of parliamentary accountability (which is the opposite of being manipulated and subservient to the executive). The International Budget Partnership's Open Budget Survey[19] measures how much information the government provides to the public in its budget documents ('to obtain a clear understanding of the budget and to provide a check on the executive').

Regarding judiciaries, data on the rule of law are easily available, and data on the ability of the judiciary to hold the executive to account (judiciaries' check and balances capability) can be found. There are individual country reports of quality, such as the US Department of State Human Rights Country Reports, and some comparative and longitudinal data on the rule of law such as the WGI indicator Rule of Law and the World Justice Project's Rule of Law Index.[20] The Electoral Integrity Project[21] measures perceptions of electoral integrity, which can indicate manipulations if the values are low.

In sum, however, most of these existing datasets cover slightly different aspects of and either narrower or broader issues than power-preserving political corruption. Again, a strategic choice and a combination of methods can nevertheless shed much light on the issue.

Implications for Anti-Corruption Work

Persson et al. (2013) argue that despite a worldwide increase in awareness of the detrimental effects of corruption and increased priority given to the fight against systemic corruption, few successes have resulted. Like Marquette and Peiffer (2015), they argue that part of the explanation as to why anti-corruption reforms fail is that they are based on the theoretical misconceptualisation of

---

[19] See: http://survey.internationalbudget.org/.

[20] See: www.state.gov/j/drl/rls/hrrpt/index.htm and http://worldjusticeproject.org/rule-of-law-index.

[21] See: https://www.electoralintegrityproject.com.

corruption as a principal-agent problem. This theoretic lens presupposes non-corruptible and 'principled' so-called principals, which is not necessarily the case. Too often, the principals are corrupt and not acting in the interest of the society but instead pursuing their own narrow self-interests (Persson et al. 2013: 451). This is entirely in line with our understanding of political corruption.

Khan (2016: 3) has argued that anti-corruption strategies often wrongly assume that aggregate levels of corruption can be reduced through a top-down combination of policies that improve enforcement of the rule of law and changes to the expected returns of corruption (for example, through bureaucratic pay increases, greater transparency or harsher punishments). These strategies have generally delivered modest reductions in corruption in contexts of entrenched political corruption, which Khan calls a 'configuration of social power [that] does not support the enforcement of generalized rule-following behaviour' (ibid.: 3).

Political corruption cannot be tackled by a technical and/or technical/bureaucratic approach alone, by capacity-building interventions and technical support, and it cannot be treated only as another problem of market regulation or good governance. Political corruption is when the ruling elite/government is corrupt, when individuals with political power are corrupt and therefore – of course – lack the political will to address corruption. This means that the country's policies and priorities as well as individual politicians' actions will directly contradict and/or annihilate most anti-corruption efforts.

Sometimes, there will be political resistance to anti-corruption, as corrupt politicians will defend their vital interests vehemently and sometimes even violently. At other times, corrupt politicians will pick and choose what anti-corruption measures to implement, and these will typically not be the ones that will reduce their own opportunities for extraction and power preservation, but rather those that will increase government legitimacy and efficiency, and preferably, simultaneously reduce the influence of political rivals and opponents.

Political corruption calls for political solutions. Deepened democracy is to a large extent a question of the institutional capability of public and private institutions to control and withstand the pressures for elite extraction and elite reinvestment in power.

The solution to the problems lies particularly in the institutionalisation of public control mechanisms and in the 'ring-fencing' of informal practices. That is, the solution will have to include institutional checks and balances, free and fair elections, human rights, and horizontal and vertical accountability mechanisms.

REFERENCES

Amundsen, I. (2006), 'Political corruption', Bergen: Chr. Michelsen Institute, U4 Issue 6:2006.

Amundsen, I. (2014), 'Drowning in oil. Angola's institutions and the "resource curse"', *Journal of Comparative Politics*, 46(2): 169–89.

Andvig, J.C., O-H. Fjeldstad, with I. Amundsen, T. Sissener and T. Søreide (2001), 'Corruption: a review of contemporary research', Bergen: Chr. Michelsen Institute, CMI Report R 2001:7.

Argandoña, A. (2017), 'The changing face of corruption in the Asia Pacific', in M. dela Rama and C. Rowley, *The Changing Face of Corruption in the Asia Pacific*, Oxford/UK: Elsevier Ltd.

Bachelard, J.Y. (2010), 'The Anglo-Leasing corruption scandal in Kenya: the politics of international and domestic pressures and counter-pressures', *Review of African Political Economy*, 37(124): 187–200.

Baskin, M. and M.L. Mezey (eds) (2014), *Distributive Politics in Developing Countries: Almost Pork*, London: Lexington Books.

Booth, D. and F. Golooba-Mutebi (2012), 'Developmental patrimonialism? The case of Rwanda', *African Affairs*, 111(444): 379–403.

Brusco, V., M. Nazareno and S.C. Stokes (2004), 'Vote buying in Argentina', *Latin American Research Review*, 39(2): 66–88.

Cain, G. (2015), 'Bad governance in Zimbabwe and its negative consequences', *The Downtown Review*, 2(1).

Cohen, N. (2007), 'The politics of sleaze', *The Guardian*, 16 November 2003.

Corntassel, J. (2007), 'Partnership in action? Indigenous political mobilization and co-optation during the first UN indigenous decade (1995–2004)', *Human Rights Quarterly*, 29(1): 137–66.

della Porta, D. and A. Vannucci (1999), *Corrupt Exchanges: Actors, Resources, and Mechanisms of Political Corruption*, New York: Walter de Gruyter Inc.

Demir, F. (2010), 'A political economy analysis of the Turkish military's split personality: the patriarchal master or crony capitalist?' in T. Cetin and F. Yilmaz (eds), *Understanding the Process of Economic Change in Turkey: An Institutional Approach*, New York: Nova Science Publishers.

Easton, D. (1965), *A Framework for Political Analysis*, Englewood Cliffs: Prentice-Hall.

Encyclopædia Britannica: *Public Administration*, https://www.britannica.com/topic/public-administration (accessed 17 August 2018).

Fish, M.S. and M. Kroenig (2009), *The Handbook of National Legislatures: A Global Survey*, New York: Cambridge University Press.

Fraud Magazine (2018), '5 most scandalous fraud cases in 2018', *Fraud Magazine*, November 2018, https://www.fraud-magazine.com/2018Top5Frauds/ (accessed 15 April 2019).

Frederickson, H.G. (ed.) (2015), *Ethics and Public Administration*, New York: Routledge.

Glaesera, E., J. Scheinkmanb and A. Shleifera (2002), 'The injustice of inequality', *Journal of Monetary Economics*, 50 (2003): 199–222.

Global Witness (2008), *StatoilHydro's Libyan Corruption Scandal Shows Need For Oil Industry Disclosure Laws*, London: Global Witness, Report November 2008.

Heidenheimer, A.J. and M. Johnston (eds) (2002), *Political Corruption: Concepts and Contexts*, 3rd edn, New Brunswick/NJ and London: Transaction Publishers.

Hessami, Z. (2014), 'Political corruption, public procurement, and budget composition: theory and evidence from OECD countries', *European Journal of Political Economy*, 34: 372–89.

Heywood, P.M. (2015), *Routledge Handbook of Political Corruption*, London: Routledge.

Hjellum, T. (2007), *Politisk korrupsjon som demokratisk problem*, Oslo: Cappelen Forlag.

Huntington, S.P. (1968), *Political Order in Changing Societies*, New Haven, Conn.: Yale University Press.

Johnston, M. (ed.) (2011), *Public Sector Corruption* (4 vols), Thousand Oaks/CA: SAGE Publications Ltd.

Kaufmann, D., A. Kraay and M. Mastruzzi (2010), *The Worldwide Governance Indicators Methodology and Analytical Issues*, Washington: World Bank (World Bank Policy Research Working Paper 5430).

Khan, M. (2016), '*Corruption Spotlight*', London: Department of Economics, SOAS, University of London, Background Note for the 2017 World Development Report.

Lambsdorff, J.G. (2007), *The Methodology of the Corruption Perceptions Index 2007*, Berlin: Transparency International, www.stt.lt/documents/soc_tyrimai/KSI_methodology_2007.pdf (accessed 29 March 2017).

Loftis, M.W. (2014), 'Deliberate indiscretion? How political corruption encourages discretionary policy making', *Comparative Political Studies*, 48(6): 728–58.

Marquette, H. and C. Peiffer (2015), *Corruption and Collective Action*, Bergen and Birmingham: U4 Anti-Corruption Resource Centre and The Developmental Leadership Program (DLP), Research Paper 2, https://www.u4.no/publications/corruption-and-collective-action.pdf (accessed 17 August 2018).

Moody-Stuart, G. (1997), *Grand Corruption: How Business Bribes Damage Developing Countries*, Oxford: WorldView.

Nattrass, N. (2014), 'A South African variety of capitalism?', *New Political Economy*, 19(1): 56–78.

Nye, J.S. (1967), 'Corruption and political development: a cost-benefit analysis', *American Political Science Review*, 61(2): 417–27.

Olken, B.A. (2007), 'Monitoring corruption: evidence from a field experiment in Indonesia', *Journal of Political Economy*, 115(2): 200–49.

Persson, A., B. Rothstein and J. Teorell (2013), 'Why anticorruption reforms fail – systemic corruption as a collective action problem', *Governance*, 26(3): 449–71.

Tangri, A. and A.M. Mwenda (2013), *The Politics of Elite Corruption in Africa: Uganda in Comparative African Perspective*, Oxon/UK: Routledge.

The Economist (2017), 'Beware the taxman: tax authorities are the latest tools of repression in Africa', 30 September 2017, https://www.economist.com/middle-east-and-africa/2017/09/30/tax-authorities-are-the-latest-tools-of-repression-in-africa (accessed 21 August 2018).

The Guardian (2015), 'Malaysian taskforce investigates allegations $700m paid to PM Najib', 6 July 2015, https://www.theguardian.com/world/2015/jul/06/malaysian-task-force-investigates-allegations-700m-paid-to-pm-najib (accessed 15 April 2019).

TI (2004), *Global Corruption Report (Special Focus Political Corruption)*, London/Sterling VA: Pluto Press, Transparency International, http://www.transparency.org/research/gcr/gcr_political_corruption (accessed 28 March 2017).

TI (2006), *Global Corruption Report 2006*, Berlin: Transparency International.

Tóth, I.J. and M. Fazekas (2014), 'New ways to measure institutionalised grand corruption in public procurement', U4 Brief 2014:9, Bergen: U4 (Anti-Corruption Resource Centre).

V-Dem Institute (2016), 'The role of legislative powers for executive corruption', Stockholm: V-Dem Institute, Policy Brief No. 3, 13 January 2016.

Villoria, M., G.G. Van Ryzin and C.F. Lavena (2013), 'Social and political consequences of administrative corruption: a study of public perceptions in Spain', *Public Administration Review*, 73: 85–94.

World Bank (1997), *Helping Countries Combat Corruption: The Role of the World Bank*, Report, Washington: World Bank.

Zaum, D. (2013), *Political Economies of Corruption in Fragile and Conflict-Affected States: Nuancing the Picture*, U4 Brief 2013:4, Bergen: U4 (U4 Anti-Corruption Resource Centre).

2. Political corruption and the limits of anti-corruption activism in Ghana

Kofi Takyi Asante and Moses Khisa

POLITICAL CORRUPTION AND ANTI-CORRUPTION ACTIVISM IN A 'CHOICELESS DEMOCRACY'

This chapter analyses four high-profile political corruption cases in Ghana's fourth republic. We focus on the post-Rawlings era, which marked a decisive break from the military dictatorship of the 1980s and the 'authoritarian democracy' of the 1990s. The end of the Rawlings era was welcomed as a watershed moment in Ghanaian politics. John Agyekum Kufuor's New Patriotic Party (NPP) won power on an anti-corruption platform and declared zero tolerance for corruption in his inaugural speech. The NPP government repealed the criminal libel law six months after assuming the reins of government, a move enthusiastically welcomed by the press and Civil Society Organisations (CSOs). The liberalisation of the media continued under the new government, and civil society activism flourished. Indeed, students of corruption observed that transitions from authoritarian governance intensifies the fight against corruption, as an erstwhile informal or loosely connected civil society institutionalises and consolidates itself (Setiyono and McLeod 2010).

Over the past two decades, Ghana has evolved a tradition of ruling-party alternation which has contributed to democratic consolidation (Asamoah 2014, Boafo-Arthur 2007, Gyimah-Boadi 2009), without, however, any significant reduction in the prevalence of corruption. A vibrant electoral democracy in the context of a generally unproductive economy may fuel political corruption by creating incentives for politicians with short time horizons (Whitfield 2011).

With two parties dominating the electoral system, Ghana's political settlement has been described as a 'choiceless democracy' (Ninsin 2006: 7).[1] The NPP defeated Rawlings's National Democratic Congress (NDC) at the polls in 2000 and again in 2004. The NDC won back power from 2008 to 2016, when they again lost to the NPP. While in opposition, both parties have raised charges of corruption against their opponents in power and made strong commitments to transparent and accountable governance, yet they find themselves equally tainted with the same allegations when in power (Josiah-Aryeh 2008: 286–7).

Given the failure of electoral politics to effectively curb the prevalence or scale of corruption, civil society activism is believed to impose more effective checks on public office holders. This belief is premised on the optimism that direct engagement by citizens, whether in their individual capacities or as members of CSOs, has the ability under certain conditions to help 'transform 'basic state–society relations [...] thereby reducing clientelism, empowering citizens and enhancing the quality of democracy' (Wampler 2012: 341).

Nonetheless, the analysis of CSOs in the fight against corruption needs to be placed within a larger country-specific institutional and political context. Scholars such as Setiyono and McLeod (2010) have expressed scepticism about the ability of CSOs to make a meaningful impact in the fight against corruption without first tackling its root causes.

Mushtaq Khan (1998) argues that developing countries are prone to political instability stemming from the social dislocations and inequalities that result from the process of development. In this context, political corruption is a constituent part of 'a wider set of exchanges within patron–client networks through which incumbent elites construct political compromises with clients who would

[1] The term 'choice-less democracy' was first used by Thandika Mkandawire to describe the relationship between democratising African countries and their 'development partners' wherein strings attached to aid entrammels national governments, making them more responsive to the demands of donors and international financial institutions than to their citizens (Mkandawire 1999; 2010).

otherwise threaten the political stability of the system' (ibid.: 112). From this perspective, power-preserving political corruption – and the extractive corruption that usually sustains it – is extremely difficult to control because the very structure of state–society relations encourages those kinds of malfeasance. Framing the problem in this manner enables us to better evaluate the prospects as well as limits of CSO activism in the fight against corruption.

The political power exploited to commit corrupt acts also exercises considerable control over the existing institutional mechanisms to curb corruption. This severely constrains the ability of CSOs to effectively wage war against corruption. As we will attempt to show below, CSO anti-corruption efficacy requires a delicate combination of strategic mobilisation and appropriate knowledge of institutional procedures.

The rest of the chapter proceeds as follows. The next section summarises the case selection and the methodology used, followed by a presentation and analysis of four case studies of political corruption, both extractive and power preserving, in governments led by both NDC and NPP. The concluding sections draw the broad implications of political corruption and anti-corruption activism in a competitive clientelist political settlement.

CASES, SELECTION AND ANALYSIS

Corruption studies are notoriously plagued with methodological problems. This is compounded in our case by the small number of cases upon which our analysis is based. Nonetheless, our careful selection of cases and systematic analysis allow us to generate some general insights about political corruption in Ghana. We have selected cases that capture both extractive and power-preserving political corruption, and that straddle both NDC and NPP governments.

In our selection, we made sure that the cases included corruption at both individual and institutional levels in both administrations. We use the term individual-level corruption for instances of corruption in which one individual, or a few individuals working in concert, plan and carry out corrupt acts. In contrast, we use the term institutional-level corruption for instances where the involvement of an entire organisation is necessary to undertake corrupt acts. Although both individual and institutional levels of corruption have extractive and regime-preserving elements, individual-level corruption tends to be more extractive while institutional corruption maintains elements of both extraction and power preservation.

Another challenge confronting studies on corruption is quality of data. The covert nature of corruption, coupled with the natural tendency towards denial when cases come to light, generates obstacles for rigour in corruption studies. This is more so for cases of grand corruption where the accused always default to denial. However, these obstacles are not insurmountable. Reports from administrative or judicial enquiries are sources of high-quality data, as are the outcomes of investigative journalism and reports arising from civil society activism. Depending on the purpose of a study, even denials, and the consequences of such denials, can be important sources of information.

For our analytical purposes, we constructed a unique dataset of news articles, press releases and official reports. Using this dataset, we provide a narrative of the four selected cases of corruption (see Table 2.1) and drawn out the salient features of each case, the level and types of corruption, and the parties involved. In all cases there were both intense media scrutiny, civil society activism and official inquiries. Documents arising from these sources constituted our main data. We supplemented these with more than thirty in-depth interviews and informal conversations with political actors, civil society activists and keen observers in media and academia. Using this dataset, we can uncover the prospects and limits of anti-corruption activism in Ghana's fourth republic.

Table 2.1 The cases and their characteristics

CASES	**Kickback**	**Anane**	**Smarttys**	**GYEEDA**
Power preserving	Yes	No	Partly	Partly
Extractive	Partly	Yes	Yes	Yes
Individual/group level	Yes	Yes	Partly	Yes
Institutional level	Maybe	No	Partly	Yes
Anti-corruption activism	Yes	Yes	Yes	Yes
Anti-corruption victories	No	Partial	Yes	Yes

Haruna Esseku and the Kickback Saga

CSOs and the media are crucial in generating awareness about corruption, especially when it comes to the exposure of corrupt deals. But this does not necessarily result in major anti-corruption victories. The 'kickback saga', which is an example of institutional-level, power-preserving political corruption, is a case in point. It hinted at the submerged structure of patronage relationships of incumbent and previous governments, political parties and private economic actors. These patronage networks had a bearing on both the nature of corruption and the possibility of anti-corruption victories (Khan 1998).

The case started with an exposé in November 2005 by the *Enquirer* newspaper, which published an explosive allegation of corruption reaching up to the very pinnacle of government. The paper's editor, Raymond Archer, claimed to have a secret tape recording in which the NPP chairman, Haruna Esseku, admitted that the president took bribes at the Osu Castle (then the seat of government)[2] on behalf of the ruling party. Mr Esseku, then seeking re-election in the party's upcoming congress, reportedly told some party delegates that the 'Castle is financially suffocating the NPP by hijacking kickbacks meant for the administration of the party' (The Enquirer 2005a).

The party chairman alluded to the fact that 'kickback' money, meant to run the party and thus to preserve power, was hijacked by state house and the presidency – pointing to extraction by individuals around the presidency. He was reported to have said that it was the president himself who always authorised party expenditure requests:

> I don't know who keeps the money, the only thing I know is that when I go to the Castle, I present the budget to the President, I wait in the President's office, he reads through the budget and he signals his men […] Before I go, the money is dumped at the back of my car in bags (The Enquirer 2005b).

Earlier, during the voter registration exercise in 2004, party chairman Esseku reportedly received 10 billion cedis (1 million US

---

[2] The seat of government was moved to Jubilee House in 2013.

dollars at the time)[3] from the Castle to help the party mobilise its base to register (ibid., Africa Confidential 2005). The money was apparently to pay for party militants deployed to counter threats from its main rival, the NDC. The NPP national organiser, Lord Commey, boasted that the party had the potential to deploy 1,200 party 'vigilantes' or militants, whom he called 'action troopers', to fight back harassment from the NDC (Ghanaian Chronicle 2005a).

The Enquirer also reported that there was dissatisfaction among contractors affiliated with the NPP. Kufuor's declaration of zero tolerance for corruption had reportedly generated apprehension among his ministers, discouraging them from extorting bribes from contractors affiliated with the NPP to avoid the risk of exposure. They thus awarded the juiciest contracts – running into billions of cedis – to contractors affiliated with the NDC, giving NPP contractors bids worth 'only' hundreds of millions of cedis (The Enquirer 2005b).

Haruna Esseku denied uttering the term 'kickback' (The Enquirer 2005d), but admitted that the Castle did receive 'contributions and donations' from party 'organs', including members of the presidency itself. He also admitted that the party was facing a funding crisis, and that 'I do send people to receive money from the Castle. Sometimes I go there myself. The monies were from several organs of the party including the presidency' (Myjoyonline 2005a).

The presidency and senior party officials insisted that the party was transparently funded. O.B. Amoah, Deputy Minister of Education and Sports, claimed that the Castle actively discouraged party financiers from directing their contributions to the Castle (GNA 2005b, The Statesman 2005b). However, the NPP-affiliated newspaper *The Statesman* seemed to give some credence to *The Enquirer* story, arguing in an editorial that if the party chairman had indeed solicited for cash donations from contract winners, he had not committed any illegality, even if this was 'perhaps regrettable' (The Statesman 2005a).

This scandal highlights the interconnection of party financing and political corruption. Party financing is key to winning and holding on to political power, and, given the intense competition between

---

[3] In 2007, the cedi was redenominated, knocking off three zeros, and renamed the Ghana cedi (GH₵); 1,000 old cedis became GH₵1. The current (August 2019) value is approximately US$0.18.

the two major parties, it has become critical in the electoral calculations. In opposition, members readily pay dues and make donations, but winning power discourages further contribution because of the assumption that the ruling party has state resources at its disposal (The Enquirer 2005c).

There were also extractive elements to this case. An implicit revelation from the scandal was the understanding among politicians and private businesses that bribes needed to be paid in exchange for government contracts. For instance, Esseku said he 'asked several contractors why they have not been paying (the kickbacks) and they laughed at me and said, how can we be doing this business and would not be paying' (The Enquirer 2005b). The previous NDC government was said to have demanded 10 per cent kickback on contracts, but the NPP apparently fixed its rate on a case-by-case basis (The Statesman 2005b).

Like all the cases of corruption discussed in this chapter, this scandal generated widespread public condemnation and media scrutiny. The Ghana Anti-Corruption Coalition, an umbrella body of anti-corruption groups, called for an investigation, a call that was endorsed by the state anti-corruption agency, the Serious Fraud Office (SFO, now Economic and Organised Crimes Office, EOCO), although the boss of the SFO admitted that the law on reporting requirements for the funding of the political parties 'do not have much push' (Myjoyonline 2005b).

The political opposition at the time, notably the Convention People's Party (CPP) and the NDC, also demanded investigations. The NDC claimed that nothing but a parliamentary inquiry will satisfy them, because they could not rely on the SFO, a state agency, to conduct an objective probe. More extreme critics called for the impeachment of the president (Ghanaian Chronicle 2005b, GNA 2005a, 2006e). However, none of these translated into concrete remedial action.

The 'kickback saga' was a case of power-preserving political corruption at the institutional level. The network of corruption that it unveiled included the presidency, political parties and private economic actors. It showed an institutionalised pattern of corruption, in which the presidency controlled the flow and distribution of funds, causing friction between factions of the ruling elite. Although CSOs spoke out against the ruling party, no major anti-corruption victory was recorded.

Richard Anane's Abuse of Office

The Anane scandal was a case of political corruption involving abuse of power perpetrated at the individual level. Although the extraction in this case can only be inferred, and the amount involved rather small, it casts light on the protection of seemingly corrupt officials, and the impunity that this subsequently engenders. This case also shows how easily anti-corruption victories can be eroded.

The scandal exploded during Dr Richard Anane's ministerial vetting in parliament, which under normal circumstances should have been a mere formality. However, he was forced to respond to media reports of an affair with an American woman which had allegedly taken place while he was on an official trip and which had resulted in a baby. He allegedly remitted about US$90,000 to her, an amount he could not have afforded on his declared income, as well as hotel bills and other costs that he had charged to the account of state institutions.

The stakes became high as moral outrage over a sexual affair was combined with allegations of illegal use of government money. In his response, Anane claimed to have remitted only about US$10,000. He claimed, much to public scepticism, that he got 'money from my brothers, friends, among others anytime I travel, they give me money' (Ghanaian Chronicle 2005c). The minority in parliament decided to defer confirmation of his appointment until questions regarding the affair had been answered. The Minority Leader, Alban Bagbin, hinted at the possibility of flying the woman, Alexandra O'Brien, to Ghana to testify (Ghanaian Chronicle 2005d).

Anane initially enjoyed the support of the government and his party. In fact, the media referred to him as the president's 'darling boy', and he got solidarity from a youth group calling itself Friends of Dr Richard Anane, organising a demonstration on his behalf. One placard read 'every human is fallible' (GNA 2005c). The government also used its parliamentary majority to push his appointment through, but the ensuing pressure became a source of unease in government circles to the extent that a presidential spokesperson declared on radio that 'all of us have felt uncomfortable' about the controversy (Ghanaian Chronicle 2005e).

Public pressure continued after further damning media reports. Raymond Archer, the journalist who broke the story, claimed he had records of financial transactions indicating the minister had lied under oath to the vetting committee (The Enquirer 2005g). Archer's newspaper, *The Enquirer*, alleged further that Anane had been involved in a case of conflict of interest by using his influence, while Minister of Health, 'to persuade' the Attorney General to award O'Brien a government contract (The Enquirer 2005e).

In June 2005, the Commission on Human Rights and Administrative Justice (CHRAJ) instituted investigations into the matter, focusing on the allegations of corruption, abuse of office and conflict of interest (The Enquirer 2005f). During the CHRAJ proceedings, a friend of Anane, Collins Kwame Duodu-Bonsu, claimed to have remitted over US$72,000 to O'Brien 'because of his friendship with the minister' (GhanaWeb 2006). Attributing ownership of property or sources of income to family or friends is a familiar strategy for politicians to deflect allegations of financial malfeasance. In fact, Anane claimed to have been unaware of the remittances (GNA 2006d). When O'Brien testified via video-conferencing, she confirmed that she indeed received several transfers adding up to US$90,000 from Anane (Ghanaian Chronicle 2005c).

In a much-anticipated ruling after an 18-month investigation, CHRAJ cleared the minister of the corruption allegations, but upheld the charges of abuse of office and conflict of interest and also found him guilty of perjury (GNA 2006b, 2006c). In its recommendations, CHRAJ advised the president to dismiss the minister. While the public awaited the presidency's actions, the Ghana Integrity Initiative, a non-government organisation (NGO), advised Anane to resign as a matter of public decency and to avoid 'unnecessary confusion about the standards of good governance observed in Ghana and by our government' (GNA 2006a).

Although Anane fought to hold on to his job, the weight of public opinion was decidedly against him and there was widespread speculation about his impending dismissal (Ghanaian Chronicle 2006, The Statesman 2006a, 2006b). At this point, even the president's patronage could no longer save him. In the end, he decided, or was compelled, to resigned.

But his resignation turned out to be a tactical move. Free from the trammels of office, he challenged the CHRAJ ruling in court and got the adverse decisions against him quashed on technical grounds. The court ruled that because the commission had initiated the proceedings on its own contrary to its mandate, the investigations lacked legal backing (Ghana Heritage Post 2007).

True to public speculations after his legal victory, Anane got nominated back to the Ministry of Transport in February 2008. Despite protests by the opposition NDC, his appointment was approved by parliament (Ghanaian Chronicle 2008, GhanaWeb 2008), an event described by an NDC leader as 'a classic case of getting away with murder'.[4]

In the Anane case, anti-corruption activism by the media achieved a short-lived victory. It set in motion institutional anti-corruption measures and the pressure from the SFO and other bodies made the minister's continued stay in office untenable. However, the fact that he could hold on to his position that long, and the ease with which he was reinstated, speaks to the limits of anti-corruption victories. The fact that Anane was able to successfully get the court to squash the CHRAJ verdict indicates that, in the fight against corruption, successful action requires a balance between skilful activism and knowledge of institutional procedure. This will be illustrated further in the next two cases.

Smarttys Bus Branding

The bus branding contract between Smarttys Management and Productions (SMP Ltd) and the Ministry of Transport combined power preservation for the NDC, in power at the time, and extraction for individuals connected to it. It also blurred the lines between individual- and institutional-level corruption. A crucial anti-corruption victory was won in this instance because the lead CSO, OccupyGhana, had lawyers and other professionals who brought their knowledge of institutional procedure to bear on the anti-corruption fight.

In July 2015, Smarttys, a movie and event management company owned by Selassie Ibrahim, a celebrity with connections to the NDC government, was awarded a contract to brand 116 new Metro Mass Rapid Transit buses with the images of the president – who

[4] Interview with Kwamena Ahwoi, former Minister of Local Government and senior NDC party official, 26 June 2018, Accra.

was running for re-election the following year – and three former presidents. The GH₵3,649,004 used to brand the vehicles was taken from the country's oil fund. The revelation was made by the minority leader in parliament who condemned the expenditure as 'too huge and unacceptable' and chastised the government for misplacing its priorities (Myjoyonline 2015a).

The revelation generated an immediate public uproar (GhanaWeb 2015). In a radio interview, the manager of the company sub-contracted to do the actual branding claimed to have been paid only GH₵100 as labour cost per bus, and not GH₵2,000 as recorded in the pro forma invoice (Myjoyonline 2015b). The majority in parliament then tried to block attempts by the minority to initiate a probe into the matter (Citifmonline 2016).

Public outrage eventually became so intense that the Minister of Transport, Dzifa Attivor, who initially defended the contract with the claim that 'artistic work is generally expensive', buckled under pressure and resigned (GhanaWeb 2015). A review of the contract concluded that the contract sum was inflated by GH₵1.9 million, which Smarttys was ordered to refund. Smarttys reached an agreement with the Attorney General's department to refund the money in instalments and to revise the amount down to a little over GH₵1.5 million (Citifmonline 2015a).

However, these steps did little to assuage public outrage. Not satisfied with the resignation and refund, the political pressure groups OccupyGhana and Citizen Ghana Movement pursued the government for full accountability and won a High Court judgement ordering the government to make full disclosure of the contract. The court ruled that even in the absence of a Right to Information law,[5] people still possessed inviolable rights to information. Following this ruling, the Attorney General delivered the documents covering the transactions to OccupyGhana, but left out the report her office had prepared for the presidency (GraphicOnline 2015).

These documents uncovered an orchestration to give the semblance of legality to what was simply an act of official plunder. Ace Ankomah, a lawyer and high-ranking member of OccupyGhana,

[5] Parliament passed the Right to Information (RTI) bill on 26 March 2019.

described the deal as 'an illegal sweetheart transaction' (OccupyGhana 2016c). The sole-sourced contract, which was barely a page long, had been put together after the fact and was approved by the Public Procurement Authority (PPA) within 24 hours. The PPA cited urgency and threats to national security as justification for the use of sole sourcing (TV3 2016).

In addition to the Ministry of Transport and the PPA, the abetment of the Office of the President, the Ministry of Finance, the Controller and Accountant General's Department, and the Bank of Ghana helped to push the deal through. For instance, the Ministry of Transport paid Smarttys from the Consolidated Annual Budget Funding Amount (ABFA) even before the Accountant General had authorised the transfer. Even though the use of the ABFA requires parliamentary approval because it is covered by the Petroleum Revenue Management Act of 2011, Smarttys was paid without recourse to parliament (OccupyGhana 2016a, 2016b).

Thus, the Smarttys deal could not have gone through without a well-coordinated collusion between key accountability institutions, which should have prevented this deal in the first place. In a public forum in November 2016, OccupyGhana stated that it had prepared and submitted a 20-page dossier to the Attorney General, parliament and other stakeholders for the retrieval of 'every *pesewa* (penny) paid to Smarttys', and for the prosecution of the officials involved (GhanaWeb 2016). A year after they lost the 2016 presidential elections, calls came from within the NDC party for Dzifa Attivor, the minister under whose term the deal was made, to be prosecuted. Some in the party even blamed the deal for their defeat at the polls (GhanaWeb 2017).

The GYEEDA Scandal

The Ghana Youth Employment and Entrepreneurial Development Agency (GYEEDA) scandal is arguably the most audacious of all the cases examined in this chapter. It was an instance of grand corruption with only partial elements of power preservation. This case occurred at the institutional level, and provided rare glimpses of government–private business relationships which in Esseku's case described above could only be inferred. Here again, skilled activism by CSOs resulted in modest anti-corruption victories.

The NPP government established a National Youth Employment Programme (NYEP) in 2006, which the NDC government rebranded as GYEEDA in 2012 and expanded by consolidating all government programmes targeting youth. The main task of the agency was to recruit unemployed youth and give them training in, for instance, sanitation, education, agri-business, and information and communications technology (ICT).

Less than a year after its rebranding, the agency was shaken by revelations of monumental corruption and official misconduct. The news of the scandal was broken by a reporter with the Accra-based radio Joy FM, and was subsequently taken up by critical private media and the minority in parliament. The radio reporter uncovered the misappropriation of funds running into hundreds of millions of cedis and the signing of 'questionable contracts' between the agency and private-sector partners (Myjoyonline 2013a).

There was widespread public condemnation of the way the agency was administered, and there were calls for the contracts to be terminated. Some civil society actors went as far as demanding that the entire agency be scrapped, but this call was opposed by other civil society bodies and commentators, with one proposing that the agency be instead decentralised (Citifmonline 2015b, CPR 2013).

Official attempts to rebuff the allegations proved futile (Myjoyonline 2013c). Facing mounting public pressure, the sector minister, Elvis Afriyie Ankrah, instituted a committee to undertake a comprehensive review of the agency's operations. He told the media that the outcome of the committee's work would vindicate him (GNA 2013, Myjoyonline 2013b). However, the media reported that the investigation had resulted in hostilities between Ankrah and the former Minister of Youth and Sports, Kofi Humado, under whose tenure the most egregious parts of the scandal had taken place, and who feared the current minister was trying to absolve himself at his (Humado's) expense (The Scandal 2013).

The ministry-instituted committee found that a combination of weak institutional capacity and poorly trained workforce had enabled and exacerbated the corruption that rocked the agency. The findings revealed that three businessmen, Roland Agambire, Joseph Siaw Agyapong and Seidu Agongo, controlled virtually all the contracts given out by the agency, and had exerted influence to the extent of dictating the terms of the contracts and getting rid of

GYEEDA officials who dared question them. The committee also found evidence of official complicity in the creation of 'ghost names' on the payroll and fraudulent withdrawals. The overreliance on sole sourcing in the agency's procurement practices came up for special criticism (Ministry of Youth and Sports 2013)

The committee made a number of recommendations, including review of some contracts, retrieval of up to GH₵200 million and, where criminal violations had occurred, for the Attorney General to take necessary action. In fact, the report tasked the Attorney General to take these steps, but the Attorney General's department later claimed that, since it was not a partner in these transactions, it was not in a position to cancel the contracts or to retrieve the money (GhanaWeb 2013).

The Economic and Organised Crimes Office (EOCO) was later ordered by the president to recover the money fraudulently paid to the service providers, and to take steps on the criminal aspects of the committee findings (Myjoyonline 2013d). The national coordinator, Abuga Pele, and later Philip Akpeena Assibit, a representative of one of the service providers, were accused on charges of wilfully causing financial loss to the state and were subsequently sentenced to a combined jail term of 18 years.

As in the Smarttys case, OccupyGhana pressed statutory bodies to fully apply the law against all individuals involved in the fraud at GYEEDA. They demanded that the Auditor General exercise its legal statutory authority to disallow the fraudulent payment made by the agency and to surcharge it (GraphicOnline 2016). The matter ended up at the Supreme Court after the Auditor General's refusal to exert its authority in this regard, and the Auditor General was ordered to surcharge not only the individuals involved in the GYEEDA case, but all those found to have misappropriated public funds as stated in its annual reports (Myjoyonline 2017).

BROADER THEORETICAL AND EMPIRICAL IMPLICATIONS

These four cases throw light on some aspects of political corruption in Ghana. The explosion of the media landscape and expansion in the civil society arena have enabled greater scrutiny and intensified anti-corruption activism. Yet, no major dent seems to have been made in the prevalence of political corruption in Ghana. A long-standing observer and analyst of Ghanaian politics summed up the problem as 'the corrupt elite' and the nature of the institutional landscape where the public ethic of restraint in the exercise of power is not deep-rooted.[6]

Political corruption in Ghana is embedded in the country's competitive clientelist political settlement (Oduro et al. 2014, Whitfield 2011). The two parties have the same modus operandi of rent extraction for political purposes. The effect of the absence or weakness of constraining formal rules is exacerbated when it interacts with the actual power distribution in Ghana – that is, the nature of the existing political settlement as laid down by several scholars (Golooba-Mutebi and Booth 2013, Khan 2010, Kjaer 2015, North et al. 2009).

The persistence of political corruption is in part due to elite compromises and accommodations, but also due to the composition of the ruling coalitions. Power alternation between the two main parties does not alter the underlying norms that structure interactions between the main political actors. From a political settlement perspective, clientelist systems are characterised by informal channels of rent distribution to different factions that constitute ruling coalitions (Khan 2010). Under conditions of rapid social or economic change, political leaders are willing to make such illicit distributions in order to strengthen their hold on power.

Ghana has for long been hailed as a leading African country in implementing economic and political reforms in Sub-Saharan Africa following the myriad crises of the 1970s and 1980s (Bleck and van de Walle 2019, Boafo-Arthur 2007, Gyimah-Boadi and Daddieh 1999, Herbst 1993). The economic and political reforms of the 1980s and 1990s that produced a neoliberal economy and a liberal-democratic state simultaneously embedded a system of clientelist politics. In addition to enabling power consolidation during periods of rapid change, political corruption is also fuelled by the high cost of running an electoral campaign and the lack of enforcement of campaign financing laws. Conservative estimates put the cost of running for a parliamentary seat in Ghana at

---

[6] Interview with Kwame Ninsin, Professor Emeritus of Political Science, University of Ghana, Accra, 25 June 2018.

US$86,000 (WF & CDD 2018: 5). Consequently, political corruption can serve as a form of resource mobilisation, and there are expected rewards for financial contributions after winning power.[7]

Like many African electoral democracies, Ghana has an array of institutional and legal measures aimed at curbing corruption. Yet, embedded clientelism militates against bureaucratic efficiency and state capacity (van de Walle 2001). Previous attempts to harshly clean-up the Ghanaian political system by the two military interventions of Jerry Rawlings in 1979 and 1981 delivered only temporary successes, and elite rent-seeking and political corruption was reproduced in successive governments in part due to politicisation of the state institutions (Mbaku 2010: 51, 1997: 122).

Many of the measures to curb corruption in Ghana are enshrined in the 1992 constitution (Ayee 2000: 191–4), but despite this and even after successive power-alternations and turnovers, political corruption remains prevalent and, as we have shown above, public confidence about government commitment to transparency and accountability remains low. The stiff competition between the two main political parties has propelled the wheels of democratisation, responsiveness and accountability in quite important ways, but it has also simultaneously contributed to reproducing the old structures of financial malfeasance underpinned by largely informal patron–client relations.

CONCLUSIONS

The four cases analysed in this chapter reveal several legal and institutional lacunae in the political corruption landscape in Ghana. First, the regulatory and institutional frameworks fail to tackle political corruption. The existing laws are inadequate, and implementation is weak. For instance, the party financing law could not be brought to bear on the 'kickback' case. Also, Anane was able to get the courts to quash the CHRAJ's findings and conviction on purely procedural grounds. As shown in the GYEEDA case, procurement rules are easily violated when contractors have close connections to powerful political actors.

---

[7] Interview with Isaac Owusu, Lecturer of Political Science, University of Ghana, Legon, 25 June 2018.

We can, however, also interpret these cases as instructive of the shortcomings of formal rules in the context of a clientelist political settlement. Democratic consolidation in Africa, which in the past was hailed as a boon in the fight against corruption (Hope and Chikulo 2000: 13), has unfolded together with routinised political corruption even when there is power alternation. Because political corruption serves both personal and political purposes, fighting it is inherently a political matter.

Political corruption takes place at the behest of the powerful in government. The party in government preserves power through success at the ballot by raising campaign funds from private sector contractors and from powerful government officials with access to the public purse. In sum, despite the vibrancy of Ghana's democracy, the vibrancy of its media and the activism of anti-corruption civil society, political corruption continues to be a serious problem. However, our cases also show that with the right combination of strategic mobilisation and skilled utilisation of institutional procedures, it is possible for anti-corruption activists to win some victories in the fight against corruption.

REFERENCES

Africa Confidential (2005), 'Money-go-round', 46(25), 16 December 2005.

Asamoah, O.Y. (2014), *The Political History of Ghana, 1950–2013: The Experience of a Non-Conformist*, London: Author House.

Ayee, R.A.J. (2000), 'Ghana: the continuing search for cures in the fight against corruption', in K. Hope and B. Chikulo (eds), *Corruption and Development in Africa: Lessons from Country Case-Studies*, London: Palgrave Macmillan.

Bleck, J. and N. van de Walle (2019), *Electoral Politics in Africa Since 1990: Continuity and Change*, Cambridge: Cambridge University Press.

Boafo-Arthur, K. (ed.) (2007), *Ghana: One Decade of the Liberal State*, London: Zed Books.

Citifmonline (2015a), 'Bus branding saga: Smarttys ordered to refund GH₵1.9 million', 18 January 2016 (accessed 7 February 2019).

Citifmonline (2015b), 'Shut down YEA, YES programmes – Franklin Cudjoe to gov't', 13 December 2015, http://citifmonline.com/2015/12/13/shut-down-yea-yes-programmes-franklin-cudjoe-to-govt/ (accessed 7 February 2019).

Citifmonline (2016), 'CID must investigate Dzifa Attivor – PNC', 29 April 2016, http://citifmonline.com/2016/04/29/cid-must-investigate-dzifa-attivor-pnc/ (accessed 2 February 2019).

CPR (2013), 'Calls for government to stop running GYEEDA is misplaced and premature', *Center for Policy Research* (CPR) press release 24 May 2013, https://www.modernghana.com/news/465455/calls-for-government-to-stop-running-gyeeda-is-misplaced-and.html (accessed 7 February 2019).

Ghana Heritage Post (2007), 'Court quashes CHRAJ ruling against Anane', 13 March 2007, https://www.ghanaweb.com/GhanaHomePage/NewsArchive/Court-quashes-CHRAJ-ruling-against-Anane-120704 (accessed 8 February 2019).

Ghanaian Chronicle (2005a), 'Lord Commey fights back', 7 December 2005, https://www.ghanaweb.com/GhanaHomePage/NewsArchive/Lord-Commey-fights-back-95659 (accessed 7 February 2019).

Ghanaian Chronicle (2005b), 'We have to believe Esseku – Kofi Wayo', 30 November 2005, https://www.ghanaweb.com/GhanaHomePage/NewsArchive/We-have-to-believe-Esseku-Kofi-Wayo-95256 (accessed 7 February 2019).

Ghanaian Chronicle (2005c), 'Anane is Hot!', 6 December 2005, https://www.ghanaweb.com/GhanaHomePage/NewsArchive/Anane-is-Hot-95594 (accessed 7 February 2019).

Ghanaian Chronicle (2005d), 'Woman at the centre of Anane's scandal to testify', 1 February 2005, https://www.ghanaweb.com/GhanaHomePage/NewsArchive/Woman-At-The-Centre-Of-Anane-s-Scandal-To-Testify-74506 (accessed 7 February 2019).

Ghanaian Chronicle (2005e), 'Govt uncomfortable with 'darling boy' Anane', 6 May 2005, https://www.ghanaweb.com/GhanaHomePage/NewsArchive/Govt-Uncomfortable-With-Darling-Boy-Anane-80835 (accessed 7 February 2019).

Ghanaian Chronicle (2006), 'End of the road for Anane?', 29 September 2006, https://www.ghanaweb.com/GhanaHomePage/NewsArchive/End-of-road-for-Anane-111340 (accessed 7 February 2019).

Ghanaian Chronicle (2008), 'Anane to make a comeback', 5 February 2008, https://www.ghanaweb.com/GhanaHomePage/NewsArchive/Anane-to-make-a-comeback-138748 (accessed 7 February 2019).

GhanaWeb (2006), 'Anane's friend admits remitting Ms O'Brien', 20 March 2006, https://www.ghanaweb.com/GhanaHomePage/SportsArchive/Anane-s-Friend-Admits-Remitting-Ms-O-Brien-101239 (accessed 7 February 2019).

GhanaWeb (2008), 'NDC rejects Anane's nomination', 29 February 2008, https://www.ghanaweb.com/GhanaHomePage/NewsArchive/NDC-rejects-Anane-s-nomination-140068 (accessed 7 February 2019).

GhanaWeb (2013), 'Zoomlion, Rlg and others to refund over GH₵200 million to state', 22 July 2013 https://www.ghanaweb.com/GhanaHomePage/NewsArchive/Zoomlion-Rlg-and-others-to-refund-over-GH-200-million-to-State-280174 (accessed 7 February 2019).

GhanaWeb (2015), 'NDC girl grabs GH¢ 3.6 million bus branding contract', 18 December 2015, https://www.ghanaweb.com/GhanaHomePage/NewsArchive/NDC-girl-grabs-GH-3-6-million-bus-branding-contract-401816 (accessed 7 February 2019).

GhanaWeb (2016), 'OccupyGhana demands prosecution in Smarttys bus deal', 23 November 2016, https://www.ghanaweb.com/GhanaHomePage/NewsArchive/OccupyGhana-demands-prosecution-in-Smarttys-bus-deal-489450 (accessed 7 February 2019).

GhanaWeb (2017), 'Bus branding scandal cost us 2016 election – Twum Boafo', 23 March 2017, https://www.ghanaweb.com/GhanaHomePage/NewsArchive/Bus-branding-scandal-cost-us-2016-election-Twum-Boafo-521608 (accessed 8 February 2019).

GNA (2005a), 'CPP calls for investigation into "Kickback at Castle"', *Ghana News Agency*, 30 November 2005, https://www.ghanaweb.com/GhanaHomePage/NewsArchive/CPP-calls-for-inquiry-into-Kickback-at-Castle-95278 (accessed 8 February 2019).

GNA (2005b), 'Presidency denies taking kickbacks', *Ghana News Agency*, 23 November 2005, https://www.ghanaweb.com/GhanaHomePage/NewsArchive/Presidency-denies-taking-kickbacks-94806 (accessed 8 February 2019).

GNA (2005c), 'NPP youth demonstrate in support of Anane', *Ghana News Agency*, 14 February 2005, https://www.ghanaweb.com/GhanaHomePage/NewsArchive/NPP-youth-demonstrate-in-support-of-Anane-75401 (accessed 8 February 2019).

GNA (2006a), 'Ghana integrity initiative urges Anane to quit', *Ghana News Agency*, 18 September 2006, https://www.ghanaweb.com/GhanaHomePage/NewsArchive/Ghana-Integrity-Initiative-urges-Anane-to-quit-110758 (accessed 8 February 2019).

GNA (2006b), 'Judgement day postponed!', *Ghana News Agency*, 24 August 2006, https://www.ghanaweb.com/GhanaHomePage/NewsArchive/Judgement-Day-Postponed-109490?channel=D1 (accessed 8 February 2019).

GNA (2006c), 'Anane probe ends: ruling on August 24', *Ghana News Agency*, 8 July 2006, https://www.ghanaweb.com/GhanaHomePage/NewsArchive/Anane-Probe-Ends-Ruling-on-August-24-107012 (accessed 8 February 2019).

GNA (2006d), 'I later got to know about money transfer – Anane', *Ghana News Agency*, 27 April 2006, https://www.ghanaweb.com/GhanaHomePage/entertainment/I-later-got-to-know-about-money-transfers-Anane-103337?channel=D1&channel=D1&channel=D1 (accessed 8 February 2019).

GNA (2006e), 'CPP calls for investigation into 'Kickback' allegation', *Ghana News Agency*, 6 January 2006, https://www.ghanaweb.com/GhanaHomePage/NewsArchive/CPP-calls-for-investigation-into-Kickback-allegation-97192 (accessed 8 February 2019).

GNA (2013), 'Five member committee to review operations of GYEEDA inaugurated', *Ghana News Agency*, 13 April 2013, https://www.modernghana.com/news/458370/five-member-committee-to-review-operations-of-gyeeda-inaugur.html (accessed 8 February 2019).

Golooba-Mutebi, F. and D. Booth (2013), 'Bilateral cooperation and local power dynamics: the case of Rwanda', Commissioned Study, September 2013, London: ODI (Overseas Development Institute).

GraphicOnline (2015), 'Dzifa Attivor resigns over 116 branded buses', 23 December 2015, https://www.graphic.com.gh/news/general-news/dzifa-attivor-resigns-over-116-branded-buses.html (accessed 7 February 2019).

GraphicOnline (2016), 'A-G presents bus branding documents to OccupyGhana', 10 May 2016, https://www.graphic.com.gh/news/general-news/a-g-presents-bus-branding-documents-to-occupyghana.html (accessed 7 February 2019).

Gyimah-Boadi, E. and C. Daddieh (1999), 'Economic reform and political liberalisation in Ghana and Cote d'Ivoire: a preliminary assessment of implications for nation building, in K. Mengisteab and C. Daddieh (eds), *State Building and Democratisation in Africa: Faith, Hope and Realities*, Westport, CT: Praeger.

Gyimah-Boadi, E. (2009), 'Another step forward for Ghana', *Journal of Democracy*, 20(2): 138–52.

Herbst, J. (1993), *The Politics of Political Reform in Ghana: 1982–1991*, Berkeley and Los Angeles: University of California Press.

Hope, R.K. Sr. and B. Chikulo (2000), 'Introduction', in K. Hope and B. Chikulo (eds), *Corruption and Development in Africa: Lessons from Country Case-Studies*, London: Palgrave Macmillan.

Josiah-Aryeh, N.A. (2008), *Inside Ghana's Democracy*, Central Milton Keynes: AuthorHouse.

Khan, M.H (1998), 'The role of civil society and patron–client networks in the analysis of corruption', in OECD/UNDP (ed.), *Corruption and Integrity Improvement Initiatives*, New York: UNDP, Management Development and Governance Division: 111–28.

Khan, M.H. (2010), *Political Settlements and the Governance of Growth-Enhancing Institutions*, Working Paper, London: SOAS.

Kjaer, A.M. (2015), 'Political settlements and productive sector policies: understanding sector differences in Uganda', *World Development*, 68.

Mbaku, J.M. (1997), *Institutions and Reform in Africa: The Public Choice Perspective*, Westport/CO: Praeger.

Mbaku, J.M. (2010), *Corruption in Africa: Causes, Consequences, and Clean-ups*, Lanham/MD: Lexington Books.

Ministry of Youth and Sports (2013), *Report*, Accra: Ministerial Impact Assessment & Review Committee on Ghana Youth Employment and Entrepreneurial Agency (GYEEDA).

Mkandawire, Thandika. 2010. 'Aid, Accountability, and Democracy in Africa', *Social Research*, 77(4): 1149-1182.

Mkandawire, Thandika. 1999. 'Crisis Management and the Making of "Choiceless Democracies" in Africa.' *The State, Conflict and Democracy in Africa.* Ed. R. Joseph. Boulder: Lynne Rienner.

Myjoyonline (2005a), 'I will not resign – Esseku', 29 November 2005, https://www.ghanaweb.com/GhanaHomePage/NewsArchive/I-Will-Not-Resign-Esseku-95181 (accessed 7 February 2019).

Myjoyonline (2005b), 'Esseku's allegations beyond doubt', 28 November 2005, https://www.modernghana.com/news/90999/essekus-allegations-beyond-doubt.html (accessed 7 February 2019).

Myjoyonline (2013a), 'Ghana losing millions every month through questionable contracts at GYEEDA', 20 May 2013, https://www.modernghana.com/news/464796/ghana-losing-millions-every-month-through-questionable-contr.html (accessed 7 February 2019).

Myjoyonline (2013b), 'Corruption at GYEEDA: I will prove sceptics wrong, Minister assures', 12 April 2013, https://www.ghanaweb.com/GhanaHomePage/NewsArchive/Corruption-at-GYEEDA-I-will-prove-skeptics-wrong-Minister-assures-270843 (accessed 7 February 2019).

Myjoyonline (2013c), 'GYEEDA: parliament has details on how 200m was spent – Sports Minister', 26 March 2013, https://www.modernghana.com/news/455139/gyeeda-parliament-has-details-on-how-about-200m-was-spent-.html (accessed 7 February 2019).

Myjoyonline (2013d), 'EOCO to retrieve all monies last through GYEEDA scandal', 25 November 2013, https://www.myjoyonline.com/news/2013/November-25th/eoco-to-retrieve-all-monies-lost-through-gyeeda-scandal.php (accessed 7 February 2019).

Myjoyonline (2015a), 'Govt spends over 3.6 million on re-branding of metro mass buses', 16 December 2015, https://www.myjoyonline.com/news/2015/December-16th/govt-spends-over-36-million-on-re-branding-of-metro-mass-buses.php (accessed 7 February 2019).

Myjoyonline (2015b), 'Audio: we charged ¢ 100 to brand 1 Mahama bus, not ¢2000', 18 December 2015, http://www.myjoyonline.com/news/2015/december-18th/audio-we-charged-100-to-brand-1-mahama-bus-not-2000.php (accessed 7 February 2019).

Myjoyonline (2017), 'Supreme Court orders A-G to surcharge public officers', 14 June 2017, https://www.myjoyonline.com/news/2017/june-14th/supreme-court-orders-a-g-to-surcharge-public-officers.php (accessed 7 February 2019).

Ninsin, K.A (2006), 'Introduction: the contradictions and ironies of elections in Africa,' *African Development*, 31(3): 1–10.

North, D.C., J.J. Wallis and B.R. Weingast (2009), *Violence and Social Orders: A Conceptual Framework for Interpreting Recorded Human History*, New York: Cambridge University Press.

OccupyGhana (2016a), 'Smarttys documents – how the Ministry of Finance, Ministry of Transport, Accountant General and Bank of Ghana breached the Constitution and the law, just to pay Smarttys', media release, 22 May 2016, http://www.occupygh.org/education/smarttys-documents-how-the-ministry-of-finance-ministry-of-transport-accountant-general-and-bank-of-ghana-breached-the-constitution-and-the-law-just-to-pay-smarttys/ (accessed 7 February 2019).

OccupyGhana (2016b), 'Smarttys deal – role of the Office of the President (Flagstaff House)', media release, 15 May 2016, http://www.occupygh.org/civil-rights/smarttys-deal-role-of-the-office-of-the-president-flagstaff-house/ (accessed 7 February 2019).

OccupyGhana (2016c), 'Behold the Smarttys bus branding "contract"', media release, 12 May 2016, http://www.occupygh.org/media-release/behold-the-smarttys-bus-branding-contract/ (accessed 7 February 2019).

Oduro, F., A. Mohammed, and M. Ashon (2014), 'A dynamic mapping of the political settlement in Ghana', *ESID Working Paper*, No. 28.

Setiyono, B. and R.H. McLeod (2010), 'Civil society organisations' contribution to anti-corruption movement in Indonesia, *Bulletin of Indonesian Economic Studies*, 46(3): 347–70.

The Enquirer (2005a), 'Castle in crisis over kickback scandal', 24 November 2005, https://www.ghanaweb.com/GhanaHomePage/NewsArchive/Castle-in-crisis-over-kickback-scandal-94899 (accessed 7 February 2019).

The Enquirer (2005b), 'NPP's looting brigade', 28 November 2005, https://www.modernghana.com/news/90949/npps-looting-brigade.html (accessed 7 February 2019).

The Enquirer (2005c), 'Castle hijacks kickbacks', 22 November 2005, https://www.ghanaweb.com/GhanaHomePage/NewsArchive/Castle-Hijacks-Kickbacks-94785 (accessed 7 February 2019).

The Enquirer (2005d), 'We have the tapes to prove it', 24 November 2005, https://www.ghanaweb.com/GhanaHomePage/NewsArchive/We-Have-the-Tapes-To-Prove-It-Enquirer-94902 (accessed 7 February 2019).

The Enquirer (2005e), 'Anane's senseless apocalypse', 8 July 2005, https://www.ghanaweb.com/GhanaHomePage/NewsArchive/Anane-s-Senseless-Apocalypse-86039 (accessed 7 February 2019).

The Enquirer (2005f), 'CHRAJ probes Anane', 2 June 2005, https://www.ghanaweb.com/GhanaHomePage/NewsArchive/CHRAJ-Probes-Anane-82826 (accessed 7 February 2019).

The Enquirer (2005g), 'More Wahala for Anane', 16 May 2005, https://www.ghanaweb.com/GhanaHomePage/NewsArchive/More-Wahala-for-Anane-81570 (accessed 7 February 2019).

The Scandal (2013), 'Ministers clash over GYEEDA probe', 2 July 2013, https://www.ghanaweb.com/GhanaHomePage/NewsArchive/Ministers-clash-over-GYEEDA-probe-278450 (accessed 7 February 2019).

The Statesman (2005a), 'What crisis?', 30 November 2005, https://www.ghanaweb.com/GhanaHomePage/NewsArchive/What-crisis-95257 (accessed 7 February 2019).

The Statesman (2005b), 'Esseku to resign', 25 November 2005, https://www.ghanaweb.com/GhanaHomePage/NewsArchive/Esseku-to-resign-94957 (accessed 7 February 2019).

The Statesman (2006a), 'Anane's men attack The Statesman', 24 September 2006, https://www.ghanaweb.com/GhanaHomePage/NewsArchive/Anane-s-Men-Attack-The-Statesman-111042 (accessed 7 February 2019).

The Statesman (2006b), 'Anane demands apology from CHRAJ', 21 September 2006, https://www.ghanaweb.com/GhanaHomePage/NewsArchive/Anane-demands-apology-from-CHRAJ-110895 (accessed 7 February 2019).

TV3 (2016), 'GHS3.6m Smarttys bus branding contract approved within 24 hours', TV3 Network, 13 May 2016, https://3news.com/ghs3-6m-smarttys-bus-branding-contract-approved-within-24-hours/ (accessed 7 February 2019).

van de Walle, N. (2001), *African Economies and the Politics of Party Crisis, 1979–1999*, Cambridge: Cambridge University Press.

Wampler, B. (2012), 'Entering the state: civil society activism and participatory governance in Brazil,' *Political Studies*, 60: 341–62.

WF & CDD (2018), 'The cost of politics in Ghana', Westminster Foundation for Democracy and Centre for Democratic Development (Ghana), Accra: Centre for Democratic Development.

Whitfield, L. (2011), 'Growth without economic transformation: economic impacts of Ghana's political settlement', DIIS Working Paper, No 28.

3. 'Big Men' and poor voters: political corruption and elections in Kenya

Michelle D'Arcy

NYORO VS KABOGO

In the 2013 gubernatorial election in Kiambu County, Kenya, the voters had a choice between two main candidates who could not have been more contrasting. One, James Nyoro, was an academic with policy experience at the national level, who had managed the Rockefeller Foundation office in Nairobi and been involved in drafting the country's 'Vision 2030' development plan. The other, William Kabogo, was a sitting MP and 'self-made' millionaire, whose money was alleged to have come from drug trafficking (Mayoyo 2010). Nyoro ran a policy-focused campaign, outlining his vision for transforming Kiambu into the 'Singapore of East Africa'. Kabogo engaged in vote-buying and highlighted his record of delivering clientelist goods (Cornell and D'Arcy 2014). In the election Kabogo won the governorship with 487,631 votes to Nyoro's 241,658 (IEBC 2013).

In a pattern that is seen again and again in Kenya, and indeed in elections in many developing countries, an educated policy professional and newcomer is beaten by the incumbent politician, an alleged criminal who is using vote-buying and clientelist tactics in his campaign strategy. Why is this the case? Why do voters endorse corrupt candidates? These questions, at the level of voter choice, are part of a broader puzzle: why has the introduction of democratic institutions in Africa been status quo attenuating, rather than a stimulus for reform and change? Why has the introduction of democratic institutions not led to reduced corruption?

The first half of this chapter will analyse the uses of power-preserving corruption in election campaigns in Kenya and examine the reasons why it is a successful strategy for winning elections. Against the expectations of those who believe democracy should decrease corruption (Lake and Baum 2001, Chang et al. 2010, Persson et al. 1997), and in line with those who argue that corruption increases after democratic transitions (Bäck and Hadenius 2008, Montinola and Jackman 2002, Sung 2004), it will show how many forms of power-preserving corruption – especially clientelism and vote-buying – are common in Kenyan elections, and argue that this is because both voters and politicians are trapped in a collective action problem where this behaviour is rational for both actors. In addition to these rational choice explanations that emphasises the incentives for poor voters to engage in clientelism (Collier and Vicente 2012, Gutiérrez-Romero 2014), it will emphasise how winning an election in Kenya, is also explained by the need to fulfil culturally determined expectations: the 'Big Man' image. The 'Big Man' acts as a patron within the community, dispensing favours and looking after members of the community in return for their political support (de Sardan 1999: 43–5).

The second half of this chapter will explore the ways in which creating this image requires very significant amounts of money. In a context of poor campaign funding for parties and weak party finance controls, there are strong incentives for politicians to engage in extractive corruption to finance their campaigns. To give an example, in 2013 the winning candidate in the gubernatorial election in Kilifi spent an estimated 40 million Kenyan shillings (approximately 480,000 US dollars at the time) on his campaign, more than half the total amount of public funding given to his party, the Orange Democratic Movement.[1] The enforcement of the law regulating political financing is poor: in an assessment of seven African states the Institute for Democracy and Electoral Assistance (IDEA) found that Kenya had the largest discrepancy between law and practice (Ohman 2016: 3). Thus, the power-preserving forms of corruption witnessed during elections fuel extractive corruption before elections. Cumulatively, these observations suggest that

[1] Data on public funding of parties is available from the Office of the Registrar of Political Parties (http://www.orpp.or.ke/index.php/en/services/funding-and-political-parties).

elections – through the expectations of voters and the need for extensive campaign financing – are one of the significant drivers of political corruption in Kenya.

The argument is illustrated with evidence provided from interviews conducted in Kenya shortly after the 2013 gubernatorial elections. The interviews were held in July 2013 with candidates, campaign officials, experts and journalists in four counties: Kiambu, Nakuru, Mombasa and Kilifi. These were chosen because of their diverse socio-economic, ethnic and political profiles (for more detail on case selection see Cornell and D'Arcy 2014, D'Arcy and Cornell 2016). These were the inaugural elections of governors following the introduction of devolution under the 2010 Constitution.

The interview data was analysed using qualitative content analysis, whereby interview audio records were transcribed and coded to uncover major themes. Most of the interviews were recorded, and the majority of the interviewees requested anonymity. The interviews provided a rich description of the ways in which elections are won in Kenya. Interviews are quoted at some length to preserve the original wording and meaning of interviewees, and to fully exploit the strength of this kind of data in shedding light on the ground reality of the elections in Kenya, which can be overlooked by the use of other methods.

Observers expected these gubernatorial elections to mark a change in Kenyan politics, attracting candidates with more managerial and professional experience, who would focus on delivering development (Chome 2015: 300). However, these elections followed existing patterns of political mobilisation, and lend support to the suggestion that these trends are general. While acknowledging the limitations of the interview material in terms of generalisability, other studies have found similar patterns in other African, and indeed developing, countries (Cheeseman 2015, Cheeseman and Klaas 2018, Lindberg 2003, Persson 2017).

POWER-PRESERVING CORRUPTION

The most visible form of corruption in Kenyan elections is vote-buying, which, as discussed in the introduction to this volume, is a power-preserving form of corruption. This section will argue that engaging in vote-buying is key to electoral success in Kenya, and later sections will argue that the funds used for campaigning are most likely stemming from compromised sources. While the literature has often presented vote-buying as a straightforward, targeted, strategic and rational transaction between the politician and the voter (Collier and Vicente 2012, Gutiérrez-Romero 2014), the reasons behind it are, according to our interviewees, a complex interaction between the rational incentives created by poverty and wealth disparities, and a political culture that is connected to projecting the image of being a 'Big Man'.

Vote-Buying and Creating the Image of a 'Big Man'

> When we go there, hoping that I could help them learn how to fish. But they wanted fish and they wanted to be promised more fish.
>
> Gubernatorial candidate, Kilifi

Poverty obviously creates the opportunity for the politician to engage in vote-buying, as people with very little are willing to sell their vote. However, it also enables voters to make demands from politicians. As a candidate in Mombasa said of his experience on the campaign trail: 'When you try to persuade a voter to "go out and vote" he says "ah wapi pesa?" – give me money, I go and vote.' According to another candidate: 'Without having money to hand out, politicians cannot go "down to the grass roots" and campaign among the voters.' Poverty and wealth disparities create both the incentive and the opportunity for voters to ask for money from politicians.

This highlights a striking paradox: the relatively cheap cost of a vote versus the very significant cost of winning an election. Votes in Kilifi, according to the local journalist quoted above, could be bought for as little as 50–100 shillings (½–1 US dollar), but the winning candidate used 10 million – one quarter of his total campaign spending – for distribution on the last day of the election.[2] The cheapness of an individual vote highlights the significant resource gap between the voters and those seeking to be their representatives. Vote-buying has been found to be common in

---

[2] Campaign funding figures were reported by a local journalist. Without public reporting mechanisms on campaign spending it is impossible to verify these figures.

African democracies and to be especially prevalent in poor areas (Jensen and Justesen 2014: 220).

These demands are reinforced by the political culture. Africanists have long observed that many African societies are socially and politically constructed around 'Big Man' politics, where certain men within the community act as patrons, dispensing favours and looking after members of the community in return for their political support (Bayart 1993). This political culture has its origins in the traditional institutions of the pre-colonial period, and it has been reinforced by colonial and post-colonial strategies of rule (on Kenya, see de Smedt 2009: 583–6). In particular, Kenya's first president, Jomo Kenyatta, harnessed established practices of patronage in a manner that reinforced and legitimised his rule, but this had the consequence of solidifying 'the impression that the suitability of a leader was related to their wealth' (Cheeseman 2015: 64).

While culturalist arguments can be seen as problematic for their essentialist character, multiple interviewees reported that, from their point of view, cultural expectations were a central factor in shaping politicians' behaviour. As one candidate in Mombasa explained:

> You know it's our tradition in the Mijikenda. When you go somewhere, you have to give something to the elders, the mothers. It's not even bribery … when you come, you will not come empty-handed. You will come with something in your hand. So, this African culture that we had has also affected our politics in the sense that you cannot go and see people down there and talk to them and leave them empty-handed.

The need to project an image as a 'Big Man' was visible in the election campaigns of most of the candidates in the cases, and in all of the winning ones. A key part of the role of a 'Big Man' is to be the person in the community that people can approach to fix their problems, and candidates must find ways to signal to voters that they are such a 'Big Man'. To create this image, they engaged in power-preserving forms of corruption – especially vote-buying and clientelism – both of which required very large amounts of money.

Vote-buying was the most common strategy as it solved voters' survival problems, at least for one day. As one of the candidates for election in Kilifi, one of the poorest counties in Kenya, expressed it:

> The community is very poor. They have immediate needs. So, anybody who is poor is desperate, and anybody who is desperate and has despaired, they like quick-fix kind of solutions. But at that moment they are talking to a political candidate and he says 'Fine, I've just had your request but for now hold here 500 bob, maybe you can.' (The voter) says 'thank you very much I did not even have some meal for the evening'. So that kind of person is remembered more and has already the quick-fix solution, and he is the hero for the day.

As a result, according to interviewees, vote-buying is an integral part of Kenyan elections. As a local journalist put it: 'How do you influence them (the voters)? You just give them 50 shillings, 100 shillings, and you get the vote. It's just simple like that.'

A critical significance of handing out money in campaigns, in a context where poverty puts a premium on survival today and wealth disparities make it rational for voters to demand money, is to signal to voters what kind of candidate you are: a candidate who is a 'Big Man' who will solve their immediate problems. As the candidate in Kilifi put it, even if you promise to 'help them learn how to fish' it is not persuasive because 'they wanted fish and they wanted to be promised more fish'. His opponent in Kilifi literally undertook this approach as he was handing out pieces of fish and bags of maize the day before the election.

Money matters, as shown in these examples, because it enables politicians to signal to voters that they are 'Big Men' who can solve their basic survival needs today, and so might be more likely to do so in the future. This leads to a political culture where candidates are judged by their financial resources. It becomes the metric used by voters to judge the extent to which candidates are able to 'sort out their problems'. Experimental studies have supported this conclusion that money handouts matter as a signalling device for future clientelist intentions (Kramon 2016).

Clientelism and Patronage

The second form of power-preserving corruption employed in Kenyan elections is clientelism and patronage. As in the previous section, this section will argue that these practices are essential to winning elections in Kenya. Emphasising their record of delivering clientelist goods and patronage for the community was a key message in the incumbents' campaigns. As a campaign official in Kiambu said:

> We used to remind our people; let's go within the track record of Kabogo. Since 1997 what did Kabogo do for you guys? He used to supply you guys with water, roads, electricity, and so on and so and so. Kabogo used to do other projects also to women, in terms of collecting about ten ladies, giving them finances to start their own businesses, the youths to start their car wash, the small, small projects.

One of the most critical forms of patronage in the African context is jobs (van de Walle 2007: 3). As a campaign official in Nakuru explained it: 'Maybe you don't have job, or you are a widow. You have your kid, he has performed well in high school. Maybe you don't have a job, you go there, "Mzee, I want to ask for a request, just give my guy a job."' The winning candidate in Nakuru was able to say he had responded to such requests in his role as chief of the Administration Police. According to one of his campaign officials, he had 'taken people to the police force' and 'employed so many people'.

Having a clear track record of delivering patronage goods for the community is a key advantage for incumbent politicians. At the same time, those who had held positions in government and not delivered were at a disadvantage. For example, a journalist in Kilifi, discussing an experienced politician running for the governorship, said:

> Francis Baya is not new, but Francis Baya had a record that he had not delivered on his constituency level. People expected that while he had served as an administrator at the level of provincial commissioner and as assistant minister for immigration, he was in a better position to have influence and bring development down to his constituency. But the time that he was serving he did not fare well. So that was his disadvantage at that time.

The cultural expectation that politicians act as 'Big Men' makes accessibility and visibility on the ground premium qualities for candidates. If you want a politician capable of solving problems, you need someone who is visible to you and easy to access. As a candidate in Mombasa expressed it: 'If the voters say of a candidate "no I've not heard of him" then that will play against you because even if you are good, we don't know you.' People must know you and you must be approachable to them. In Mombasa, one of the disadvantages that the runner-up candidate faced was that he was seen to be too 'aloof' and, according to a local journalist, people felt that: 'If he comes to power, then people will not now be able to greet him easily.' In Nakuru, according to a campaign official, tribal elders (wazee) objected to a candidate within their party because they saw him as too young and educated, with the consequences that if he became deputy governor, according to a campaign official, 'the doors to those wazees will be closed'.

Building up this level of visibility and an image of accessibility requires extensive and expensive grass-roots campaigning. You must begin investing early in spreading the word about your candidature. As a senior party official planning to run in the next election explained:

> If I want to stand, definitely I will start by talking to the people. You know in Kenya, you buy someone a drink like Tusker then you tell him 'My friend can you go and tell your people in the village I want to be your MP next elections.' So that's how it spreads.

Candidates try to tap into existing social networks by targeting youth groups, women's groups and traders' associations. They make donations to churches in return for the chance to address congregations. Although these may be standard campaigning activities in many polities, their purpose in the Kenyan context is to persuade voters that the candidate is known to them personally and is accessible to them through their social networks.

This kind of campaigning, to build up the visibility and the impression of accessibility, requires very large amounts of money because of the large distances and large populations involved. This necessitates well-resourced campaign teams and adequate transport to move them around. For example, as one candidate explained in relation to one of the most populous counties in Kenya:

> Kiambu County has 12 constituencies with a population of close to 860,000 people. There are 60 wards, so there are about 5 wards in every constituency so there are 60 wards. So, in a ward there will be several villages, so you imagine that you have to be known and touched and seen and heard in any of those villages, I think the financial requirements really is beyond what you can imagine.

In Mombasa, a local party chairman reported that they needed at least 360 people and 108 vehicles to run a campaign in the city. There are also the usual costs of publicity, such as posters (which your opponent may repeatedly tear down, and you will have to replace). Overall, this leads to a situation where, according to a civil society representative: 'When you have money, you are able to reach more people more frequently.'

Carrying out the deep, penetrative grass-roots mobilisation of the nature necessary to convince voters that you are a 'Big Man' of the people, able to solve their problems, visible and accessible, is very challenging and expensive. In a context where, as described above, the areas candidates need to cover can be huge, substantial sums of money are needed to approach people. Cultural expectations and the context of poverty, where everyone wants their politician to be a 'Big Man' who can solve their problems, perpetuates the importance of money in elections. As later sections argue, this need for large amounts of money to win re-election creates incentives for extractive corruption.

Bribery

In addition to the use of vote-buying and clientelism, as demanded by voters, bribing public officials and the media was another key form of power-preserving corruption employed in the elections, according to our interview sources. This included the bribing of party officials for party nominations; bribing the media to 'sing your praises twenty-four hours a day' (according to a civil society representative); and the bribing of officials from the Independent Elections and Boundary Commission (IEBC).

In Mombasa, for example, the chairman of one of the opposing political parties alleged that the winning candidate had used his influence to get two of his associates onto the IEBC. According to him, this meant that when complaints were directed to the IEBC: 'Tomorrow morning a bag of money goes to him and the guy goes on rigging.' A gubernatorial candidate in Mombasa reported being approached a number of times with offers to pay their campaign expenses if they either joined their opponent's campaign or withdrew from the race.

This illegal use of money can increase the need for money for legal purposes even further, in an escalating cycle. Candidates must ensure that their agents are adequately paid, because if they are not there is the risk that they may be bought by their opponent and then they will not monitor the voting and tallying at the polling stations correctly.

Perhaps the most serious example of this illegal use of money and the need for money to respond is the use of violence and intimidation, requiring serious security on the campaign trail. In its mildest form, a journalist in Mombasa gave an example of a meeting where one of the candidates hired men to chant his name at the meeting so loudly that the other candidate could then not take the stage. In its most sinister form, the serious violence in Kilifi in the run-up to the election, where a number of police officers and IEBC officials were killed, was without doubt politically motivated (Willis and Chome 2014). In this context, all candidates need to invest in security, both to protect themselves, and to signal to their rivals that they are not to be messed with.

Overall, various forms of power-preserving corruption have become an integral part of elections in Kenya. Some of these practices are demanded by voters, and candidates not engaging in them are punished at the polls. As has been observed elsewhere in Africa (and beyond), these practices are driven by a combination of cultural expectations within the 'Big Man' mould of African politics (Bayart 1993, Cheeseman and Klaas 2018) and the rational incentives facing poor voters (Kitschelt and Wilkinson 2007).

EXTRACTIVE CORRUPTION: FUNDING ELECTION CAMPAIGNS

> If you want to join politics, you must know how to play to the rules of the game.
> National campaign official.

As the above analysis makes clear, it is expensive to run the kind of campaign necessary to create the image of the kind of candidate that ordinary voters want. Although it is difficult to get precise figures for campaign financing, according to interviewees, they spent very considerably on their campaigns. The winning gubernatorial candidate in Kilifi, according to a rival candidate, spent 40 million Kenyan shillings (480,000 US dollars). In Nakuru, the winning candidate is alleged by his rival to have spent 100 million shillings (1.2 million US dollars), while in Mombasa the winning candidate spent 600 to 700 million shillings (7.1 to 8.3 million US dollars). Although these estimates come from rival candidates, who might be expected to inflate numbers, it has been reported that to become a governor a candidate should have at least 600 million shillings (7 million US dollars) to mount a successful campaign (Oduor 2017, see also Ng'etich 2013). As one candidate put it: 'The more endowed resource-wise, then the more you are likely to win.'

The context of low public campaign financing and lax implementation of spending limits helps to explain these very high figures. The levels of public funding of parties are determined by a formula, and the levels are low. For instance, for the year 2013–14, the largest party, the National Alliance (TNA) received 90 million shillings (1.1 million US dollars) (ORPP n.d.), less than what two candidates in the case studies are estimated to have spent. In terms of regulation of camp campaign financing, while the legal framework set out in the Election Campaign Financing Act 2013 is sound, detailing how parties should regulate spending internally, report on their spending, and giving the IEBC the ability to set overall spending limits, the law seems not to be properly implemented (Ohman 2016: 4, 9). This means that politicians must either be independently wealthy or be able to persuade some rich patron (an owner of private businesses) to back them. Usually they need to be and do both.

In the absence of sufficient public financing and of effective campaign financing limits, there are strong incentives for politicians to maximise their income between elections. As argued persuasively by Persson, the need to build a 'war chest' to fight elections increases the incentives for politicians to engage in corruption between elections (Persson 2017). In a context of crony capitalism – defined as 'the use of connections to public authority to facilitate private capital accumulation' (Beresford 2015: 230) – some of the main means of wealth accumulation in Kenya are the mechanisms of extractive corruption. Candidates engage in extractive corruption directly or indirectly via support of rich patrons/business people. These patrons are most likely to back candidates who they know will play by the existing patrimonial and crony capitalist rules of the game, whereby material goods are exchanged for political support. This further reinforces the advantages of those with the most resources and preserves the status quo.

Since Kenya's independence, as in most African countries, the state has played an important role in the economy and in access to economic goods, a condition that structural adjustment attempted but failed to reform (Swamy 1994: 1–3). As noted generally in the African context, high levels of state intervention in the economy has allowed politicians to use public resources both to enrich themselves and as the key currency in patrimonial relationships (van de Walle 2001: 113–52). The close relationship between political and economic power means that there is both dependence in the relationship between business and political elites – doing business on a day-to-day basis in Kenya requires strong patrimonial relationships with those in power – and opportunity, whereby both collude to extract resources from the state and via the state for their mutual benefit.

Extractive corruption has always been used to fund parties and elections but has increased after the introduction of multi-party democracy in 1992 (Mwangi 2008: 271). Four main forms of corruption have been identified as means of financing parties in the 1990s. First, Moi used parastatals as a source of political patronage and a way of funnelling money to his campaign (CGD 2005: 7–8). Second, the infamous Goldberg scandal showed how politicised banks, including the Central Bank of Kenya, were co-opted to channel funding for Moi's KANU party through payments to a shell company for fictious imports (Mwangi 2008: 273–4). Third, white elephant projects, such as the Turkwell Gorge project, have been a way for politicians to amass wealth for their political activities (CGD 2005: 8). Finally, the Ndungu report (from a commission established in 2003 to investigate the extra-legal allocation of public land to individuals and corporations) documented the ways in which land – the foundational economic resources in an agriculturally based economy – was used as a currency in inter-elite patronage through the illegal allocation of public land to powerful individuals and families (Southall 2005: 142–51).

Although Mwai Kibaki's defeat of Moi's chosen successor in 2002 raised hopes that corruption would decrease, this did not happen. One of the most infamous examples of extractive corruption in Kenya was the Anglo-Leasing scandal, which involved collusion between politicians and private sector actors in order to perpetrate fraud in public procurement. John Githongo, the former Permanent Secretary for Governance and Ethics turned whistleblower, who exposed the scandal, was told that the main purpose of the scheme was to raise money for Kibaki's party and election campaigns (Githongo 2005: 15). While other forms of extractive corruption used by Moi, such as white elephants, have been less visible under Kibaki and Kenyatta, procurement scandals continue to come to light.

Although the new 2010 constitution designed a number of mechanisms to reduce corruption, there is little evidence that it has reduced. Recently, an even bigger fraud case has come to light, as US$100 million is alleged to have been siphoned off through the manipulation of procurement contracts related to the National Youth Service (NYS) (Aglionby 2018). Since 2013, devolution is also alleged to have widened the scope and scale of fraud by adding an additional layer of public procurement at the county level (BTI 2016: 33).

The close connection between extractive corruption and election financing has at least two important implications for politics and society. First, the cost of campaigns has advantaged the political families in Kenya who have used their political power to amass wealth. An estimated half of total private wealth in Kenya is in the hands of influential political families (Nzioka and Namunane 2014). The most important of these is the Kenyatta family. Kenya's first president, Jomo Kenyatta, used his position as president to become one of the largest landowners in the country. The vast economic resources this gave his family (according to Forbes 2011, the Kenyatta family owns about 500,000 acres of prime land in different parts of the country) has translated into sustained political influence. His son Uhuru has been president of the republic since 2013. In the most recent election, the disparities in funding and wealth between Uhuru and his opponent, Raila Odinga, were influential factors in determining the August 2017 election and the rerun in October.

The Kenyatta family initially used its political position to gain economic wealth, which it now uses to preserve access to political power, which in turn is important for maintaining their economic position. For example, as president, Uhuru Kenyatta has fought against the implementation of land redistribution reforms that threaten his family's assets (D'Arcy and Nistotskaya 2019). The 2010 Constitution proposed introducing a ceiling for the amount of land an individual could hold, an obvious threat to the Kenyatta family. Kenyatta's government has used a range of tactics to stymie the implementation of this provision by blocking the necessary legislation and laying out an unclear and vague timeline for addressing the issue.

Second, elections have, I would argue, increased the mutual interdependence of politicians and wealthy patrons/businessmen. Often what is demanded in return is influence, something that is common to most polities. As a candidate in Mombasa put it: 'When somebody supports you, he wants to be your king-maker.' This candidate went on to elaborate how, in a previous campaign, 'some men came to me. They are telling me that, we are going to stand by you. We are going to fund you. But you do what we want.'

In the Kenyan context, what these expectations often consist of is receiving preferable deals, tenders and state contracts after the election. This seems to suggest that power lies in the hands of business, with politicians being no more than puppets. However, the fact that much wealth creation comes through the close relationship between politics and economics means that while politicians need business to fund their campaigns, business also needs willing political partners on the inside to collude with. As suggested by the examples cited above, such as the Anglo-Leasing scandal, business extracts public money with the collusion of politicians.

Furthermore, although elections have given business elites increased leverage through their campaign financing, they are also moments of insecurity as businesses must try to ensure they are backing the right candidate. If you back the wrong candidate, then, as a candidate in Kiambu explained, 'your [the patron's] business is put at stake'. This means that wealthy patrons prefer to work with incumbents who they know and have already worked with. Incumbents are known to know the rules of the game and to play by them. This is a disadvantage for non-incumbents, as a new candidate in Kilifi explained:

> Because I think as a new candidate, there is always a degree of uncertainty of the people who are the professionals.[3] Uncertainty to the extent that what policy are you going to come out with, how is it going to impact on what we are already enjoying for example. But if you are the incumbent you have got kind of an advantage because people know them.

However, the stakes are such that wealthy businesspeople will hedge their bets and give some support to all the leading candidates. According to a journalist in Mombasa, the brother of the winning candidate (and a wealthy businessman in his own right) also gave money to his brother's main rival. According to a gubernatorial candidate: 'In the final stages of the campaign they are looking at trends. They wait until the end and see who is the most popular and they start giving him more money.' Thus, the candidate perceived to be the likely winner gathers momentum in the final stages of the campaign, turning the perception into a reality.

The very large amount of money needed to win elections, and the available ways of getting it, explain why elections are status quo attenuating in poor countries such as Kenya. Money from businesses give advantage to incumbents and perpetuate the entrenchment of extractive corruption in the system. You must be rich and/or get access to the rich to win, and to do so you must either be playing by the existing patrimonial rules already or commit to do so in the future. Where the rules of the game involve close relationships between business and politics, this increases extractive corruption.

CONCLUSIONS

William Kabogo was the kind of politician the electorate in Kiambu wanted (and elected): a man who was very wealthy, albeit from dubious sources, who was known to dispense loans, cash and favours widely among the ordinary Kiambu voters. One of the most damning points made against his rival, James Nyoro, was that his

---

[3] Here, 'professionals' refers to academics, teachers, doctors and so on, people generally peripheral to the patrimonial relationships between politicians and business.

own brother was still a watchman. As a local journalist said: 'If Nyoro could not help his own brother get a better job how could he be expected to help anyone else in their daily struggles?'

This example, confirmed by the evidence from the other cases, makes clear how and why political corruption in Kenya is self-reinforcing and self-reproducing. Voters expect that their politicians conform to the prevailing cultural norms and the rational incentives within the system, demanding a certain kind of politician: one who actively engages in power-preserving corruption.

Nyoro also did not have the confidence of the local business community: they could not be assured he knew how to play by the rules of the game. To enter politics successfully you need very significant amounts of money, either from the business elite, or from your own personal resources (as in, you have to be a member of the business elite yourself). In either case you are yourself a beneficiary of the status quo or incentivised into relationships of mutual interdependence with those who are, and so have incentives to preserve it. Thus, for the most part, in Kenya the introduction of elections did not serve to challenge the entrenchment of political corruption but rather preserved it.

This unfortunate situation does not only arise because of flaws in the electoral process (although these certainly exist), but because, in a context of poverty and economic inequality, this is what voters demand, what is culturally prescribed and what is rational for them in the short term.

However, this does not mean either that democracy is not a desirable set of institutions for poor and unequal countries, or that further measures could not be taken to improve the quality of democracy. Having the right to choose, and to hold politicians accountable to whatever criteria the electorate sees fit, is undoubtedly preferable to having no choice at all. Measures to cap campaign spending could, if implemented properly, at least create a more equal playing field for a greater range of candidates from outside of the business elite. Nonetheless, we must acknowledge the ways in which elections serve to further entrench rather than challenge corruption in poor, unequal societies.

ACKNOWLEDGEMENTS

Sincere thanks to Ngala Chome, for excellent research assistance while conducting fieldwork, to Agnes Cornell, with whom I collaborated in conducting the interviews used in this chapter, and to Deric Chondo for help with transcription. I would also acknowledge the contribution, across the generations, of the women in my family: Bridget Smyth, Margot D'Arcy and Kay D'Arcy. The fieldwork was carried out with the aid of a grant from the Swedish International Centre for Local Democracy (ICLD).

REFERENCES

Aglionby, J. (2018), 'Senior Kenya officials arrested in $100m corruption probe', *Financial Times*, New York, 28 May 2018, https://www.ft.com/content/5b0d5dec-625b-11e8-90c2-9563a0613e56 (accessed 28 May 2018).

Bäck, H. and A. Hadenius (2008), 'Democracy and state capacity: exploring a J-shaped relationship', *Governance* 21(1): 1–24.

Bayart, J.-F. (1993), *The State in Africa: The Politics of the Belly*, London: Longman.

Beresford, A. (2015), Power, patronage, and gatekeeper politics in South Africa, *African Affairs*, 114(455): 226–48.

BTI (2016), 'Kenya Country Report', Bertelsmann Stiftung's Transformation Index (BTI), Gütersloh: Bertelsmann Stiftung, http://www.bti-project.org/fileadmin/files/BTI/Downloads/Reports/2016/pdf/BTI_2016_Kenya.pdf (accessed 4 April 2018).

CGD (2005), 'New law: political parties to be funded by the state', Nairobi: Centre for Governance and Democracy (CGD), Policy Brief 01/03.

Chang, E.C.C., M.A. Golden and S.J. Hill (2010), 'Legislative malfeasance and political accountability', *World Politics*, 62(02): 177–220.

Cheeseman, N. (2015), *Democracy in Africa: Successes, Failures and the Struggle for Political Reform*, Cambridge: Cambridge University Press.

Cheeseman, N. and B. Klaas (2018), *How to Rig an Election*, New Haven, CT: Yale University Press.

Chome, N. (2015), '"Devolution is only for development"? Decentralization and elite vulnerability on the Kenyan coast', *Critical African Studies*, 7(3): 299–316.

Collier, P. and P.C. Vicente (2012), 'Violence, bribery, and fraud: the political economy of elections in Sub-Saharan Africa', *Public Choice*, 153(1–2): 117–47.

Cornell, A. and M. D'Arcy (2014), 'Plus ça change? County-level politics in Kenya after devolution', *Journal of Eastern African Studies*, 8(1): 173–91.

D'Arcy, M. and A. Cornell (2016), 'Devolution and corruption in Kenya: everyone's turn to eat?', *African Affairs* 115(459): 246–73.

D'Arcy, M. and M. Nistotskaya (2019), 'Intensified local grievances, enduring national control: the politics of land in the 2017 Kenyan Elections', *Journal of Eastern African Studies*, 13(2): 294–312.

de Sardan, J.P.O. (1999), 'A moral economy of corruption in Africa?', *Journal of Modern African Studies*, 37(1): 25–52.

de Smedt, J. (2009), '"No Raila, No Peace!" Big Man politics and election violence at the Kibera grassroots', *African Affairs*, 108(433): 581–98.

Forbes (2011), 'Uhuru Kenyatta', Forbes.com, https://www.forbes.com/lists/2011/89/africa-billionaires-11_Uhuru-Kenyatta_FO2Q.html (accessed 4 April 2018).

Githongo, J. (2005), 'Report on findings of graft in the government of Kenya', http://news.bbc.co.uk/2/shared/bsp/hi/pdfs/09_02_06_kenya_report.pdf (accessed 4 April 2018).

Gutiérrez-Romero, R. (2014), 'An inquiry into the use of illegal electoral practices and effects of political violence and vote-buying', *Journal of Conflict Resolution*, 58(8): 1500–1527.

IEBC (2013), 'Summary of results for governor. March 4th 2013 General Election', Nairobi: Independent Electoral and Boundaries Commission (IEBC), Updated 18 July 2013.

Jensen, P.S. and M.K. Justesen (2014), 'Poverty and vote buying: survey-based evidence from Africa', *Electoral Studies*, 33: 220–232.

Kitschelt, H. and S.I. Wilkinson (eds) (2007), *Patrons, Clients and Policies: Patterns of Democratic Accountability and Political Competition*, Cambridge: Cambridge University Press.

Kramon, E. (2016), 'Electoral handouts as information: explaining unmonitored vote buying', *World Politics*, 68(3): 454–98.

Lake, D.A. and M. Baum (2001), 'The invisible hand of democracy: political control and the provision of public services', *Comparative Political Studies*, 34: 587–621.

Lindberg, S.I. (2003), '"It's our time to chop': do elections in Africa feed neo-patrimonialism rather than counter-act it?', *Democratization*, 10(2): 121–40.

Mayoyo, P. (2010), 'Revealed: US dossier on Kenyan drug-lords', *Daily Nation*, Nairobi, 28 November 2010, https://www.nation.co.ke/news/politics/US-dossier-on-Kenya-drug-lords-/1064-1062196-7laonm/index.html (accessed 4 April 2018).

Montinola, G.R. and R.W. Jackman (2002), 'Sources of corruption: a cross-country study', *British Journal of Political Science*, 32: 147–70.

Mwangi, O.G. (2008), 'Political corruption, party financing and democracy in Kenya', *Journal of Modern African Studies*, 46(2), 267–85.

Ng'etich, J. (2013), 'Campaigns could cost Sh36 billion', *Standard Digital*, Nairobi, 6 January 2013, https://www.standardmedia.co.ke/article/2000074352/campaigns-could-cost-sh36-billion (accessed 4 April 2018).

Nzioka, P. and B. Namunane (2014), 'Political families own half of private wealth', *Daily Nation*, Nairobi, 20 February 2014, https://mobile.nation.co.ke/news/Kenyans-Wealth-Families-Politicians/1950946-2215578-format-xhtml-rdamn6/index.html (accessed 4 April 2018).

Oduor, E. (2017), 'Millions of dollars at play as Kenyans go into their most expensive election yet', *The East African*, Nairobi, 22 May 2017, https://www.theeastafrican.co.ke/news/ea/Millions-of-dollars-at-play-as-Kenyans-go-to-the-polls/4552908-3937572-qbjthez/index.html (accessed 21 November 2018).

Ohman, M. (2016), 'The state of political finance regulations in Africa', Stockholm: International IDEA, IDEA Discussion paper 16/2016.

ORPP (n.d.), 'Funding of political parties', Nairobi, Office of the Registrar of Political Parties (PRPP), http://www.orpp.or.ke/index.php/en/services/funding-and-political-parties (accessed 22 November 2018).

Persson, A. (2017), 'The democratic roots of corruption: how competitive elections without rule of law shape opportunities and incentives for corrupt exchange', paper presented at the Anxieties of Democracy workshop, Oxford, May 2017.

Persson, T., G. Roland and G. Tabellini (1997), 'Separation of powers and political accountability', *The Quarterly Journal of Economics*, 112(4): 1163–202.

Southall, R. (2005), 'The Ndungu report: land and graft in Kenya', *Review of African Political Economy*, 32(103): 142–51.

Sung, H.-E. (2004), 'Democracy and political corruption: a cross-national comparison', *Crime, Law and Social Change*, 41, 179–94.

Swamy, G. (1994), Kenya: structural adjustment in the 1980s, Washington: World Bank Publications, vol. 1238.

van de Walle, N. (2001), *African Economies and the Politics of Permanent Crisis, 1979–1999*, New York: Cambridge University Press.

van de Walle, N. (2007), 'The path from neopatrimonialism: democracy and clientelism in Africa today', Cornell: Cornell University, Mario Einaudi Centre for International Studies, Working Paper Series No. 3–07.

Willis, J. and N. Chome (2014), 'Marginalization and political participation on the Kenya coast: the 2013 elections', *Journal of Eastern African Studies*, 8(1): 115–34.

4. Congenitally conjoined and inseparable: politics and corruption in Nigeria

Emmanuel Oladipo Ojo, Vaclav Prusa and Inge Amundsen

FLAGRANT SYSTEMIC CORRUPTION

Nigerians claim, with a mixture of pride and embarrassment, that Nigeria is famous for three things: vast oil deposits, the Super Eagles football team and corruption. Nigeria has become a synonym for dysfunctional governance, systemic corruption, spam and scams. On a daily basis, Nigerian and international media report on mind-blowing cases of flagrant corruption that are hardly concealed and happen in plain sight.

Transparency International's Corruption Perceptions Index consistently ranks Nigeria as one of the most corrupt in the world, with little improvement over the last decade (TI 2018). Corruption is entrenched, systemic, and ranging from high-level political corruption down into the state bureaucracy and service delivery. Page (2018a: 1) argues that 'the scope and complexity of corruption in Nigeria is immense'.

One recent example of a high-level corruption case took place in October 2018, starting with the governor of the northern state of Kano being filmed when receiving (allegedly) US$5 million from some construction contractors. When an investigative online journal made the video public (Jaafar 2018), the governor denied all allegations and sued the journalists for doctoring the video and making false accusations. The law enforcement authorities then investigated the journalist not the governor, and the Kano House of Assembly set up an investigative panel to scrutinise the journalist.

Then, President Muhammadu Buhari openly endorsed the governor's second-term bid (Onwuka 2019), probably because the governor belongs to his party and the state was important for his re-election.

This episode is a good example of how political considerations shape the trajectory of corruption scandals in Nigeria. It also underscores the resilience of political corruption in the country, where the problem is inflated by the size of the economy (second biggest economy in Africa), population size (roughly 200 million), and an export-oriented economy with vast revenues from oil and gas (Africa's largest oil exporter). Despite some positive trends, like the relatively free media, a vibrant civil society, reasonably free elections, and so on, the justice system is twisted and gives the perpetrators impunity. Political corruption is a 'quasi-legitimised' tool to advance party, personal and political gains, and frequently all at the same time. The many corruption scandals support the often-repeated statement by Nigerians that 'corruption is in the national DNA' (Onomuakpokpo 2019).

Colonial and Dictatorial Corruption

Political corruption is not a recent phenomenon in Nigeria. A cursory glance at some colonial records shows that political office holders in colonial Nigeria did not only corruptly enrich themselves and engage in widespread nepotism; they used the instruments of power to perpetuate themselves and their cronies in office. In fact, the colonial 'bundling' of Nigeria, in blatant disrespect of the ethnic and tribal differences, laid the foundations for post-independence political corruption as the different tribes had to fight for influence and resources in this artificially created state.

For instance, in mid-1955, a series of allegations of political corruption were levied against the Eastern Region Government, and a commission of inquiry was appointed to 'make a formal inquiry into allegations of bribery and corruption in all branches of public life in the Eastern Region of Nigeria and to consider measures for the eradication of such bribery and corruption as may be found' (NAI 1955: 194). Some Eastern Region ministers were also indicted by the Colonial Office, which opined that 'the tradition of these people [ministers] is one in which public power is exercised for personal profit' (NAI 1955: 201).

Nigeria's last colonial Governor-General pointed out that 'Nigeria's great handicap is the rifeness of graft and corruption […] in every walk of life' (NAI 1960: 151). Indeed, in 1956, the Colonial Office opined that because of 'corruption of much of its political life, Nigeria will be unfit for independence for many years' (NAI 1956: 43).

With independence in 1960, Nigeria soon fell into civil war and military dictatorships, which further laid the foundations for weak governance and poor rule of law. There was a civilian interlude with President Shehu Shagari from 1979 to 1983, a civilian regime that launched huge industrial and infrastructure projects that quickly proved to be unsustainable and economically irrational, and reckless spending. Oil income and growing foreign debts allowed the civilian rulers to dole out contracts and favours and to siphon off profits and build political alliances. The Shagari administration was called 'the government of the contractors by the contractors and for the contractors' (Bagura 1986: 31).

From 1985 until 1998 the different military dictatorships only further entrenched the patterns of corruption, in addition to human rights abuse. One commentator lamented at the time that in Nigeria, 'corruption isn't part of government, it's the object of government' (Rupert 1998).

Current Political Corruption

Following the death of General Sani Abacha in June 1998 and a successful transition to civil rule midwifed by a military-led interim government, Olusegun Obasanjo became Nigeria's second democratically elected president in May 1999. Nigeria has since held five general elections, in 2003, 2007, 2011, 2015 and 2019. The first-ever handover of power from one elected civilian president to another took place in 2007 (within the same ruling party), and in 2015, Mohammadu Buhari, presidential candidate of the All Progressives Congress, defeated Goodluck Jonathan, marking the first time in the history of Nigeria an incumbent lost an election.

The general elections of 1999, 2003 and 2007 (plus a large number of by-elections) were all marred with irregularities, manipulations, fraud, violence, thuggery and armed gangs. However, as the Electoral Law was revamped and the Independent National Electoral Commission (INEC) was reformed by former

President Goodluck Jonathan, the elections of 2015 were considered relatively (in the Nigerian context) free and fair. The European Union (EU) observer mission reported that 'elections were marred by incidents of violence, abuse of incumbency [...] and attempts at manipulation [...] however no centralised systemic fraud was observed' (EUEOM 2015: 4).

The 2015 electoral change of government is, to some extent, explained by the prior fall in oil prices and the ensuing massive fall in government revenues and thus reduced possibilities for patronage prior to the elections (Amundsen 2017: 21). This demonstrates the importance of oil revenues for preserving power in Nigeria: when oil revenues fell and the extraction from this wealth fell with it (although temporarily), this contributed to the fall of the government.

For the 2019 general elections, the EU's observer mission cited 'serious operational shortcomings', and the level of violence was probably as high as in 2011 (officially 39 people were killed on election day and in addition more than 800 were killed during the campaigns and state elections). Vote-buying was more widespread than ever, with Buhari's All Progressives' Congress (APC) and his challenger Atiku Abubakar's People's Democratic Party (PDP) both being culpable (The Economist 2019).

In the following, we will outline some of the extractive political corruption mechanisms used in oil-rich Nigeria over the years of civilian rule from 1999 to date, with emphasis on the characteristically 'Nigerian way' of extractive political corruption, such as stealing from the vast oil revenues, the 'oaths of secrecy' and the 'security votes'. After this, we will in some more detail analyse the main forms of power-preserving political corruption mechanisms in Nigeria, as these are less known: vote-buying, the 'war chests' and the use of anti-corruption.

THE RESOURCE CURSE

There is little doubt that Nigeria's immense oil wealth has fuelled corruption in Nigeria. Thus, the 'resource curse' and subsequent 'rentierism' is one of the main factors pointed to in the literature explaining the persistently high levels of corruption in the country.

Among the other explanations forwarded are the related factors of clientelism, patronage, power concentration and secrecy in politics.

Most of the literature on the 'resource curse' has viewed Nigeria as a quintessential example of a resource-cursed country (see for instance Collier and Hoeffler 2001, Mähler 2010, Onapajo et al. 2015). According to Heller, what explains the resource curse are weak political institutions (2006: 24), and according to Mehlum et al. (2006: 1119) the main difference between 'the resource-blessed' and 'the cursed' is in the quality of institutions. Basically, the rents generated from mineral extraction and other easily accessible resources can either be channelled into the productive economy or be captured by the ruling elite for personal enrichment, status gain and power purposes.

Political scientists working on the theory thus emphasise that an abundance of natural resources tend to produce not only weak economic growth but also weak government institutions and weak mechanisms of checks and balances. This is because natural resource windfalls lead to an overexpansion of the public sector, patronage and clientelism (Robinson et al. 2005: 464). The resource rents provide power holders with both the incentives and the means to hold on to power (Amundsen 2014: 171).

In 2012, the respected former chairman of the Economic and Financial Crimes Commission (EFCC) Nuhu Ribadu described in a report how US$35 billion was lost to corruption in the oil sector over the preceding ten years (or more than an entire year's government spending). He described how officials from the Ministry of Petroleum, and representatives of state-owned and international oil companies such as Shell and Sinopec, created a closed system where oil concessions and profits were diverted to private and political use (Allison 2012).

A TAXONOMY OF EXTRACTIVE CORRUPTION

Mathew T. Page has recently developed 'A New Taxonomy for Corruption in Nigeria' (2018a), where he lists 20 vulnerable sectors and identifies and exemplifies 28 corruption tactics in Nigeria. Although his 'taxonomy' is not strictly analytical, it points to a number of methods of extraction that other researchers have also highlighted.

Security Votes and 'Treasonable Stealing'

One of the least sophisticated but most powerful strategies of extractive corruption in Nigeria is embezzlement of state funds. Nigerian elected officials, public servants and military leaders use state funds as 'personal ATMs' with little or no distinction between personal and official resources (Ijewereme 2015: 9, SaharaReporters 2015).

The problem with embezzlement is particularly severe at the subnational level as vast funds (about half of all government spending, some estimates say up to 60 per cent) are transferred from the federal government and managed by the 36 state governments. Although the governments at the federal level have made some steps towards political and economic reform to better control the use of state funds, federal authorities exercise minimum checks and balances. Many federal states resemble rather feudal states where governors rule with autonomy and spend the state funds as they please (Adeyemi 2012: 194–5).

One example of systemic embezzlement at the state level is so-called Security Votes. This is a relic of military rule, and the Security Vote funds are monthly allowances allocated to the 36 states for the purpose of funding security services. However, certain officials are disbursing the funds at their discretion, as the use is not subject to legislative oversight or independent audit because of its ostensibly sensitive nature (Page 2018b: 1, see also Egbo et al. 2012 and Meers 2018).

Given the lack of transparency of this fund, it is impossible to know how much is privately embezzled, how much is used for advancing political agendas and how much is used for legitimate security expenditures. Two examples can illustrate this.

In the early 2000s, the governor of Amambra state, besides embezzling funds directly, used Security Votes funds for his so-called 'Bakassi Boys', militants who spread political violence and were responsible for hundreds of extra-judicial killings and torture (Isaacs 2002). In 2014 in Bayelsa State, the 'Special Advisor to the Governor for Beautification' and the 'Senior Special Assistant for Research and Social Media' received from the 'security fund', clearly without any 'security' in mind but political patronage (Page 2018b: 14).

Military procurement fraud involves larger sums of money, as 'phantom contracts' in defence have included helicopters, fighter jets, and bombs and ammunition worth billions of dollars that were never supplied (Ogala 2018). One witness describes that he was paid for navy boats that had been already delivered by another supplier, but directly approved by two political presidential national security advisors (ibid.).

Inflating military contracts is another method of embezzling funds, also called 'treasonable stealing'. According to one news report:

> Within months after he resumed office, President Muhammadu Buhari set up the Committee to probe arms procurement in the Armed Forces. The committee, made up of serving and retired military officers, quickly went to work; investigated defence procurement from 2007 and unravelled large scale sleaze in the arms procurement process. The committee found that billions of dollars meant for the procurement of arms in the heat of the war against Boko Haram terrorists, were eventually traced to retired military officers, influential politicians, phantom contractors and others (Rabiu 2017).

A large volume of corrupt extraction also stems from non-military public procurement, especially large infrastructure projects. Between 60 and 75 per cent of the graft and corruption cases in Nigeria are procurement-related (Onwubiko 2018). One insider (a former minister) estimated that corruption in the country's public sector procurement process accounts for over 70 per cent of the total budgets (Vanguard 2017).

Procurement fraud can be found in all government procurement from a few paper boxes to multibillion infrastructure projects. Despite the enactment of the Public Procurement Act and increased fiscal responsibility through the Fiscal Responsibility Bill, and through the establishment of the Bureau of Public Procurement (all in 2007), which in theory should eliminate the direct influence of elected politicians in procurement, senior government officials retain direct or indirect procurement power.

Another extractive corruption strategy is awarding lucrative contracts to anonymous entities or shell companies. Despite the existence of the Public Procurement Act (2007), which amongst others stipulates conditions for single sourcing and for the involvement of political figures, these rules are blatantly ignored, and many public contracts end up with politically exposed persons. It is a widely held perception in the business community in Nigeria that in almost every contract bid at least one decision maker already has a preferred candidate. The business community has even publicly advised bidders to 'obtain insider contacts' to increase their chances (StartupTipsDaily 2017).

'Big Men' and 'Godfathers'

The Nigerian version of democracy is a case-example of neopatrimonialism, which is seen by many scholars as a defining feature of post-colonial African governance structures (see for instance Chabal and Daloz 1999, Eisenstadt 1973). Neopatrimonialism is the pervasive culture of one-man rule that concentrates de facto powers to the top of the hierarchy, disrespecting formal rules and procedures.

At the lower level, it is easy to spot crowds of 'petitioners' in front of the private houses, offices, or places of the *ogas* ('Big Men') of the Nigerian elite. A deliberate lack of devolution of power and near absence of delegation of even the simplest tasks to subordinates is a strategy to preserve the monopoly of influence at the top. This patron–client system bypasses the official bureaucracy through a system of personal connections at both the high and lower levels of power. The patrons profit directly by extracting money for the privilege of opening access to clients.

In addition, there are ethnic and other forms of clientelism. In the religiously divided, ethnically segregated and tribally structured power-houses of Nigerian politics, clientelism is much more than a localised handout of state resources. Clientelism penetrates the Nigerian political economy as a strategy to build a circle of dependents within an institution, elected office, private company, or even non-governmental organisations (NGOs).

Clientelism is a major driver behind growing inequality in Nigeria, as a rich class of well-connected individuals grow richer while the rest of the country stays desperately poor. As Oxfam (2017: 8) reported, 'the combined wealth of Nigeria's five richest men – US$29.9 billion – could end extreme poverty at the national level'.

In the same vein, 'godfatherism' is a form of clientelism that is a foundational feature of Nigerian politics (HRW 2007, Sule et al.

2018). A godfather is a billionaire sponsoring anointed candidates for elections at all levels in return for political favours and advantages. The intention of the godfather is to rule by proxy. Sometimes, godfathers are not qualified to hold office as prescribed by the law, and therefore they install a 'godson', a protégé. The relationship between godfather and godson is sometimes written and often sealed spiritually with an oath. It is a patron–client relationship because of the symbiosis between them (Ayoade 2008: 89–90).

The godfather gives financial support to install his godson, sometimes by paying the campaign bill, sometimes by bribing party structures, election officials and police units, and sometimes by financing and mobilising violent 'militants'. The 'godson', when having taken office, returns the gestures manifold. He will protect the interests of the godfather in many ways; he will provide government services, appointments, policy decisions and (in particular) grant contracts for the godfather's companies. The initial support given by the godfather is an investment with substantial returns (if not, the godfather will choose another protégé).

Godfatherism is an ideology based on the idea that certain individuals can unilaterally determine who wins party primaries and who wins the electoral contest (Gambo 2006), but the influence of the godfathers spreads beyond the electoral process; they are an elite that have created a parallel informal system of governance. Otigbu (2013) states that:

> [T]he ills of godfatherism has continued to stare us in the face with no remedy in sight. Civil servants, those in the private employ, and even teachers in remote villages know that having a godfather helps put food on the table and move up in the social strata of life.

Lack of Transparency and the Oath of Secrecy

Another defining principle of political corruption in Nigeria is secrecy and lack of transparency. Until the passage of the Freedom of Information Act in 2015, nearly all governmental business was secret and governmental information of any sort inaccessible to the public. Since 2015, access to information has partly improved, but the financing and ownership structures in most strategic sectors such as oil and gas, defence, construction and so on, are still shrouded in near darkness.

One example of the level of secrecy is the Halliburton bribery scandal. The Okiro Report (called so after the investigation headed by former Inspector General of Police Mike Okiro) was sent to President Umaru Yar'Adua in May 2009 with a list of 80 individuals, foreigners and Nigerians, including four former heads of state as well as former governors and ministers (and some of their wives). These people were indicted in the United States for taking part in the 27 billion Nigerian naira bribe that Halliburton gave to win contracts in the Niger Delta. Though the report was submitted in 2009, it was not made public for a very long time, and no legal action has been taken in Nigeria against any of the accused (Independent 2010).

The Nigerian elite love showing off their wealth without disclosing how they gained their fortunes. Even some legitimate salaries and entitlements are in Nigerian politics so outrageous that they are rather kept secret. Nigerian lawmakers, for example, are the best-paid lawmakers in the world, earning annually US$540,000, with generous fringe benefits added. A campaign to disclose salaries and entitlements was carried out by BudgIT and other Nigerian NGOs, but it took many years before it was finally disclosed in 2017, to the shock and disbelief of the Nigerian public (Yomi 2017).

Furthermore, the 'oath of secrecy' is part of the civil service tradition for civil service employees; they take this oath of secrecy or allegiance before their assumption of duty. This is not so unusual, but the manner, timing and wordings of the oath as administered by the Peoples' Democratic Party, National Assembly and presidency indicates an unambiguous phobia and deep-seated disdain for the free flow of information (Madubuike-Ekwe and Mbadugha 2018: 105, Oji et al. 2014).

CORRUPT POWER PRESERVATION

Smythe and Smythe (1960: 194) pointed out already in 1960 with reference to Nigeria that 'those who are in power are likely to join in a conscious [...] attempt to consolidate their position and protect their claim to elite status'. This aside, and despite the diverse and massive literature on extractive corruption in Nigeria, there is a noticeable paucity of scholarly work on how political office holders in Nigeria have deployed corruptly acquired resources (and other state funds) to preserve their political parties and themselves in power.

However, as with corruption and power abuse, there are overlaps between extractive and power-preserving political corruption, as we will see in the following examples. However, corrupt power-preservation methods are often combined with secrecy, the manipulation of institutions, intimidation and even violence, and we will try to outline the methods that entail fraudulent use of corruptly (and not so corruptly) acquired resources.

Building a 'War Chest' to Stay in Power

Power-preserving corruption inevitably relies on diverting public resources into the political arena (parties and campaigns) to win elections. These resources are referred to in Nigeria as the 'war chest' of a political party or candidate. The war chest is spent on legitimate campaigning (on rallies, security, posters, ads and so on), but also on buying supporters to win primaries, buying votes, buying 'militants', and buying election officials and public control bodies.

Nigeria's legislators often monetise their constitutional roles, enriching themselves and building up their campaign war chests. In the words of one state legislator:

> We control the operation of the money, that's all anybody's looking for. You may appropriate it rightly or wrongly. But there are certain things, even if they are wrong, they are conventional. (Cited in Page 2018a: 8)

One of the most damaging and brazen cases of spending on campaigning involved the national security adviser Sambo Dasuki, who has been investigated since 2015 for allegedly diverting around US$2 billion to political campaigning for the ruling party, as well as for his private use. The diverted funds were allegedly meant to prop up Goodluck Jonathan's campaign and rig elections (Abati 2018, Olumhense 2019).

Without substantial financial resources (usually accumulated through a long political career and the utilisation of state resources for political and personal gains), the ascent to power is close to impossible. The failed 2019 presidential candidacy of the anti-establishment female candidate Obiageli 'Oby' Ezekwesili may illustrate this. Ezekwesili presented an alternative programme, in many respects technically more detailed and evidenced compared to the two top candidates. However, without the political backing of important patrons and godfathers and their financial resources, she never stood a chance (Webb 2019). Technical competency and international experience could not substitute for a 'war chest'.

With a well-filled war chest, ascent to power is possible, although incumbency is the primary source of financial strength. Thus, one of the factors that made the 2019 elections so uncertain was the fact that the incumbent's main contender, Atiku Abubakar, is one of Nigeria's richest men. He had his private, bountiful 'war chest'.

Rigging and Electoral Corruption

Election rigging in Nigeria used to be so commonplace that it arguably became a part of the political culture. Indeed, elections in Nigeria are for the purposes of 'reproducing regimes in power' (Tar and Zack-Williams 2007: 540). Except for the 2015 presidential election, Nigeria has not conducted a single election that was not rigged or bought.

Individuals and political parties who control the system often seek to hold on to power by 'personalising' state institutions, including paying bribes to government agencies saddled with elections-related duties. Indeed, in 2012, Attahiru Jega, the then chairman of Nigeria's electoral body, the Independent National Electoral Commission (INEC), lamented that in Nigeria 'political parties budget to bribe security and INEC officials' (cited in Onapajo et. al. 2015: 1).

Election rigging assumed unprecedented proportions in 2007. Determined not to lose and relinquish power, the ruling PDP invested heavily in their candidate Umaru Yar'Adua. The outgoing PDP President Obasanjo declared the election as a 'do or die affair'. It is therefore not surprising that the 2007 elections were 'blatantly rigged' (Ashby 2007, see also Tenuche 2009). The EU described Nigeria's 2007 elections as the worst they had ever seen anywhere in the world (according to CNN 2011).

The PDP won these elections, and Yar'Adua became president. When he died in 2010, his vice-president Goodluck Jonathan took over, and again in 2011 the PDP and the incumbent president invested enough funds to secure Jonathan's election. The elections were generally praised for being well managed, as there was a new legal framework, greater public confidence in the leadership of election authorities, and a higher level of engagement by political parties and civil society (NDI 2012: 7).

The 2015 general elections were managed even better, and tolerably free and fair. Several observers, including the ECOWAS Observer Mission and the Commonwealth Observer Group described the elections as fair, credible and transparent. The fact that the election, for the first time in the nation's history, saw an opposition candidate dislodging a sitting president through the ballot box, indicated a departure from what was the norm.

It must be noted, however, that while the 2015 elections may not have been rigged, the Jonathan administration, at all levels, deployed huge private and public funds to remain in power. For example, it now seems incontrovertible that his administration, for instance through the office of the National Security Adviser, diverted several millions of dollars into funding the 2015 elections (Adinde 2019).

Using the 'War Chest': Vote-Buying

Today, elections in Nigeria seem to be more characterised by vote-buying than by rigging and falsification of results. Simply defined, vote-buying is the act of offering rewards, especially money, to voters in exchange for voting for a particular candidate or party. Vote-buying is not new to Nigeria, but it has gone from a minor to a major political tool. Vote-buying 'is everywhere', it is getting more brazen, and party agents are openly offering people cash for votes (Ejike 2018).

The Osun and Ekiti state governorship elections in July and September 2018 are probably indicative of this shift to vote-buying. A cursory glance at Nigerian newspapers after the 2018 governorship elections in Ekiti and Osun states (south-west) confirms this assertion: 'INEC decries vote-buying in Ekiti governorship election' (Akinkuotu 2018); 'Ekiti Election: APC chieftain confesses to vote buying on national TV' (Egbas 2018); 'Ekiti vote buying: Rewarding emerging electoral fraud with victory' (Atoyebi 2018); 'Politicians woo voters with ₦10,000 on WhatsApp as Osun elects new governor' (Atoyebi et al. 2018); and 'Analysis: How vote buying may make or mar Osun polls' (Onyeji 2018).

There were variations in the amounts of cash paid for votes, but it ranged between 3,000 and 10,000 Nigerian naira (between 8 and 27 US dollars) per person per vote.[1] Indeed, security operatives provided cover while agents of the ruling party publicly dispensed cash for votes at polling centres (Ripples 2018). Both the Ekiti and Osun governorship elections were 'won' by the candidates of the ruling party.

Vote-buying was also widespread at the 2019 general elections, according to *The Economist* (2019). For instance, the EFCC arrested party agents with 1.5 million naira (4,200 US dollars) in cash prepared for vote-buying at polling units in Maiduguri, and one of the Ogun State House of Assembly candidates was arrested by the EFCC with 1.7 million naira (4,700 US dollars) 'neatly arranged in white envelopes' (Akinrujomu 2019, SaharaReporters 2019).

Impunity and Pardon

It is indubitable that the holders of the reins of power in Nigeria engage in extensive manipulation of state institutions to gain impunity and to preserve themselves in power. While it is practically impossible to chronicle the endless instances of this, several examples validate this assertion.

One example is that of Diepreye Alamieyeseigha, a former governor of Bayelsa State, who probably stole more than US$5 billion in state funds between May 1999 and September 2005 (Mayah 2016, Ovuakporie 2009). Investigations by the Proceeds of Corruption Unit of the London Metropolitan Police led to Alamieyeseigha's arrest in London in September 2005, charged with money laundering. The Metropolitan Police had found about £1 million in cash at his London home.

After three weeks in custody, Alamieyeseigha was released on bail on conditions including the surrender of his passport, the payment of US$2.6 million to the English High Court in sureties,

---

[1] Ekiti is the state of origin of one of the authors, Emmanuel Ojo, who participated in the election and observed first hand some of the money-for-vote deals. See also Omorotionmwan 2018.

and daily reporting to the police. Then, in November 2005, Alamieyeseigha donned disguise, fled England and returned to Nigeria, only to be arrested by the EFCC and charged with corruption. He pleaded guilty to all the charges and was sentenced to two years in prison, effective from the day of his arrest two years earlier, and therefore released a few hours later.

Then, in March 2013, President Goodluck Jonathan granted Alamieyeseigha presidential pardon. Indeed, Jonathan described the latter as his 'political benefactor' (Murdock 2013), apparently because Jonathan served as Alamieyeseigha's deputy between 1999 and 2005 and became governor following the former's removal from office. This is what has been referred to as 'unpardonable pardon' (Edukugho 2013).

Another episode also underlines the fact that many political office-holders enjoy impunity. In late 2018, just ahead of the last elections, eight powerful politicians faced corruption investigations. After they 'defected' to the ruling party, their charges were either dropped or were not being pursued further (Akinkuotu et al. 2018).

To assert it further, Adams Oshiomhole, the national chairman of the ruling party APC, said in a recent public declaration at his party's presidential electioneering campaign in Edo State, that 'once you join APC your sins are forgiven' (Sunday 2019). The story of this felonious declaration, published under the caption 'Once you join APC, your sins are forgiven', was carried by most Nigerian dailies on 18 or 19 January 2019.

In a new report entitled 'Letting the Big Fish Swim' by SERAP, a leading anti-corruption NGO in Nigeria, it is argued that among the 'high-profile' people accused of corruption only a handful have been convicted, and none have gone to prison (SERAP 2018: 6). The SERAP study further argues that of the more than 1,500 convictions made between 2000 and 2017, only ten cases can be ranked as 'high profile', and out of these almost none were convicted, let alone went to prison. Cases were either 'inexplicably withdrawn', dismissed because of legal immunity clauses (also called 'impunity clauses'), and most corruption cases against high-profile defendants witnessed 'delays tactics and tricks by defendants to truncate fair trial' (ibid.: 8).

Finally, some convicts have received presidential pardon, like Alamieyeseigha, and some have been reinstalled in political positions.

Anti-Corruption Corruption

Another method of institutional manipulation in Nigeria is the use of anti-corruption agencies (ACAs) as a political weapon. The executive power (presidency) has in some cases been using the Independent Corrupt Practices and Other Related Offences Commission (ICPC), the Economic and Financial Crimes Commission (EFCC), and the Code of Conduct Bureau and Tribunal (CCB) as state-coercive tools to intimidate political opponents and rivals.

On assuming the presidency, Obasanjo declared that ‘corruption, the greatest single bane of our society today will be tackled head on at all levels […] and […] stamped out’ (The Guardian 1999). This led to the launch of ICPC and the EFCC in September 2000 and April 2003, respectively. These agencies were empowered to identify, investigate, prosecute and secure convictions of individuals who engaged in corruption and other economic crimes. On the surface, they did tolerably well in stemming some of the corruption excesses, which had assumed a pandemic proportion as the military exited from the political scene in 1999.

Ironically, however, these agencies became potent weapons of vendetta and retribution by the Obasanjo administration as they readily harassed, ‘investigated’ and cowed real and imagined foes of the administration (Odunsi 2015). Likewise, in 2018 as he was out of power, Obasanjo accused the Buhari administration of using the EFCC and ICPC to the same end, to ‘witch-hunt political opponents’ (Opejobi 2018).

In the Nigerian context, the ruling elite is controlling and using the ACAs through their direct control over key appointments and their indirect control of the strategic management of the agencies. Projecting direct control is mostly the privilege of the president and his cronies. The power to direct corruption-related investigations and persecutions, to drop charges and forfeit assets is one of the most powerful weapons in the corrupt power-preserving arsenal.

The mere threat to press charges against an individual is a very simple strategy to subdue political opponents or co-opt them into their own political camp. As one commentator pointed out, the presumption of innocence in corruption-related charges does not exist in Nigeria: ‘When the message is out that when law enforcement agencies investigate, you are guilty no matter what the investigation proves or not.'[2] Especially in the pre-election time, when alliances are built and resources collected to keep or capture power, impartial and objective investigation seems close to impossible.

The primary interest across the Nigerian elite spectrum seems to be to control the ACAs' powers, in contrast to frequent proclamations to genuinely fight corruption. This is seen in the proliferation of anti-corruption institutions with no tangible evidence that corruption has been actually reduced.

The ACAs' independence has been directly or indirectly undermined by this political 'weaponising'. The ACAs have become crucial in consolidating political power, usually by the incumbent administration, as their control serves to cement own power basis or weaken political and power opponents. The ineffectiveness of the anti-corruption fight in Nigeria is unlikely to be solved by increased capacity building, increment of financial resources, greater international assistance and so on, as long as it clashes with the primary objective of the Nigerian elite: to remain in power.

CONCLUSIONS

In this chapter, we have attempted to show that politics and corruption in Nigeria are congenitally conjoined and inseparable. Political corruption has not only grown in leaps and bounds; it has become systemic, diversified and variegated (Ojo 2016: 2097-98).

Today, Nigeria does not only rank among the most corrupt countries of the world; its power preservation methods rank among the crudest and cruellest. The occupiers of political power deploy all available weapons in their political armoury – fair, foul, constitutional, extra-constitutional, judicial or extra-judicial – to perpetuate themselves and their political parties in power and thus continue to preside over the system of rents and rewards.

Arguably, the 'change' mantra – the campaign slogan of the APC – was the magic wand that led to an unprecedented disruption of the political status quo in the country in 2015: for the first time in the nation's history, an opposition candidate dislodged a sitting

---

2 Personal interview with a programme manager, CISLAC, Abuja, 28 December 2018.

president through the ballot box. According to the APC, the 'change' mantra was to strengthen democracy, rejuvenate and revolutionise the Nigerian socio-economic and political landscape by engendering a radical and clean break with the past.

However, many relatively objective observers of the Nigerian situation since 2015 argue that nothing substantial has changed (see: Adedokun 2018, Amaefule et al. 2017, Igbokwe 2016, Ogundele and Iroanusi 2018, Ojomoyela 2015, Omokri 2016). According to Roy (2017: 30), the need for inclusion of ever-wider social groups in a system of 'competitive clientelism' will make Nigeria's 'informal redistribution' a likely feature of the political settlement also in the future, meaning that rent capture will continue and that rent recipients 'will be difficult to discipline'. With heavily personalised state institutions and agencies, unrestrained manipulation of the electoral process and pervasive vote-buying, political corruption and power preservation are Nigeria's Siamese twins.

REFERENCES

Abati, R. (2018), '2019 and the politics of campaign finance', proshareng.com, 15 May 2018, https://www.proshareng.com/news/Politics/2019-And-The-Politics-Of-Campaign-Finance/40034 (accessed 8 March 2019).

Adedokun, N. (2018), 'Can Buhari still bring the change?', *Punch* (Nigeria), 4 January 2018, https://www.thecable.ng/can-buhari-still-bring-change (accessed 26 March 2019).

Adeyemi, O.O. (2012), 'Corruption and local government administration in Nigeria: a discourse of core issues', *European Journal of Sustainable Development*, 1(2): 183–98.

Adinde, S. (2019), 'Excess crude account: the oil fund paying for Nigerian elections', Stears Business, 4 March 2019, https://www.stearsng.com/article/excess-crude-account-the-oil-fund-paying-for-nigerian-elections (accessed 26 March 2019).

Akinkuotu, E. (2018), 'INEC decries "vote-buying" in Ekiti governorship election', *Punch*, 18 July 2018, https://punchng.com/inec-decries-vote-buying-in-ekiti-governorship-election/ (accessed 22 March 2019).

Akinkuotu, E., G. Adeoye and J. Alagbe (2018), 'Eight politicians with N232bn corruption cases working for Buharis re-election', *Punch*, 1 September 2018, https://punchng.com/eight-politicians-with-n232bn-corruption-cases-working-for-buharis-re-election/ (accessed 10 March 2019).

Akinrujomu, A. (2019), 'Vote-buying: EFCC arrests party agents with N1.5m cash at polling units', NAIJ.com, 9 March 2019, https://www.legit.ng/1226513-vote-buying-efcc-arrests-party-agents-n15m-cash-polling-units.html (accessed 10 March 2019).

Allison, S. (2012), 'Nigeria: how to lose $35bn', The Guardian (UK), 13 November 2012, https://www.theguardian.com/world/2012/nov/13/nigeria-oil-corruption-ridabu (accessed 24 February 2019).

Amaefule, E., O. Fabiyi, A. Adepegba and I. Onuba (2017), 'Four million Nigerians have lost their jobs this year – NBS (Nigerian Bureau of Statistics)', Punch, 23 December 2017, https://punchng.com/four-million-nigerians-have-lost-their-jobs-this-year-nbs/ (accessed 26 March 2019).

Amundsen, I. (2014), 'Drowning in oil: Angola's institutions and the "resource curse"', *Comparative Politics*, 46(2): 169–89.

Amundsen, I. (2017), 'Nigeria: defying the resource curse', in Aled Williams and Philippe le Billon (eds), *Corruption, Natural Resources and Development. From Resource Curse to Political Ecology*, Cheltenham/UK: Edward Elgar, ch. 1, pp. 17–27.

Ashby, T. (2007), 'Yar'Adua declared winner of Nigeria poll "charade"', Reuters, 23 April 2007, https://www.Reuters.com/article/us-nigeria-election/yaradua-declared-winner-of-nigeria-poll-charade-idUSL2149632920070423 (accessed 26 March 2019).

Atoyebi, O. (2018), 'Ekiti vote buying: rewarding emerging electoral fraud with victory', Punch, 22 July 2018, https://punchng.com/ekiti-vote-buying-rewarding-emerging-electoral-fraud-with-victory/ (accessed 22 March 2019).

Atoyebi, O., F. Makinde, S. Nwogu, J. Alagbe, O. Aluko and D. Ojerinde (2018), 'Politicians woo voters with N10,000 on WhatsApp as Osun elects new governor today', Punch, 22 September 2018, https://punchng.com/osun-2018-politicians-devise-new-tactics-of-vote-buying-woo-pvc-holders-on-whats app/ (accessed 22 March 2019).

Ayoade, J.A.A. (2008), 'Godfather politics in Nigeria', in V.A.O. Adetula (ed.), *Money, Politics and Corruption in Nigeria*, Arlington/VA: IFES (International Foundation for Electoral Systems), pp. 85–96.

Bagura, Y. (1986), 'The Nigerian economic crisis', in P. Lawrence, *World Recession and the Food Crisis in Africa*, London: James Curry, pp. 40–58.

Chabal, P. and J.-P. Daloz (1999), *Africa Works: Disorder as Political Instrument*, Oxford: Currey.

CNN (2011), 'Nigerian election pushed back a week', 4 April 2011, http://edition.cnn.com/2011/WORLD/africa/04/03/nigeria.election/index.html?eref=ft (accessed 25 February 2019).

Collier, P. and A. Hoeffler (2001), *Greed and Grievance in Civil War*, Washington DC: The World Bank.

Edukugho, E. (2013), 'Alamieyeseigha: unpardonable pardon', *Vanguard* (Lagos), 23 March 2013, https://www.vanguardngr.com/2013/03/alamieyeseigha-unpardonable-pardon/ (accessed 27 February 2019).

Egbas, J. (2018), 'APC chieftain confesses to vote buying on national TV', Pulse (Nigeria), 19 July 2018, https://www.pulse.ng/news/politics/ekiti-election-apc-chieftain-confesses-to-vote-buying-on-national-tv/hbs7djy (accessed 10 March 2019).

Egbo, O., I. Nwakoby, J. Onwumere and C. Uche (2012), 'Security votes in Nigeria: disguising stealing from the public purse', *African Affairs*, 111(445): 597–614.

Eisenstadt, S. (1973), *Traditional Patrimonialism and Modern Neopatrimonialism*, Beverly Hills: Sage Publications.

Ejike, P.E. (2018), '"It's everywhere": vote-buying gets more brazen in Nigeria ahead of 2019', blogpost, African Arguments, 4 September 2018, https://africanarguments.org/2018/09/04/everywhere-vote-buying-more-brazen-nigeria-2019/ (accessed 10 March 2019).

EUEOM (2015), *Federal Republic of Nigeria, FINAL REPORT, General Elections 28 March 2015, 11 April 2015*, July 2015, Brussels: European Union Election Observation Mission (EUEOM).

Gambo, A.N. (2006), 'Godfatherism and electoral politics in Nigeria', in V.A.O. Adetula (ed.), *Money, Politics and Corruption in Nigeria*, Arlington/VA: IFES (International Foundation for Electoral Systems), pp. 88–105.

Heller, T.C. (2006), 'African transitions and the resource curse: an alternative perspective', *Economic Affairs*, 26(December): 24–33.

HRW (2007), *Criminal Politics, Violence, 'Godfathers' and Corruption in Nigeria*, 19(16)(A), October 2007, New York: Human Rights Watch (HRW).

Igbokwe, J. (2016), 'Opinion: the real meaning of change APC promised Nigerians', The Will, 2 September 2016, https://thewillnigeria.com/news/opinion-the-real-meaning-of-change-apc-promised-nigerians/ (accessed 22 March 2019).

Ijewereme, O.B. (2015), 'Anatomy of corruption in the Nigerian public sector: theoretical perspectives and some empirical explanations', *SAGE Open*, 5(2), 4 June: 1–16.

Independent (2010), 'Nigeria: Obasanjo, Atiku, Kupolokun got U.S.$74 million – Okiro Report', 18 April 2010, https://allafrica.com/stories/201004190070.html (accessed 24 February 2019).

Isaacs, D. (2002), 'Gang rule in Nigeria', BBC World, 20 May 2002, http://news.bbc.co.uk/2/hi/africa/1998624.stm (accessed 24 February 2019).

Jaafar, J. (2018), 'Exclusive video: Kano governor, Abdullahi Ganduje, caught receiving bribe', Daily Nigerian, 14 October 2018, https://dailynigerian.com/exclusive-video-kano-governor-abdullahi-ganduje-caught-receiving-bribe/ (accessed 23 February 2019).

Madubuike-Ekwe, N.J. and J.N. Mbadugha (2018), 'Obstacles to the implementation of the Freedom of Information Act, 2011 in Nigeria', *Nnamdi Azikiwe University Journal of International Law and Jurisprudence*, 9(2): 96–109.

Mähler, A. (2010), *Nigeria: A Prime Example of the Resource Curse? Revisiting the Oil-Violence Link in the Niger Delta*, GIGA WP 120/2010. Hamburg: German Institute of Global and Area Studies (GIGA).

Mayah, E. (2016), 'Panama papers: how Alamieyeseigha began looting of Bayelsa 3 months after becoming governor', Premium Times (Abuja), 4 May 2016, https://www.premiumtimesng.com/panama-papers/202875-panamapapers-how-alamieyeseigha-began-looting-bayelsa-3-months-after-becoming-governor.html (accessed 27 February 2019).

Meers, J. (2018), *Increase of Nigerian Security Money Graft Destabilizing Country*, Report 29 May 2018, Maryland: OCCRP (Organized Crime and Corruption Reporting Project).

Mehlum, H., K. Moene and R. Torvik (2006), 'Cursed by resources or institutions?', *The World Economy*, 29(August): 1117–31.

Murdock, H. (2013), 'Nigeria pardons ex-governor jailed for corruption', VOA (Voice of Africa), 13 March 2013, https://www.voanews.com/a/Nigeria-president-pardons-ex-governor-convicted-of-graft/1620636.html (accessed 26 March 2019).

NAI (1955), 'Letter from C.J. Mayne to T.B. Williamson on reactions to the Ikpeazu Commission into bribery and corruption in the Eastern Region', 9 November 1955, *National Archives Ibadan*, CO554/1226, No. 4.

NAI (1956), 'Nigeria constitutional conference 1956: structure of the federal government: CO final brief', *National Archives Ibadan*, CO 554/905, No. 45.

NAI (1960), 'Dispatch no 53 from Sir J Robertson to Mr Macleod reviewing the end of British rule in Nigeria and prospects for the future', 15 Sept 1960, *National Archives Ibadan*, CO 554/2479, No. 11.

NDI (2012), *Final Report on the 2011 Nigerian General Elections*, Final Report, Washington, DC: National Democratic Institute (NDI).

Odunsi, W. (2015), 'Buhari is like Obasanjo, he is using EFCC to crush opponents – Adebanjo', Daily Post, 20 October 2015, http://dailypost.ng/2015/10/20/buhari-is-like-obasanjo-he-using-efcc-to-crush-opponents-adebanjo/ (accessed 1 March 2019).

Ogala, E. (2018), 'When generals turn bandits: inside the massive corruption in Nigeria's security contracting', Premium Times, 15 May 2018, https://www.premiumtimesng.com/investigationspecial-reports/268123-when-generals-turn-bandits-inside-corruption-nigeria-security-contracting.html (accessed 25 February 2019).

Ogundele, S. and Iroanusi, Q. (2018), 'Buhari may not win 2019 election even with massive rigging', Premium Times, https://www.premiumtimesng.com (accessed 20 February 2019).

Oji, R.E., E.C. Nwachukwa and O.I. Eme (2014), 'Oath of secrecy in the Nigerian public service', *Arabian Journal of Business and Management Review*, 2(8), 98–116.

Ojo, E.O. (2016), 'Combating Systemic Corruption in Africa: Altitudinal, Attitudinal, Confrontational or Constitutional?', *Journal of Siberian Federal University. Humanities & Social Sciences*, 9, 2092–2123.

Ojomoyela, R. (2015), 'Olujimi derides APC's change mantra', Punch, 1 December 2015, https://www.vanguardngr.com/2015/12/olujimi-derides-apcs-change-mantra/ (accessed 26 March 2019).

Olumhense, S. (2019), 'What Sambo Dasuki symbolises', Punch, 24 February 2019, https://punchng.com/what-sambo-dasuki-symbolises/ (accessed 26 February 2019).

Omokri, R. (2016), 'Buhari, Jonathan and a redefinition of change', The Cable, 4 November 2016, https://www.thecable.ng/buhari-jonathan-redefinition-change (accessed 26 March 2019).

Omorotionmwan, J. (2018), 'Vote buying taken to the limits', Vanguard, 6 September 2018, https://www.vanguardngr.com/2018/09/vote-buying-taken-to-the-limits/ (accessed 10 March 2019).

Onapajo, H., S. Francis and U. Okeke-Uzodike (2015), 'Oil corrupts elections: the political economy of vote buying in Nigeria', *African Studies Quarterly*, 15(2): 1–21.

Onomuakpokpo, P. (2019), 'Buhari, Onnoghen et al and their common DNA', The Guardian (Nigeria), 31 January 2019, https://guardian.ng/opinion/buhari-onnoghen-et-al-and-their-common-dna/ (accessed 13 April 2019).

Onwubiko, E. (2018), 'Weak public procurement breeds corruption', The Guardian (Nigeria), 7 March 2018, https://guardian.ng/issue/weak-public-procurement-breeds-corruption/ (accessed 25 February 2019).

Onwuka, A. (2019), 'Buhari was right on Ganduje but …', Punch, 5 February 2019, https://punchng.com/buhari-was-right-on-ganduje-but/ (accessed 13 April 2019).

Onyeji, E. (2018), 'ANALYSIS: how vote buying may make or mar Osun polls', Premium Times, 20 September 2018, https://www.premiumtimesng.com/news/headlines/284519-analysis-how-vote-buying-may-make-or-mar-osun-polls.html (accessed 22 March 2019).

Opejobi, S. (2018), 'EFCC, ICPC, FIRS, others directed to witch-hunt political opponents – Obasanjo', Daily Post, 11 July 2018, http://dailypost.ng/2018/07/11/efcc-icpc-firs-others-directed-witch-hunt-political-opponents-obasanjo/ (accessed 1 March 2019).

Otigbu, V. (2013), 'The ills of Godfatherism and the political elite', Vanguard, 5 November 2013, https://www.vanguardngr.com/2013/11/ills-godfatherism-political-elite/ (accessed 24 February 2019).

Ovuakporie, E. (2009), 'EFCC returns Alams' (Alamieyeseigha's) N7bn loot to Bayelsa govt.', Vanguard, 9 July 2009, https://www.vanguardngr.com/2009/07/efcc-returns-alams-n7bn-loot-to-bayelsa-govt/ (accessed 27 February 2019).

Oxfam (2017), 'Nigeria: extreme inequality in numbers', Oxfam International, Nairobi, https://www.oxfam.org/en/even-it-nigeria/nigeria-extreme-inequality-numbers (accessed 27 February 2019).

Page, M.T. (2018a), *A New Taxonomy for Corruption in Nigeria*, Washington DC: Carnegie Endowment for International Peace, https://carnegieendowment.org/2018/07/17/new-taxonomy-for-corruption-in-nigeria-pub-76811 (accessed 25 February 2019).

Page, M.T. (2018b), *Camouflaged Cash. How 'Security Votes' Fuel Corruption in Nigeria*, Berlin: Transparency International and Civil Society Legislative Advocacy Centre (CISLAC).

Rabiu, B. (2017), 'Corruption in defence procurement: any lessons from arms probe?', Leadership (Nigeria), 13 November 2017, https://leadership.ng/2017/11/13/corruption-defence-procurement-lessons-arms-probe/ (accessed 25 February 2019).

Ripples (2018), 'Dogara blames INEC, security agencies for vote-buying in Osun gov election', Ripples Nigeria, 10 December 2018, https://www.ripplesnigeria.com/dogara-blames.inec-security-agencies-for-vote-buying-in-osun-gov–election (accessed 26 March 2019).

Robinson, J.A., R. Torvik and T. Verdier (2005), 'Political foundations of the resource curse', *Journal of Development Economics*, 79(February), 447–68.

Roy, P. (2017), *Anti-Corruption in Nigeria: A Political Settlements Analysis*, ACE Working Paper 002, London: SOAS, University of London.

Rupert, J. (1998), 'Corruption flourished in Abacha's regime', *Washington Post*, 9 June 1998: A01.

SaharaReporters (2015), 'Leaders or dealers: former Nigerian governors undergoing trial for corruption', SaharaReporters, New York, 11 May 2017, http://saharareporters.com/2017/05/11/leaders-or-dealers-former-nigerian-governors-undergoing-trial-corruption-3 (accessed 23 February 2019).

SaharaReporters (2019), 'EFCC arrests Amosun's ally with N1.7m "neatly arranged in white envelopes"', SaharaReporters, New York, 10 March 2019, http://saharareporters.com/2019/03/09/efcc-arrests-amosuns-ally-n17m-neatly-arranged-white-envelopes, (accessed 21 March 2019).

SERAP (2018), *Letting the Big Fish Swim*, Lagos: Eddy Asae Press.

Smythe, H.H. and M.M. Smythe (1960), *The New Nigerian Elite*, California: Stanford University Press.

StartupTipsDaily (2017), 'How to win contracts in Nigeria from the government and large companies', 16 September 2017, http://startuptipsdaily.com/how-to-get-contracts-in-nigeria/ (accessed 25 February 2019).

Sule, B., M. Azizuddin, M. Sani and B. Mat (2018), 'Godfatherism and political party financing in Nigeria: analysing the 2015 general election', *Malaysian Journal of Society and Space*, 14(1): 1–14.

Sunday, N. (2019), '"Once you join APC, your sins are forgiven", Oshiomhole says as PDP lambasts him', Vanguard, 18 January 2019, https://www.vanguardngr.com/2019/01/once-you-join-apc-your-sins-are-forgiven-oshiomhole-says-as-pdp-lambasts-him/ (accessed 27 February 2018).

Tar, U.A. and A.B. Zack-Williams (2007), 'Nigeria: contested elections & and unstable democracy', *Review of African Political Economy*, 34(113), 540–548.

Tenuche, M. (2009), 'The language of politics and political behaviours: rhetoric of President Olusegun Obasanjo and the 2007 general elections in Nigeria', *Journal of Public Administration and Policy Research*, 1(3): 47–54.

The Economist (2019), 'Time to keep those promises: Nigeria's President Muhammadu Buhari wins a second term', The Economist, 28 February 2019, https://www.economist.com/middle-east-and-africa/2019/02/28/nigerias-president-muhammadu-buhari-wins-a-second-term (accessed 20 February 2019).

The Guardian (1999), 'Time to stop corruption?', *The Guardian*, 19 December 1999.

TI (2018), 'Corruption perceptions Index 2018', Berlin: Transparency International (TI), https://www.transparency.org/cpi2018 (accessed 23 February 2019).

Vanguard (2017), 'Corruption in procurement makes up 70% of budget, says Ex-Minister', Vanguard, 26 August 2017, https://www.vanguardngr.com/2017/08/corruption-procurement-makes-70-budget-says-ex-minister/ (accessed 25 February 2019).

Webb, R. (2019), 'Nigeria General Election 2019: female candidate creates new vision of Nigeria', *Institute for Development Studies* (IDS), opinion, 4 February 2019, https://www.ids.ac.uk/opinions/nigeria-general-election-2019-female-candidate-creates-new-vision-of-nigeria/ (accessed 24 February 2019).

Yomi, K. (2017), 'A dogged transparency campaign reveals why it pays to be a lawmaker in Nigeria', QuartzAfrica, 15 May 2017, https://qz.com/africa/983331/a-dogged-transparency-campaign-reveals-why-it-pays-to-be-a-lawmaker-in-nigeria/ (accessed 24 February 2019).

5. Inclusive co-optation and political corruption in Museveni's Uganda

Moses Khisa

THE USES AND ABUSES OF POLITICAL CORRUPTION

Political corruption is both extractive and regime preserving, quite different from petty bribery and bureaucratic thieving that has been the focus of most research about corruption. Extractive corruption can serve personal interests in the standard form, defined as the use of public office for personal gain. But extraction can also serve a broader goal of maintaining the extant political status quo – regime preservation. Here, we can locate a feedback loop. Individuals engage in political corrupt practices that preserve the regime and the existing political system, and in turn the established system provides avenues for personal enrichment that benefit individual politicians and their supporters. This is cyclical.

The focus of this chapter is on the contours of political corruption in Uganda under Yoweri Museveni's *National Resistance Movement* (NRM) government. The chapter approaches political corruption as a type or subset of corruption. Political corruption should not be conflated with other forms of corruption or with corruption as a general label. Much of the literature on corruption proceeds from the principal-agent model and the market incentives that fuel especially bureaucratic corruption (see, for example, Borges et al. 2017, Gans-Morse et al. 2018, Olken and Pande 2012, Rose-Ackerman and Palifka 2016). In contrast, this chapter construes political corruption as integral to the survivability of the political system in place. This means that political corruption goes beyond the failure of principals to supervise agents. It is an integral part of the system in which both principals and agents are implicated.

Analytically, there is also a distinction between political and bureaucratic corruption. The former is primarily driven by and serves political ends, the latter might be petty and strictly for personal enrichment. But political corruption is not the preserve of politicians only. Bureaucrats too can engage in political corruption if we define it according to the political functionality or the ends it serves. Political corruption takes place at the behest of politicians. It happens and persists because those engaged in it have the political power to pursue corrupt acts without punitive consequences.

Besides, it is theoretically plausible (and empirically testable) that some non-politicians, such as government bureaucrats and accounting officers, can engage in and execute acts of political corruption on behalf of their principals – the politicians. This is so because it is bureaucrats who directly control public finances and manage state resources generally.

In many African countries that have embraced democratic procedures and accountability systems, it is often common for political leaders to find an easy exit from allegation of corruption by deflecting scrutiny to the accounting officers – the bureaucrats. In high-profile corruption scandals in countries such as Ghana and Uganda, it is not unusual for government ministers to claim that they were not directly involved in procurement scandals, irregular financial activities, or transactions under scrutiny in their respective ministerial dockets. In reality, it is plausible to surmise that politicians often collude with accounting officers, the bureaucrats, as the latter are under the supervision of the former, yet the latter directly control funds and manage budgets.

Political corruption has become pervasive and even endemic in many poor and developing countries because of its dual functionality – first, individuals profit from it as a form of extraction, and second, the extant regimes benefit from it as a critical source of regime preservation. That is, individuals extract resources through corruption so as to preserve the regime and the regime in turn is preserved so as to maintain avenues for extraction by individuals. It is reciprocal and cyclical.

Political corruption operates at two levels, the individual and the institutional. At the individual level, political corruption takes place when politicians and state agents abuse their political power to sustain their own power, status and wealth (Amundsen 2006: 8, and Chapter 1, this volume). Individuals can use their power and possible judicial impunity and, in many countries where corruption is prevalent, powerful politicians and their cronies are literally above the law.

The resources they extract go in part to oiling the political system in order to sustain the status quo. In Uganda, as some scholars have noted, individual power-holders are able to divert public resources into their own hands and influence institutions that are supposed to enforce accountability, which in turn means that the top political leadership retains the loyalty of those who profit from the system and keeps them in the ruling coalition (Asiimwe 2016: 208, Tangri and Mwenda 2006: 104). The ruling coalition is sustained in large part through allowing corrupt practices and by making direct transfer of patronage resources to individuals and groups.

Institutionally, endemic political corruption builds a self-reinforcing dynamic that makes corruption an institution in itself, short of which the system in place would suffer shocks and possible collapse. We can conceive of political corruption as an institutional routine or a site from which individuals feed off the public purse, and from which state and governmental institutions depend for their very existence. Governmental institutions can, for example, be sustained and preserved even when decayed and dysfunctional because individuals use them to extract pecuniary benefits.

In the case of Uganda, high-level corruption has been concerned with private gain as well as political consolidation – the two go together. This chapter argues that political corruption, both extractive and power preserving, is the lifeblood of the current political system under the NRM government and President Museveni. It is the way the system works and not fails. This is not a rehashing of the lurid assertions in Chabal and Deloz's (1999) 'Africa works' thesis. Rather, it is to suggest that political corruption is a deliberate choice and tactic in a broader strategy of rule that is brought to bear on the necessity of regime survival and presidential longevity. Political actors have a choice not to instrumentalise political corruption, but when they choose to and adopt it as a part of a collage of tactics, it does not mean that political corruption is 'natural' and 'integral' to how 'Africa works'. This cynical assertion of 'Africa works' rests on a rather shaky empirical and theoretical ground.

This chapter makes two related sets of arguments with respect to Uganda. First, pervasive political corruption in Uganda evolves out of the governing strategy of inclusive co-optation of potential challengers and the need to buy loyalty from a wide spectrum of supporters. The NRM's initial strategy of 'broad-based' government had as its primary aim to reach out and build an inclusive governing coalition under a no-party 'movement' system. At the outset, this may have been a principled attempt at inclusive politics. Over time, however, broad-based became 'bread-based' as inclusion was driven by calculations of buying support for the regime and rewarding allies, and to demobilise opposition (Weekly Topic 1989).

Second, the strategy of pursuing regime survival through co-optation has fuelled factionalism, institutional fragmentation and, ultimately, 'decentralisation' (or rather 'democratisation') of corruption. Some scholars have referred to this as 'decentralised rent management', a key feature of Uganda's political settlement (Kjaer 2015: 232). The creation of an elastic and ever-expanding ruling coalition, more so at the local level than at the top, has resulted in different factions pitted against each other within the ruling party and outside (Golooba-Mutebi and Hickey 2013, Kjaer 2015).

Institutionally, the need to accommodate various groups and constituents resulted in the proliferation of state agencies and governmental bodies in the wake of the privatisation of state parastatals in the 1990s (Tangri and Mwenda 2013: 28). This invariably fragmented the state's institutional landscape but also produced 'inflationary patronage' due to the need to house people in a 'big tent' (Vokes 2016: 661).

The sum of it is a 'decentralisation' of the avenues of rent-seeking, making political corruption pervasive and normalised, routinised and institutionalised. It has become 'democratised' as the avenues of extraction are now spread out to accommodate so many actors at all levels, national and subnational. And this has been one of the downsides to the politics of inclusion and pseudo-democracy: when inclusivity and participation is instrumentalised to achieve co-optation rather than principled engagement, it leads to a rentier system where the rent management is dispersed and decentralised.

Different factions, constituencies and interest groups scramble for economic spoils in a marketplace that is mediated by political power.

The upside to the politics of inclusion based on co-optation and an instrumental use of patronage is the role it can play in state building. It can serve as a stabilising force, without which challengers would disrupt the status quo and create social disorder. As Richard Vokes noted, 'far from indicating a weak state, the massive expansion of patronage under Museveni in recent years has vastly strengthened both his own position and that of his NRM government' (Vokes 2016: 664). This is an aspect of the neo-patrimonial mode of rule that has not been fully appreciated by Africanist scholars: facilitating political stability and institutionalising authority through political corruption.[1] Here, corruption is functional in maintaining the political system and is a substitute for reform (Huntington 1968: 64). The rest of this chapter proceeds in two major sections. The next section presents some of the major extractive and regime preserving corruption scandals that took place in Uganda since the late 1990s. This period was a major turning point: it was the time when grand corruption took on a major regime preservation role. This course has endured remarkably. The last section of the chapter turns on teasing out the broader economic and political implications of the intersection of corruption and regime politics in Uganda.

POLITICAL CORRUPTION: BETWEEN EXTRACTION AND POWER-PRESERVATION

In Uganda since the late 1990s, the incidents of grand and high-level corruption have been too numerous to be studied individually or exhaustively. Grand corruption has ranged from diversion or direct theft of funds from both donor-funded projects and from budget allocations for government ministries, departments and agencies (see Asiimwe 2013, 2016, Fjeldstad 2005, Robinson 2007, Tangri and Mwenda 2013), to big-money procurement scandals in

---

[1] This point was made to the author by Andrew Mwenda, Managing Director, *Independent Publications*, Kampala, in an interview in March 2018.

the military and in the privatisation of state parastatals in the 1990s, as analysed by Tangri and Mwenda (2001, 2003).

Within a few years of capturing power in 1986, there were muted murmurs about the government being 'bread-based' and not 'broad-based' (the term was coined in *Weekly Topic* newspaper in 1989). But the two, 'broad-based' and 'bread-based', were not necessarily in conflict: being 'broad-based' made it possible for politics to be 'bread-based'. The very practice of being 'broad-based' engendered 'bread-based' politics – that is, marshalling an inclusive and broad coalition entailed creating a system of sharing access to state spoils among elites and their constituents, the 'politics of the belly' (Bayart 1993). Over time the exigencies of maintaining a broad-based coalition have contributed to the sprawling, and indeed the 'normalisation', of political corruption. By the late 1990s, grand graft in privatisation and public procurement became rampant and an integral part of the survival strategy of the regime. Corruption became an 'essential strategy for the NRM to maintain its grip on power' (Tangri and Mwenda 2013: 47).

Since then, and from the turn of the century, the scope of financial malfeasance and the extent of graft in Uganda has been too vast as to be easily quantified or exhaustively outlined. Below I will nonetheless summarise a few cases to highlight both the extractive and power preservation roles of political corruption in Uganda.

Extractive Political Corruption: the Military

Political corruption became fully manifest in Uganda in the late 1990s. The first major (publicised) scandal was in 1997–8 and involved the purchase of helicopter fighters and military uniforms for the national army Uganda People's Defence Forces (UPDF) (Tangri and Mwenda 2013: 69–71). First, the cost of the choppers was inflated. Second, it turned out that they were 'junk'. Third, the cost of the military uniforms procured from China was inflated and they were undersized.

Several individuals were involved in this case of extractive political corruption. Museveni's brother, General Salim Saleh, who at the time was senior adviser to the minister of defence (who was the president himself), confessed to taking a hefty US$800,000 bribe. President Museveni told the judicial commission of inquiry set up to investigate the scandal that Saleh had confessed to taking the bribe and that he (the president) had ordered him to use the money for operational expenses in northern Uganda (Asiimwe 2013: 135–6), where the UPDF was fighting several rebel groups. Still, corruption in the military provided an avenue for siphoning off patronage resources to oil the regime (Reno 2002: 424, Tangri and Mwenda 2003: 551).

Although it remained an important source of patronage resources, corruption in military procurement subsided somewhat with the greater professionalisation of the UPDF in the late 1990s and early 2000s. Instead of grand procurement corruption, as was the case in the 1990s, from the mid-2000s the front of extraction moved more to classified defence and intelligence budget allocations under the control of individuals close to the presidency and members of the very inner circle of the ruling coalition. The defence budget grew exponentially (against protests from major western donors), ostensibly to prosecute insurgencies in the north, from US$97 million in 1991 to US$286 million at the peak of fighting rebels in 2002–3 (Tangri and Mwenda 2013: 28).

Extractive Political Corruption: Privatisation of Parastatals

Between 1997 and 1999, two major scandals in the privatisation of government parastatals set the tone and tenor for political corruption in Uganda: the divestiture of the national carrier, Uganda Airlines Corporation (UAC) and the leading national/state bank, Uganda Commercial Bank (UCB). Both scandals involved individuals at the very highest levels of politics (see below), and in both cases there was glaring malfeasance and outright abuse of political power for private gain, which for the most part went unpunished.

These and other cases of grand corruption in the late 1990s laid the ground for full integration of political corruption in Uganda's body politic. In the case of the UCB, the key actor at the centre of a botched takeover that put an already distressed bank into deeper jeopardy was (yet again) Museveni's brother, Salim Saleh, and a prominent minister, Sam Kutesa, an in-law to Museveni (Tangri and Mwenda 2013: 57, Taylor 2012: 137). Around the same time Saleh was implicated in the fraudulent sale of UCB to Westmont Land Malaysia, a shadowy company that was a front for a local bank,

Greenland Bank, in which he was a shareholder (Tangri and Mwenda 2013: 58).

For the national carrier, UAC, its handling service, which was a lucrative section comprising 60 per cent of the company, was irregularly divested to Entebbe Handling Services (ENHAS), owned by Sam Kutesa. Again, Salim Saleh was at the centre of the initial controversial privatisation of UAC's ground-handling business. The two men (Saleh and Kutesa) worked out a deal that led to 50 per cent of handling services going to ENHAS. Subsequently, two separate companies owned by Kutesa and Saleh bought off the remaining 50 per cent of UAC's air-handling services without open competitive bidding and at far below market value (Taylor 2012: 137). A parliamentary report noted that the process had been manipulated and taken advantage of by a few politically powerful people (cited in Tangri and Mwenda 2013: 58). The takeover of 100 per cent of the ground-handling services effectively grounded the national carrier, which was eventually shut down in 2001. Efforts have been underway to revive it and it is planned to resume flights later this year.

The two scandals, UAC and UCB, took place at a time when Uganda's parliament still maintained some autonomy in performing its oversight functions. Thus, in May 1999 minister Sam Kutesa was censured by parliament, accused of abuse of office and influence peddling (Tangri and Mwenda 2013: 61, Taylor 2012: 138). Earlier, in December 1998, the minister for privatisation, Matthew Rukikaire, was forced to resign over the handling of the privatisation of UCB (Tangri and Mwenda 2001: 127). Also, the minister for primary education, Brigadier Jim Muhwezi, accused of abuse of office and embezzlement of World Bank funds for universal primary education, was censured by parliament in March 1998. In a spell of a few years, several high-profile ministers and other officials had been either censured or forced to resign over grand corruption scandals. Museveni, on his part, tactfully reshuffled Sam Kutesa and Jim Muhwezi from cabinet in 1999, but the two were reappointed back to cabinet after the March 2001 elections. Since then, the names of both men have again come up in cases of grand corruption scandals.

Regime Preservation: Grand Corruption in Ministries

Among the leading cases of grand corruption were two donor-funded projects in the Ministry of Health: Global Alliance for Vaccines and Immunization (GAVI), and the Global Fund on AIDS, Tuberculosis and Malaria (see Cocks 2007, IRIN 2006). An estimated US$800,000 was allegedly embezzled from the former and US$4.5 million from the latter (Human Rights Watch 2013: 18). An opposition leader and former member of parliament, Norbert Mao, pointed out that these embezzled funds were used to pay presidential pledges in different parts of the country.[2] The key figure involved in both scandals was, yet again, a top-level member of the inner circle of the ruling elite mentioned above: Jim Muhwezi (Tushabe 2013: 151). He had made a comeback to cabinet after a few years on the sidelines following his 1998 censure by parliament (Asiimwe 2013: 136).

In large part because of direct pressure from western donors, who momentarily suspended funding, Muhwezi was this time prosecuted along with two deputy health ministers, Mike Mukula and Alex Kamugisha, along with Alice Kaboyo, a state house official and relative to the first lady, who was in charge of youth affairs for the president. Kaboyo told the Inspector General of Government that some of the money was used in political activities including for the 2004–5 referendum campaigns (Asiimwe 2013: 136). However, all accused were acquitted by the High Court's anti-corruption division, except Alice Kaboyo who pled guilty and got away with a fine of 20 million shillings (75,000 US dollars) (Kasozi 2012, New Vision 2012).

Another senior and long-surviving minister, Sam Kutesa (cited above), was named in one exposé after another, including WikiLeaks and most recently in the Panama Papers (WikiLeaks 2009). In 2011, he was the subject of a rancorous debate in parliament, accused along with two other ministers, Amama Mbabazi and Hillary Onek, of taking bribes from multinational oil companies seeking licences in Uganda's nascent oil and gas industry.

Around the same time as the GAVI and Global Fund scandals, the Commonwealth Heads of Government Meeting (CHOGM) held

---

[2] Interview with Norbert Mao, president of the Democratic Party and former member of parliament, Kampala 13 March 2018.

in Kampala in 2007 left behind major procurement scandals (Parliament of Uganda 2007). These ranged from leasing luxury executive cars to granting deals to hotels and spending sprees on 'beautifying' Kampala ahead of a major international event. In a 'value for money audit' the Auditor General unearthed gross irregularities and misappropriations. In a follow-up investigation, the Public Account Committee of parliament found, *inter alia*, that billions had been spent on works for private hotels, including those owned by Sudhir Ruparalia, who is known to be a major source of political and campaign financing for the NRM (Biryabarema 2008, Parliament of Uganda 2007: 46).

Several high-ranking ministers including Sam Kutesa, Amama Mbabazi, Hope Mwesigye, John Nassasira, Mwesigwa Rukatana and the then vice-president Gilbert Bukenya were cited in improprieties with huge monies at stake (BBC 2011b, Parliament of Uganda 2007). They were investigated by parliament's Public Accounts Committee and by the Inspector General of Government. Four years later, in May 2011, Bukenya was sacked from his position as vice-president, and the following month he was arrested and charged with abuse of office and fraud (BBC 2011a). A few months later the charges were dropped, however, just as the trial was about to start (BBC 2011c). Bukenya had cried out loud for President Museveni to step in, arguing that only he could end what he saw as a politically motivated prosecution.

In October 2011, three ministers (Kutesa, Nassasira and Rukutana) were charged with abuse of office and causing financial loss to the government. Earlier, they had been forced to step down from their ministerial positions before being charged, but they returned to cabinet less than a year later. They were subsequently acquitted, with the presiding judge faulting the prosecution (by the government Ombudsman) for presenting a weak case that had no evidence to form a *prima facie* case and to warrant a trial (Wesaka 2012).

Around the same time that parliament investigated the above-named ministers, and predictively cleared them of wrongdoing, another high-profile minister became the subject of a big-money scandal: the then security minister Amama Mbabazi, who subsequently became the prime minister. Mbabazi was also the ruling party's Secretary General. He was investigated by a parliamentary committee for conflict of interest and influence peddling in the sale of a large swath of land to the statutory workers' pension fund, the

National Social Security Fund (NSSF). The parliamentary investigation report found Mbabazi culpable and recommended his dismissal. The report was to be voted on by the whole house, and pressure was mounting on Mbabazi as it became increasingly clear that he would be censured by parliament (The Independent 2008). Then, President Museveni stepped in to thwart what he characterised as a ploy to finish off the party by targeting its Secretary General (Nganda 2008). The censure did not happen, and Mbabazi was cleared of wrongdoing by courtesy of a minority report that contradicted the majority report findings.

In all, the individuals named above, and many others who over the years were accused of involvement in grand corruption scandals, are part of a wider network of insiders critical to regime survival. For the most part they got away with their actions, where other actors would not, precisely because they were at the centre of power and are able to exact influence on accountability and prosecutorial institutions.[3]

Regime Preservation: Financial Inducements to MPs

The rule of Museveni and the NRM has been built in part on legal and constitutional engineering, or what can be referred to as 'rule by law' – that is, the manipulation of laws and the constitution to keep a grip on power. To achieve this, parliament has been critical, so financial inducements to members of parliament to effect constitutional changes has become a routine form of regime-preserving political corruption.

The first major incident of alleged bribery of members of parliament was during the 2005 constitutional amendments that, among other things, deleted the presidential term limit from the constitution (The Observer 2012). This was a turning point in Uganda's contemporary politics and the stakes were very high. The allegations of bribing of MPs were openly confirmed by several MPs including opposition MP Odonga Otto and NRM MP Theodore Sekikubo (Mutaizibwa 2005).

At least 213 of the 307 parliamentarians in 2005 were paid 5 million shillings (about 3,000 US dollars at the time). Sekikubo

[3] I am grateful to Godfrey Asiimwe of Makerere University for pointing out this. Interview, Kampala, 24 July 2018.

publicly denounced the payments and since then, together with a couple of others, became known as 'rebel MP' for his outspokenness and going against NRM official party-positions in parliament. The money was officially meant for consultations on the government White Paper tabled in parliament, but in reality it was to support the removal of presidential term limits (Tripp 2010a: 171, see also Trip 2010b for a general analysis). If it was for consultations then all MPs would have received the money, yet payments were selectively and clandestinely made to only those MPs known to have been in support of the proposed amendment of the constitution to removal presidential term limits.

Most recently, the controversial and chaotic removal of the age limit from the constitution in December 2017 was realised through a combination of force and finance.[4] In October 2017 the Ministry of Finance released approximately US$3.5 million ostensibly for MPs to conduct consultations on an issue that had already been reported as unpopular among the public (The Observer 2017, VOA 2017). Each of the 445 MPs was paid US$8,000, although some opposition MPs returned the money to parliament in protest.

More generally, since around 2005 parliament has been a key institutional site for buying loyalty and dispensing patronage. According to an outspoken NRM MP, Museveni has become increasingly reliant on using financial inducements to mollify MPs and assure cohesion within the NRM.[5] In particular when there is a controversial legislation before parliament, MPs are paid money under the guise of 'consultation', even when there is no necessity for consultations and when the MPs do not carry out any consultations. It is also striking that financial inducements to MPs involve money that often comes directly from the Central Bank and the Ministry of Finance, as was the case, for example, on the eve of the 2011 elections through a 30 per cent 'supplementary budget', which according to one scholar 'made political corruption overt and official'.[6]

---

[4] Interview with Felix Okot-Ogong, NRM MP for Dokolo South County in Northern Uganda, Kampala, 24 July 2018.

[5] Interview with Okot-Ogong.

[6] Interview with Oloka-Onyango, Professor of Law at Makerere University, Kampala, 14 March 2018.

This practice of relying on patronage resources is a major departure from Museveni's early years and the 'broad-based' arrangement when he depended more on persuasion than coercion and bribery to win over critics and opponents.[7] In the early years, Museveni's initial ruling coalition primarily aimed at state building. However, in recent years co-options and financial compromise are some of the ways for assuring regime survival and power preservation than pursuit of a common good for the country.

POLITICAL AND ECONOMIC IMPLICATIONS

What are the implications of the fact that political corruption has become integral to the very survivability of the Museveni regime?

There are implications for politics and for the economy. Economically, a system of decentralised (and 'democratised') corruption is also a system of decentralised rent-seeking and individualised extraction at the expense of the public good (Kelsall 2013). Aside from the fact that corruption can generally be detrimental to investment and growth by, among other things, frustrating investors, it also can pose a problem for the mobilisation of public funds for national development (Asiimwe 2016).

When individuals have a free hand to extract resources for personal benefit, and to fund the continuation of the political system, it becomes difficult to productively deploy state revenue towards social transformation. The perverse incentives of neo-patrimonial politics undermine the transformative productivity as rent allocations are not underpinned by a system that is committed to a development agenda (Booth and Golooba-Mutebi 2012, Kelsall 2013). In this case, economic activity may be productive but not inclusive, growth might take place without transformation, and basic social services can be adversely undermined (IMF 2016: 13, Kjaer and Katusiimeh 2012).

If we approach this from an institutionalist conceptual angle, a system undergirded by pervasive political corruption produces a rentier political economy. The system, and especially its underlying institutions, are reproduced through a feedback loop between the

---

[7] Interview with Augustine Ruzindana, former government Ombudsman and former MP, Kampala, 13 March 2018.

institutions in place and the economic outcomes they generate (North 1982). From the point of view of historical institutionalism, different scholars have variously identified such economic systems as extractive and limited access orders (Acemoglu and Robinson 2012, North et al. 2009).

The empirical implications of such systems, historically, have been the absence of structural transformation, and growth in wealth inequality. This was the case with colonial economies that were outrightly extractivist. Many African economies have remained trapped in these extractive systems for most of the post-independence times, only that the power of economic extraction shifted from colonial actors to independent patrimonial ruling classes.

The record of African economic performance over the past half century of independence has been underwhelming, and Uganda is no exception despite attempts to present it as a 'success story' (Kuteesa et al. 2010). Economic reforms in much of Africa have tended to stumble, and the recorded growth from the 1970s through the 1990s was very disappointing with limited industrialisation and economic diversification (van de Walle 2001, Whitfield et al. 2015).

In Uganda, scholars have aptly underlined the paradox of economic growth without structural transformation (Golooba-Mutebi and Hickey 2013: 24, Kjaer 2015: 231, Kjaer and Katusi-imeh 2012: 10). Part of the explanation for this is the structure of the economy itself and the fact that growth has not been in the crucial sectors like manufacturing, which can make an overall structural difference.

However, another explanation has to do with grand and pervasive political corruption that compromises public sector efficiency and undermines prudent resource allocation and utilisation (Asiimwe 2013). There has been a lack of government investment in strategic sectors that can bring about long-term change precisely because such investments may not provide immediate rents to powerful figures in charge of the system. Where there have been exceptions, like in the dairy sector, there was political support for this productive sector as it helped build a stronger political support base and established close ties between the ruling elite and dairy-sector actors (Kjaer 2015: 237).

An important dynamic of political corruption is the extent to which public resources haemorrhage into the hands of individuals both in politics and in the private sector. In Uganda, as is undoubtedly the case in other African countries, some of the key actors in the politics tend to be either the same individuals in private business or at least they have their agents there, thus engaging in inside trading and using their political power to pursue business. Sam Kutesa, for example, named in many corruption scandals, is one of the most powerful politicians in Uganda at the same time as he is a leading businessman. This collusion between political actors and business players can result in the privatisation of public policy altogether (IMF 2016). More generally, corruption undermines the quality and increases the cost of public goods and services (Olken and Pande 2012: 492).

Politically, a system underpinned by political corruption necessarily engenders institutional decay and the deepening of personalist rule.[8] This has been the case in Uganda in recent years, where the incumbent president has used his access to patronage resources to secure his grip on power. As one scholar noted, a perverted system of patron-clientelism 'has thrived as those in power pursue narrow political and sectional interests for survival, reward, and reproduction of their inner-circle and socio-political power bases' (Asiimwe 2013: 131). Asiimwe further notes that in much of the political corruption cases under the NRM, 'the main actors have largely been inner-circle political and military cronies and first-family members who are closely interrelated through ethno-kinship links, alliances, loyalty, collegiality, and clientele relations' (ibid.).

The Ugandan political system has evolved with a contradictory logic of factional fragmentation side by side with a centralised, personalised system of power in what is increasingly an imperial presidency (Khisa 2013). Factional struggles at the lower levels are mediated by a patrimonial structure of power at the top level (Kjaer and Katusiimeh 2012: 13). Even at the centre, there is a simultaneous centralisation along with fragmentation geared at meeting the contending factional demands for access to economic spoils and political inclusion (Khisa 2013, Kjaer 2015). Some scholars have referred to this as a clientelist political settlement (Golooba-Mutebi and Hickey 2013: 4). But rather than a political 'settlement' it is perhaps better conceptualised as a system of political uncertainty

[8] Interview with Ruzindana.

(Khisa 2015), characterised by short-term compromises and manoeuvres to maintain a coalition necessary for regime survival.

On the whole, over the years, cases of grand corruption in government ministries, departments and statutory agencies have become part of regular news-reporting and the subject of endless probe-committees, commissions of inquiry, and investigations by a slew of accountability bodies and prosecutorial agencies. The late 1990s were the watershed period when grand corruption broke into the political schema, but also the time when a plethora of legal and institutional initiatives were brought to bear on political corruption (Flanary and Watt 1999, Tangri and Mwenda 2006). Several committees of parliament have been at work, especially the Public Accounts Committee, drawing on annual reports filed by the Auditor General. The Inspectorate of Government (IG) and Criminal Investigations Department of the police have investigated and attempted to prosecute countless cases. Ad hoc committees and bodies have been set up in the president's office and state house.

These measure and initiatives have for the most part produced a contradictory outcome: political corruption has become far more pervasive, and even regularised, despite the creation of numerous agencies and bodies ostensibly to curb it (Asiimwe 2016, Tangri and Mwenda 2013). The IG, the frontline body in investigating and prosecuting corruption, has for the most part been supine, especially when it comes to big cases involving the powerful people at the top (Ruhweza 2008). The actions and efficacies of all these bodies and institutions are effectively undermined by the top political leadership. Because elite corruption is an important means of consolidating the government in power, the 'top political leaders have influenced and controlled anti-corruption bodies whenever they threatened to expose the corrupt ways of Uganda's state elite' (Tangri and Mwenda 2006: 105).

Some government ministries have even been direct sources of regime-preserving corruption, especially when it comes to campaign financing.[9] Extraction to finance politics has entailed tapping into official government budgets by way of grand corruption that

[9] Interview with Joe Oloka-Onyango, Professor of Law at Makerere University, Kampala, March 2018.

goes unpunished.[10] Military procurement, for instance, constitutes an important source. Unlike government procurement tenders, which are subject to scrutiny and audit, 'military procurement has been classified and highly susceptible to corruption' (Tangri and Mwenda 2003: 551). Through lucrative deals involving massive overpayments, military procurement has for long:

> provided the financial wherewithal needed to fund the NRM's political patronage system (such as raising money for the president's election campaign) as well as for high ranking army officers and government officials to be rewarded personally for their loyalty to the incumbent regime. (Tangri and Mwenda 2003: 551)

CONCLUSION

Political corruption has become systemic and integral to the political system in Uganda today. It is not an unintended consequence, but a product of deliberate choices made as part of a broader strategy of regime consolidation and political survival. Deepening political corruption can trigger the disintegration of the political system, especially when resources dry up, as happened in the Congo under Mobutu. If the proposition that political corruption is the foundation for the survival and sustenance of the NRM regime is accurate, what does this tell us about corruption as a governance problem?

Grand corruption is a political issue that is not amenable to technical fixes. For as long as grand corruption services a critical political end, it can only be ameliorated through a political solution. What that solution can be in concrete terms may be difficult to state precisely, but conceding it has to be a political solution is a key starting point to finding the ultimate remedy. Unless it gets to the point where the top political class do not have to rely on patronage resources to buy their stay in power, corruption remains the leitmotif. If the immediate political payoffs outweigh the costs of political corruption, political elites will remain incentivised to

[10] Interview with Peter Wandera, Director, Transparency International (Uganda), Kampala, July 2018.

politically instrumentalise corruption and to extract rents for personal enrichment as well as 'reinvesting' in sustaining the extant system.

REFERENCES

Acemoglu, D. and J. Robinson (2012), *Why Nations Fail: The Origins of Power, Prosperity and Poverty*, New York: Crown Business.

Amundsen, I. (2006), 'Political corruption and the role of donors (in Uganda)', Bergen: Chr. Michelsen Institute (CMI), Commissioned Report.

Asiimwe, G.B. (2013), 'Of extensive and elusive corruption in Uganda: neo-patronage, power, and narrow interests', *African Studies Review*, 56(2): 129–44.

Asiimwe, G.B. (2016), 'Progress and constraints of civil society anti-corruption initiatives in Uganda, 2008–2015', in B. Davis (ed.), *Corruption: Political, Economic and Social Issues*, New York: Nova Science Publishers.

Bayart, J.-F. (1993), *The State in Africa: The Politics of the Belly*, London and New York: Longman.

BBC (2011a), 'Gilbert Bukenya: Uganda ex-VP charged with CHOGM fraud', 16 June 2011, https://www.bbc.com/news/world-africa-13789542 (accessed 22 November 2018).

BBC (2011b), 'Uganda Chogm ministers face fraud, 5 October 2011, https://www.bbc.com/news/world-africa-15190664 (accessed 22 November 2018).

BBC (2011c), 'Uganda drops Gilbert Bukenya CHOGM fraud charges, 4 November 2011, https://www.bbc.com/news/world-africa-15598628 (accessed 22 November 2018).

Biryabarema, E. (2008), 'Chogm roads inquiry causes storm', Daily Monitor, Kampala, 28 July 2008, https://allafrica.com/stories/200807280183.html (accessed 22 November 2018).

Booth, D. and F. Golooba-Mutebi (2012), 'Developmental patrimonialism? The case of Rwanda', *African Affairs*, 111(444): 379–403.

Borges, M., J. Gans-Morse, A. Makarin, A. Nickow, M. Prasad, V. Watters, T. Mannah-Blankson and D. Zhang (2017), 'Combatting corruption among civil servants: interdisciplinary perspectives on what works', USAID Research and Innovations Grants Working Paper Series. Washington/DC: USAID.

Chabal, P. and J-P. Deloz (1999), *Africa Works: Disorder as Political Instrument*, Bloomington: Indiana University Press.

Cocks, T. (2007), 'Uganda court charges ex-minister with embezzlement', Reuters, 22 May 2007, https://www.reuters.com/article/idUSL22595360 (accessed 22 November 2018).

Fjeldstad, O.H. (2005), 'Corruption in tax administration: lessons from institutional reforms in Uganda', CMI Working Paper 2005:10, Bergen: Chr. Michelsen Institute (CMI).

Flanary, R. and D. Watt (1999), 'The state of corruption: a case study of Uganda', *Third World Quarterly*, 20(3): 515–36.

Gans-Morse, J., M. Borges, A. Makarin, T. Mannah-Blankson, A. Nickow and D. Zhang (2018), 'Reducing bureaucratic corruption: interdisciplinary perspectives on what works', *World Development*, 1(105):171–88.

Golooba-Mutebi, F. and S. Hickey (2013), 'Investigating the links between political settlements and inclusive development in Uganda: towards a research agenda, ESID Working Paper No 20, 1 August 2013, Manchester: University of Manchester.

Human Rights Watch (2013), *Letting the Big Fish Swim: Failure to Prosecute High-Level Corruption in Uganda*, New York: Human Rights Watch.

Huntington P.S. (1968), *Political Order in Changing Societies*, New Haven and London: Yale University Press.

IMF (2016), *Corruption: Costs and Mitigating Strategies*, IMF Staff Discussion Note 16/05, Washington/DC: International Monetary Fund.

IRIN (2006), 'Global fund probe reveals massive graft', IRIN News, 3 April 2006, http://www.irinnews.org/report/58620/uganda-global-fund-probe-reveals-massive-graft (accessed 22 November 2018).

Kasozi, A. (2012), 'Mukula, Muhwezi charges dropped', Daily Monitor, Kampala, June 17, https://www.monitor.co.ug/News/National/Mukula–Muhwezi-charges-dropped/-/688334/1428892/-/x2tfrez/-/%2523 (accessed 07 December 2018).

Kelsall, T. (2013), *The State, Business and Politics in Africa: Challenging the Orthodoxies on Growth and Transformation*, London: Zed Books.

Khisa, M. (2013), 'The making of the "informal state" in Uganda', *Africa Development,* 38(1&2): 191–226.

Khisa, M. (2015), 'Political uncertainty and its impact on social service delivery in Uganda', *Africa Development*, 40(4): 159–88.

Kjaer, A.M. (2015), 'Political settlements and productive sector policies: understanding sector differences in Uganda', *World Development*, 68, 230–41.

Kjaer, A.M. and M. Katusiimeh (2012), 'Growing but not transforming: fragmented ruling coalitions and economic development in Uganda', Copenhagen: Danish Institute for International Studies, DIIS Working Paper 2012/07.

Kuteesa, F., E. Tumusiime-Mutebile, A. Whitworth, and T. Williamson (eds.) (2010), *Uganda's Economic Reforms: Insider accounts.* Oxford: Oxford University Press.

Mutaizibwa, E. (2005), 'Parliament in fresh Kisanja cash scandal', Daily Monitor, Kampala, 17 March 2005, https://allafrica.com/stories/200503170735.html (accessed 10 December 2018).

New Vision (2012), 'GAVI case: Kaboyo guilty, fine Shs20m', 12 June 2012, https://www.newvision.co.ug/new_vision/news/1302478/gavi-kaboyo-guilty-fined-sh20m (accessed 10 December 2018).

Nganda, S.I. (2008), 'Bit by bit account of how Museveni saved Mbabazi', The Observer, Kampala, 5 November 2008, https://www.observer.ug/news-headlines/1495-bit-by-bit-account-of-how-museveni-saved-mbabazi (accessed 22 November 2018).

North, D., J.J. Wallis and B. Weingast (2009), *Violence and Social Orders: A Conceptual Framework for Interpreting Recorded Human History*, Princeton/NJ: Princeton University Press.

North, D.C. (1982), *Structure and Change in Economic History*, New York: WW Norton.

Olken, B.A. and R. Pande (2012), 'Corruption in developing countries', *Annual Review of Economics*, 4(1): 479–509.

Parliament of Uganda (2007), 'Report of the Public Accounts Committee on the Special Audit Report of the Auditor General on the Commonwealth Heads of Government Meeting (Chogm) 2007', Kampala: Parliament of Uganda.

Reno, W. (2002), 'Uganda's politics of war and debt relief, *Review of International Political Economy*, 9(3): 415–35.

Robinson, M. (2007), 'The political economy of governance reforms in Uganda', *Commonwealth & Comparative Politics*, 45(4): 452–74.

Rose-Ackerman, S. and B.J. Palifka (2016), *Corruption and Government: Causes, Consequences, and Reform*, Cambridge: Cambridge University Press.

Ruhweza, D.R. (2008), 'Frustrated or frustrating?: The Inspector General of government and the question of political corruption in Uganda', Kampala: Makerere University, Faculty of Law, Human Rights and Peace Centre, HURIPEC Working Paper 20.

Tangri, R. and A.M. Mwenda (2001), 'Corruption and cronyism in Uganda's privatisation in the 1990s', *African Affairs*, 100(398): 117–33.

Tangri, R. and A.M. Mwenda (2003), 'Military corruption & Ugandan politics since the late 1990s', *Review of African Political Economy*, 30(98): 539–52.

Tangri, R. and A.M. Mwenda (2006), 'Politics, donors and the ineffectiveness of anti-corruption institutions in Uganda', *The Journal of Modern African Studies*, 44(1): 101–24.

Tangri, R. and A.M. Mwenda (2013), *The Politics of Elite Corruption in Africa, Uganda in Comparative Perspective*, London: Routledge.

Taylor, D.S (2012), *Globalization and the Cultures of Business in Africa: From Patrimonialism to Profit*, Bloomington and Indianapolis: Indiana University Press.

The Independent (2008), 'Why Museveni wants IGG to investigate Mbabazi', 12 November 2008, https://www.independent.co.ug/museveni-wants-igg-investigate-mbabazi/ (accessed 22 November 2018).

The Observer (2012), 'How term limits were kicked out in 2005', 13 May 2012, https://observer.ug/component/content/article?id=18710:how-term-limits-were-kicked-out-in-2005 (accessed 08 December 2018).

The Observer (2017), 'Age limit: NRM MPs to change strategy after harsh reaction,' 16 October 2017, https://observer.ug/news/headlines/55448-age-limit-nrm-mps-to-change-strategy-after-harsh-reaction (accessed 8 December 2018).

Tripp, A.M. (2010a), 'The politics of constitution making in Uganda,' in L.E. Miller and L. Aucoin (eds), *Framing the State in Times of Transition: Case Studies in Constitution Making*, Washington DC: US Institute of Peace Press, pp. 158–75.

Tripp, A.M. (2010b), *Museveni's Uganda: Paradoxes of Power in a Hybrid Regime*, Boulder/CO: Lynne Rienner Publishers.

Tushabe, C. (2013), 'Politics of change: the notion of "giving" and feminist struggles in Uganda', in M.N. Amutabi and S.W. Nasong'o (eds), *Regime Change and Succession Politics in Africa. Five Decades of Misrule*, New York/London: Routledge, pp. 142–56.

van de Walle, N. (2001), *African Economies and the Politics of Permanent Crisis, 1979–1999*, Cambridge: Cambridge University Press.

VOA, (2017), 'Uganda opposition MPs reject payments as bribes', *Voice of America*, 25 October 2017, https://www.voanews.com/a/ugandan-opposition-mps-reject-payments-bribes/4085811.html, (accessed 8 December 2018).

Vokes, R. (2016), 'Primaries, patronage, and political personalities in south-western Uganda', *Journal of Eastern African Studies*, 10(4): 660–676.

Weekly Topic (1989), 'From broad-base to bread-base government', *Weekly Topic*, Kampala, 28 June 1989.

Wesaka, A. (2012), 'Anti-corruption court acquits Uganda ministers of shs14 billion Chogm money', Daily Monitor, Kampala, 9 November 2012, https://www.monitor.co.ug/News/National/Anti-corruption-court-acquits-Nasasira–Kutesa–Rukutana/688334-1615896-26h2e0/index.html (accessed 22 November 2018).

Whitfield, L., O. Therkildsen, L. Buur and A.M. Kjaer (2015), *The Politics of African Industrial Policy: A Comparative Perspective*, Cambridge: Cambridge University Press.

WikiLeaks (2009), *Uganda: Scenesetter for Visit of Assistant Secretary Carson*, 19 October 2009, Canonical ID: 09KAMPALA1197_a, https://wikileaks.org/plusd/cables/09KAMPALA1197_a.html (accessed 29 November 2018).

6. The 'secret loans affair' and political corruption in Mozambique

Adriano Nuvunga and Aslak Orre

A DESTRUCTIVE ROLE

By early 2019, the 'secret loans affair' was ravaging Mozambique (Cotterill 2017).[1] These secret loans, most of them acquired in 2013 and totalling some US$2.2 billion, added around 30 per cent to the country's foreign debt (Castel-Branco and Massarongo 2016c: 2, Hanlon 2017: 766) – yet the Mozambican public had no known benefit from them. It was a large-scale, premeditated and cynical scheme threatening the financial stability of the country and the political life of the president and an ex-president. It involved well-known names from the country's state and party elite.

Behind the secret loans affair we find the two drivers of political corruption, that of self-enrichment and that of securing and enhancing political power. Rather than an aberration or exception we see the affair as a symptom revealing systemic traits, and as an epitome of a historical process.

The secret loans brought the destructive role of grand political corruption to the extreme. It contributed significantly to plunging Mozambique back to a situation of high debt, high poverty and low growth, shortly after the discovery of giant offshore natural gas deposits potentially worth hundreds of billions of dollars. The affair

[1] What we refer to as the 'secret loans affair' is frequently referred to in international media also as the 'hidden loans', 'hidden debt' or even the 'Tuna Bond' affair.

jeopardised the Mozambican government's standing with the public, the development partners, and potential business and finance partners.

The country's credit-worthiness plummeted to the worst in the world along with Venezuela (S&P 2019), especially as Mozambique defaulted on an interest payment on dollar-denominated bond notes in January 2017. Foreign direct investment dropped by 40 per cent, foreign grants dropped by 72 per cent, and external loans disbursements by 87 per cent from 2014 to 2017 (Orre and Rønning 2017: 12). Mozambique's net debt to gross domestic product (GDP) increased from a controlled 25 per cent in 2011 to an unsustainable 131 per cent in 2017, one of the highest in the world (S&P 2019). GNI per capita dropped from US$620 in 2014 to US$420 in 2017 (World Bank 2019).

The scandal radically altered the political and economic landscape and led to major public outcry against the country's political powers and institutions. It demonstrated a prolonged failure of the judicial and other government institutions to confront corruption in the political elite – but also timid attempts to re-establish a modicum, or appearance, of rule of law from parts of the justice system and the ruling party. Some within the regime realised that the fallout from the scandal could threaten the survival of the political regime itself.

Despite the optimism of much of the 2000s, which followed the end of the devastating post-independence civil war, Mozambique remains one of the world's poorest and least developed countries, ranking as ninth from the bottom among 189 countries (UNDP 2018). Since independence, its state finances have relied on massive transfers of capital from abroad in terms of loans and donations, and until recently development aid catered for half of the state budget (Orre and Rønning 2017: 18). Experts and the public generally assume that corruption is pervasive in Mozambique and some researchers have estimated the annual cost of corruption, at worst, to be almost equal to the size of the annual state budget (CIP&CMI 2016: 7).

All this makes it a paramount task for Mozambique to understand how the country ended up in this state of entrenched corruption that culminated with the secret loans debacle. An improved system of accountability and public integrity should build upon a clear analysis of the roots of corruption. We therefore discuss how

Mozambique came to this point by tracking the evolution of the political–economic elite at the helm of the Frelimo party in the post-independence era, and by tracing how corruption has been described and explained in the literature. Then, we look at the dual role of political corruption: as a quest for enrichment (the formation of an economic elite) and then as a means to secure political power (the consolidation of the political elite). This forms the basis for our analysis of the secret loans affair in the final section.

ELITE FORMATION AND THE ORIGINS OF CORRUPTION

Frelimo (Frente de Libertação de Moçambique) fought the Portuguese colonial power in a war for independence that started in 1964. The movement originated mainly in the black and non-white sections of colonial society, which despite systematic colonial discrimination were making a living in urban areas. Until independence, Mozambique remained a settler colony where Europeans controlled the modern industrial and urban economy, the transport infrastructure, the military, the civil state administration, the education system – in short, all levers of power. Colonial Mozambique produced no black economic elite.

Thus, the process of installing the Frelimo cadre in the cities as the country's new leadership began only after the revolution in Portugal in April 1974, when the new government in Lisbon settled for a total and hurried decolonisation. Frelimo was the only political movement able and ready to take power.

Frelimo has kept political power ever since independence, and many of the key cadre at independence are still among the most powerful politicians of the country. Not unlike what happened in other 'liberation movement states', they found it difficult to separate their movement, the state and their personal interests. The party installed itself as the 'vanguard' of a one-party state in practice shortly after independence and from 1977 by law. With staff mainly drawn from the party cadre, or subject to party leadership, Frelimo took control over the former Portuguese civil administrative apparatus and the main public enterprises. With the flight of tens of thousands of Portuguese, the party-state also nationalised privately held property. In lieu of a civil society, Frelimo organised workers, peasants, women, youth, teachers and other 'categories' of people into a number of 'mass organisations' (Hanlon 1990: 142–3) in a corporatist structure, controlled by the party (Hall and Young 1997: 69–73, Newitt 2017: 158).

After a long and bloody civil war (1977–92), Frelimo ended the one-party system in 1990. Yet the party has continued as the dominant force in state and society (Weimer and Carrilho 2017: 49–52), winning all five presidential and parliamentary elections. Mozambique is not formally a one-party state, but the ruling party is still so deeply entrenched in the state apparatus that in practice it is still hard to separate one from the other.

Upon this historical backdrop, the academic debate about the origins of corruption in Mozambique has been ongoing since corruption was identified as a major development impediment in the early 1990s. As elsewhere, the two motives of political corruption are clearly present in Mozambique: corruption for personal and group enrichment (extraction) and for the preservation of political power.

Are natural resources and the resource curse to blame for corruption in Mozambique? Without 'the fabulous oil wealth of Angola or Nigeria' it has not been 'hit by the "resource curse" – there simply isn't enough money for big corruption', Hanlon and Mosse argued (2009: 1). True, its resource endowment augmented with the discovery of giant deposits of valuable natural gas offshore. This only enabled the promiscuous borrowing that led to the major increase in national debt after 2010, which culminated with the secret loans affair (Castel-Branco and Massarongo 2016a, 2016b). But political corruption was discussed as a problem long before the Mozambican resource boom of the 2000s. Hence, the boom cannot have caused it.

The most influential line of argument is that in Mozambique corruption emerged because of two scourges. The first calamity was the civil war. It pulverised the national project of the post-independence years, including its collective and altruistic ethos that curtailed corruption. As the economy, public services and trade networks collapsed, the war pushed everyone to 'fend for himself' (Bertelsen 2016, Chingono 1996: 87).

The second calamity that befell Mozambique was the neoliberalist ideology that prescribed the 'rolling back' of the state and 'rolling out' of structural adjustment and privatisation in the late

1980s and 1990s (Abrahamsson and Nilsson 1995: 158, Hanlon 1996, Sumich 2008). This literature argued that liberalisation meant budget cuts and misery for many and opportunity for a few, and, where war had created need, neo-liberalism justified greed. Hanlon, in particular, added to this analysis by including the dominant role of the donors on the Mozambican political economy. He emphasised that the neo-liberalist ideology and politics crept in through western influence, and with it the propensity for corruption. In addition, with the heavy dependence on donor funds, the Mozambican government lost its sense of responsibility towards its own citizenry, feeling accountable to donors as much as voters (Hanlon 2004, 2017).

The common trait in this literature is that opportunity and greed motivated corruption in the political elite. In our view, this literature tends to tilt the balance of blame towards external forces, while downplaying the responsibility of the domestic elite's own responsibility. A subcategory of the corruption-for-enrichment thesis is that 'corruption' has an intentional and beneficial policy objective. Hanlon and Mosse (2009) toyed with the idea that personal enrichment of select elite members in fact served to build a national bourgeoisie, 'national champions', or a national entrepreneurial capitalist class that is gearing up to build industry and economic growth in the way the Asian Tigers developed in the second half of the twentieth century. The authors never returned to the thesis, and the actual development in Mozambique suggests this scenario was highly unlikely.

The 'corruption-in-grief-and-greed' literature did not aim to explore political corruption as a method of underpinning the political power of the party elite. Nevertheless, elite formation was a growing topic of the literature, as it became ever more obvious that one amalgamated political and economic elite consolidated itself under Frelimo's party-state system. It started in embryonic forms at independence and then solidified, as we shall see later, during the privatisation drives in the 1990s (Pitcher 2002).

The most 'successful' Frelimo politicians are also businesspeople. Not all businesspeople may be Frelimo politicians, but all of them enjoy family links – or other close ties – with the political elite. The urban 'middle classes' are also intimately linked to the Frelimo elite in an ambiguous mutual dependency (Sumich 2018: ch. 7) of patron–client relationships. Much recent literature has underscored the unity of Mozambique's political–economic elite under Frelimo, despite its frequently factious political struggles.

The fundamental tenet of Mozambique's economy is the centrality of the state in channelling resources to society – directly through public spending, through the many parastatals, or through businesses that are favoured due to their links with ruling party politicians (Cortês 2018: ch. 7, Nuvunga 2014, Weimer and Carrilho 2017: 47–9). In addition, when the party during the reign of President Armando Guebuza (2004–14) doubled down on its penchant for merging into the state, this time as a semi-official policy, the party increased its influence over the central and local state apparatus. No other political force was relevant to the distribution of wealth – although intra-elite rivalry for business opportunities ensured significant factionalism and opposition within the party (Buur and Whitfield 2014, Cortês 2018). A system was created wherein access to the state's resources was the road to economic opportunity – from the districts to the capital – and that access was negotiated through the Frelimo system.

With that came a new understanding of political corruption, departing from that of 'grief and greed'. Sumich, for instance, brought in the question of political power when observing that, 'The Frelimo elite is becoming a ruling class based on political power, which acts to defend its interests' (Sumich 2008: 124).

We shall in the following explore, as have many authors recently (Cortês 2018, Nuvunga 2014, Orre 2010, Weimer and Carrilho 2017), the possible motives behind political corruption: how the Frelimo political party and its leaders have (mis)used public resources for the party's parochial interests – that is, to maintain political power. Such parochial interests may at times also have been those of the party elite and parts or factions thereof.

CORRUPTION FOR ENRICHMENT

During Mozambique's First Republic (1975–90), which revolved around the charismatic President Samora Machel, there were cases of corruption. But the public ethic was such that when discovered the perpetrators committed suicide – or were shot in the public square. It was revolutionary ideology, moralism and fear – but not exactly integrity. It was the Frelimo ethics, that of the central figure of President Machel, and the ethics of ascetic virtue. This 'Samoraism' did not include nepotism, however, in part because the children of the party leaders were minors.

As the civil war dragged on after 1977, military leaders began to make public procurement. There are reports that, even in socialist 'Samoraist' times, some state agents received generous offers or deals from Brazilian intermediaries when purchasing public buses in the 1980s. Similar deals were reported in the business transactions for the construction of the Pequenos Libombos Dam with Italian partners in the mid-1980s.

Under Structural Adjustment, which was implemented shortly after Machel's death in 1986 and throughout the 1990s, the people who were in the lead of state-owned companies stayed with them, even when their revenues and compensations fell to symbolic value or none at all. The party-state wanted to get rid of these companies, but at the same time it wanted to ensure that they were in the hands of the comrades, both as a preparation of the economic field for political liberalisation and privatisation, and as a strategy in relation to the Renamo rebels who were anticipated to arrive in Maputo sooner or later (Sumich 2018).

The Frelimo political elite thus rushed to seize the assets of the state (Castel-Branco 2015). However, corruption was probably more driven by necessity (social security) than by the accumulation of wealth (greed). With the civil war and economic crisis, the state had almost collapsed and could not meet people's basic needs, and Frelimo elite cohesion and solidarity was eroding. For example, President Chissano's less than dignified treatment of the Machel family after the presidential succession in 1987 may have alerted the cadres that each family needed to get consolidated and fend for itself.

Also in the 1990s, the real-estate assets of the state (known by its acronym APIE) were privatised for free, as the party leaders living in state houses assigned to them for performing official duties were simply transferred to them. Some got more than one property, and some were given several. It provided opportunities on an emerging rental market that was growing with the multiplication of international non-government organisations (NGOs) operating in the country with US dollars. With very few exceptions, this accumulation (or extraction) was for consumption, including meeting the needs of their children and extended families in various provinces of origin.[2]

President Chissano (1986–2003) left a legacy on the structuring of the state and on the behaviour of the elite, much due to the ideological reorientation explained above. Under his rule came the first moments of market economy, and with it came new incentives for corruption. Not only were the 'Samorian' ethics never institutionalised, but the political leadership even made public pronouncements that were understood to normalise or legalise the global handout of state property and markets.

President Chissano did not order people to expropriate state assets in any officially proclaimed policy. He rather adapted to what was going on. His leadership focused on reconstruction, with an aim to disentangle the state and the Frelimo party, in a process that was never completed. Chissano was a professional diplomat, he believed in the market economy, so his biggest challenge was political; to maintain the state that Frelimo had built. By African standards Chissano was not corrupt, but his liberalism allowed corruption to become endemic.

Simple state officials, including teachers, nurses, medical doctors and police officers, extorted citizens in various ways to survive, as the socialist state collapsed. High-level political, public sector and state enterprise bosses, most of them former combatants and 'liberators', expropriated the state for elitist consumption and status in society. They stayed with the companies and formed the embryo of a private sector that was born dependent and umbilically linked to the power of Frelimo. Without capacity and capital, they tried but most of the time failed to keep the companies running.

Three enrichment trends emerged under President Chissano. First, national liberation leaders engaged in the expropriation of state assets. Especially Armando Emílio Guebuza, one of the most senior and controversial leaders in the early independence days, saw the opportunity for enrichment in privatisation (Hanlon 2017: 758, Mosse 2005). With no love lost, Chissano left Guebuza to 'do business' so that he would not interfere in politics. A former minister of transport and communication, Guebuza had deep knowledge of the Mozambican economy. He employed it for his ascent after the

---

2 Interviews with former Frelimo combatants, Maputo, February/March 2019.

death of Samora Machel, particularly with the new political aura he achieved after leading the peace negotiations with Renamo. He then built a business empire based on the 'privatisation' and expropriation of state assets, and through companies connected to the transport and communications sector. Guebuza was a 'liberator' made entrepreneur.

There are also other families that originated in the liberation struggle, and now flashing their wealth, that are more entrenched in the state apparatus and to a lesser extent think of themselves as business families. Some are even using façade names to front their beneficial ownership. One example is the Chipande family (Alberto Chipande was, according to the official story, the man who fired the first shot of the national liberation struggle), who now claim that 'we fought for freedom, then we have the right to be rich' (Weimer et al. 2012: 32).

The second trend is that of the children of the political elite, who are at the interface between the state and private businesses, as entrepreneurs or made entrepreneurs (Cortês 2018: 190–258). The business jargon at the time of Joaquim Chissano was 'smart partnerships' between the state and the private sector (Cortês 2018: 137–53). Thus, Nyimpine Chissano, the eldest son of President Chissano, appeared as a most successful businessman at the time when his father was president of the Republic. Allegedly, the friendship between Nyimpine Chissano with ministers, top leaders and various entrepreneurs was at the centre of the collapse of the Banco Austral (former People's Development Bank). With the pretext of privatisations, this political elite had solicited credit with the Banco Austral, which ended with non-performing loans (NPL) and the bank's collapse. This scandal probably cost the life of several people who got too close to expose the scammers (Hanlon 2002, Mosse 2006).

Furthermore, public procurement was manipulated to enrich the elite's children. The (late) daughter of President Guebuza, Valentina Guebuza, became a publicly known representative of the Guebuza business empire, which obtained lucrative contracts from the state without a public tender, and often with inflated prices. President Guebuza's two eldest sons are also implicated in the secret loans affair (PGR 2019).

The third trend is the connection between the political elite and organised crime. From the end of the 1990s, cases began to emerge of the national territory being used for drug trafficking, particularly to the Republic of South Africa (Gastrow and Mosse 2002). The northern Nampula province with its strong Muslim links to the Middle East and Pakistan was the point of entry, but, because of the extension of the country, contacts and police protection were needed to move containers without being intercepted. Allegedly, this 'protection' extended up to the higher levels of the police hierarchy, and to the political circuits of the Frelimo party. Senior Frelimo leaders received money and luxury goods from drug traffickers in return for protection (US Treasury 2010). This became so sophisticated that, according to reports, the traffickers had the 'political and police power in their hands'.[3]

CORRUPTION TO PRESERVE POWER

These tendencies were developing until 1999, when Frelimo almost lost power. It may well have been electoral fraud that ensured the maintenance of Joaquim Chissano in power (Brito 2016: 29, MPPB 2000, van Dokkum 2017), but the narrow win (52 per cent for Chissano against 48 per cent for Afonso Dhlakama, the Renamo leader) frightened the Frelimo elite and marked the beginning of the end of President Chissano and the rise of President Armando Guebuza.

After the shock of the 1999 election, Frelimo realised it needed money to secure power and win elections, and therefore created its financial and business arm, SPI – Gestão e Investimentos SARL (SPI). Soon, SPI began to receive stakes in fabulous deals, without public tender, that ensured revenues for the party (CIP 2007). SPI received joint ventures with the government, and it attracted foreign investments without paying its share. It also followed the formula of expropriation of state assets. The profits were used to pay for part of the running costs of the Frelimo party machinery, while parts remained in the hands of the top Frelimo leaders.[4]

The companies associated with the SPI holding were also politically privileged with opportunities. The following are some examples. In 2005, through an international public joint venture the

[3] Interview with former police commander, March 2019.
[4] Informal interview with a former senior party leader, Maputo, February 2018.

government had awarded the non-intrusive inspection services of harbours and borders (scanners) to a private company, Kudumba Investments Lda., in which the SPI is one of the major shareholders. Kudumba was not eligible for the tender because it had a clear conflict of interest as it imports commercial goods. Neither did it present a competitive financial offer. But the contract was awarded to Kudumba as it had business interests linked to the political elite, and its link to SPI meant a lot at the final decision-making stage (CIP 2007).

In December 2010, the SPI joined a consortium with the Vietnamese Viettel to form Movitel, which submitted a bid that won the tender for the country's third mobile-phone licence, although it did not make the best offer (Telegeography 2011). The list of SPI businesses extends even further, to the extractive industry, where it holds at least seven prospection and exploration licences, according to the mining register (GoM 2019). The list includes interests or shares in important public companies, such as Petróleos de Moçambique, the giant Cahora Bassa Hydroelectric Dam, and the Mozambican Insurance Company, as well as companies with a state participation.

While SPI represented the classic corruption formula to generate funding for the party, Frelimo also felt a need to distribute small corruption opportunities ('rents') to its political base at the local level. It then institutionalised the Local Investment Budget Initiative (OIIL), which later became the District Development Fund (FDD) in 2009, as the local community development mechanism. This facility became known as the '7 million', since initially 7 million meticais (approximately 300,000 US dollars) was distributed annually to each district, from which the District Administration granted loans to a large number of local applicants (most of it never repaid).

Various analyses and studies following this (Nuvunga 2014, Orre and Forquilha 2012, Tvedten 2016) show that the FDD was a political credit facility that distributed money to comrades while denied it to opposition party members. Personal benefit followed from being a member of Frelimo, keeping members faithful to the party hierarchy, while enticing the co-option of opposition followers. The 2009 election result, where Frelimo obtained more than two-thirds of seats in the Assembly of the Republic, can partly be explained by the effects of OIIL and then FDD, at the local level.

In the capital Maputo, one corrupt economic instrument for maintaining elite cohesion was the Confederation of Economic Associations (CTA), which is the business arm of the so-called public–private partnership. Having evolved in the context of economic reform and privatisations, CTA is the instrument that allows the organised distribution of business opportunities from the state to the private sector (Nuvunga 2014). The state is the main economic agent in Mozambique and accounts for more than 90 per cent of transactions, mainly through its procurements. The CTA ensures that state contracts go to the right hands, meaning people linked to the Frelimo party and/or a specific faction. It is also CTA that distributes opportunities for foreign direct investments.

The CTA also organises the envoys in the numerous business missions that travel with the president of the Republic. On one occasion, under President Guebuza, the CTA gave a luxurious vehicle to the president, despite the public outrage for violating the law of public probity. The CTA arranges the financial contributions to the ruling party and through it Frelimo maintains support to – and control over – the private sector.[5]

In turn, the private business sector sees Frelimo's continuity in power as structurally beneficial (Nuvunga 2014), and the government maintains a private sector that is politically docile. For fear of losing the privileges, businesses will not support opposition parties and candidates (Cortês 2018: ch. 4.3).

THE 'SECRET LOANS AFFAIR': GREED AND POLITICAL AMBITION?

In April 2016, the 'secret loans affair' sprung on to the Mozambican political scene. The International Monetary Fund (IMF) discovered that in addition to loans to the 'tuna fishing company' EMATUM (publicly known since 2014) there were two more companies apparently owned and controlled by the military and intelligence apparatus – MAM and ProIndicus – that had borrowed large sums, without informing the Mozambican parliament or its citizens, nor Mozambique's donor community. Together, they had borrowed

[5] Interviews with former CTA CEOs in Maputo, January 2019.

more than US$2 billion (Kroll 2017). None of it entered accounts in Mozambique. Credit Suisse and the Russian bank VTB provided the loans, respectively: US$500 million and US$350 million for EMATUM (ostensibly a Tuna fishing business), and US$623 and US$122 million for ProIndicus (ostensibly for maritime security). MAM received a financing of US$535 million from VTB alone (for dock installations). On top of it all, it was revealed that secret supplier's credits to the Ministry of Interior were worth another US$221 million, which had been used to buy military hardware and riot-control equipment (Hanlon 2017).

It is now clear that the key figures involved in this massive scam were very senior government officials and Frelimo politicians. The conspiracy also involved employees of the two banks. They arranged the 'loans' for the three Mozambican companies, and transferred it to the accounts of the Abu Dhabi-based naval construction company Privinvest. Privinvest sent some boats and equipment to the three Mozambican companies, but subsequent audits (Kroll 2017) and inquiries made it clear that the equipment was overpriced, and furthermore that the companies were unviable, and appeared as a mere façade to attract the loans (Comissão Parlamentar de Inquérito 2016).

Suspicion about the politicians involved soon emerged. Donors and the government hired the audit firm Kroll to investigate in 2017, but two years later the government had only published a summary of the report, though a full but anonymised version of it has leaked (Kroll 2017). The Kroll report made it clear that the key people and authorities had been uncooperative in the audit process. Senior politicians and public servants were in April 2019 officially accused of having taken bribes (PGR 2019) – some also actively conspiring – to make it possible to issue the necessary Mozambican sovereign guarantees for the loans (US Indictment 2018), in breach of the law and the Constitution (Comissão Parlamentar de Inquérito 2016). They included two former chiefs of the secret services (SISE) and some of the ruling party's top politicians and bureaucrats, including the Minister of Finance in 2013, Manuel Chang, and the then President of the National Bank, Ernesto Gove.

The involved parties appear to have split the borrowed money. One share went to the involved European banks or bankers in the form of exceptionally high fees and kickbacks. Likewise, another share went to the intermediaries and the shipbuilders of Privinvest (which resulted in the only known tangible goods procured, that is, a number of fishing vessels and patrol boats docked and rusting in the Maputo harbour since they arrived). We believe that at least US$1 billion was left with Privinvest. A third part appear to have gone to bribes to Mozambican politicians and officials in and around the ruling party, possibly up to US$300 million.

The Attorney General, drawing on information from the auditors (Kroll 2017) and the FBI (US Indictment 2018), formally accused Ndambi Guebuza (President Guebuza's son) of asking Privinvest's Jean Boustani to reserve US$50 million to 'massage the system' in Mozambique, that is, for bribes. Out of this, much appear to have been distributed and spent on items of luxury and ostentatious consumption, ranging from cattle and ranches to cars and apartments, in addition to parties (Savana 2019: 1–4).

It is also possible that these politicians channelled some of the proceeds for other purposes, such as financing the war efforts against Renamo (the conflict had once again reignited by late 2014), or to finance Frelimo's electoral campaign that same year. We will argue below however, that a significant portion of the money – the 'missing' money in the audit, to the tune of hundreds of millions of dollars – must have stayed with key people in the top leadership of the Frelimo party, but hitherto there is no proof or clarity about it.

Three years after the scandal burst in 2016, the Mozambican Attorney General formally issued a charge against former finance minister Manuel Chang following his arrest in South Africa in December 2018 (PGR 2019). South African authorities had arrested Chang after an extradition request by the USA, who wanted to put him on trial in the USA for involvement in money laundering and fraud. The timing of the Mozambican charges against him therefore appeared as a response to control the situation, rather than as a proactive search for justice and accountability. On the other hand, the Mozambican Attorney General also issued charges against two former heads of the secret services, a former governor of the National Bank, and in total 20 senior politicians and bureaucrats (PGR 2019). In Mozambique, many people strongly suspect the involvement of former President Armando Guebuza (2004–14), in particular after the arrest of both his son, his personal secretary and his political adviser (Savana 2019). Finally, as Guebuza's protégé, the case throws long shadows over current President Filipe Nyusi.

In short, the secret loans affair had drawn in the top leadership of the only party that has ruled Mozambique since independence.

Could the real motif behind the secret loans be linked to President Guebuza's ambitions to maintain his political power? Many of the involved may have wanted to enrich themselves by accepting bribes (Mozambican politicians) and kickbacks (the bribers in the banks and in Privinvest), but President Guebuza – already known as the richest man in Mozambique – had ambitions beyond enrichment alone. When the planning of the secret loans took place, Guebuza was nearing the end of his second – and according to the Mozambican constitution, final – term of his presidency. Guebuza's ambition was to bend the party into accepting him for a third term for the upcoming elections in 2014. He may have figured it would require massive amounts of money to pay for bribes and patronage to gather support for his third-term ambitions.

That plan failed in the end, whereupon Filipe Nyusi became Frelimo's candidate. Nyusi, linked to other powerful liberator politicians who are ethnic Makonde, was the Minister of Defence in Guebuza's government in 2013 – at the time when the Ministry of Defence and Security controlled the companies ProIndicus and MAM and borrowed more than 1 billion US dollars. The Frelimo elite already had a long history of stretching the banking system for credit to finance inviable projects. In short, there were few other sources available to muster fresh resources for his political ambition to stay on as president of the Republic. The hypothesis left is that the grand scheme of the hidden loans was an attempt to use the gas resources offshore as collateral and, in one blow, gather in secret an amount so huge it could not be matched by any other Mozambican politician. But, in the words of Cortês (2018: 319), Guebuza got close, but failed, to install himself as the 'big man' of Mozambican politics.

CONCLUSION

Over time, the political elite has found ways of accumulating public wealth for personal benefit, using political influence to get hold of state assets or other public goods. Senior politicians are enriching themselves and their families, and some are involved in international criminal networks. No economic elite has developed outside of the Frelimo-connected elite network.

In this clientelistic and rent-seeking political economy, access to economic opportunity is monopolised by the Frelimo party-state system. To win political support, one must wield economic clout. Thus, if our analysis is correct, one cannot be separated from the other: personal enrichment is the way to secure political power, and political power is the way to secure personal enrichment.

However, our historical analysis allows for a distinction. If, by and large, the presidency of Chissano until 2003 allowed corruption for elite enrichment alone – then Guebuza's presidency was marked by a turn towards making use of corruption to secure political power for the party and the elite – and then, in the end, to secure political power for Guebuza himself and his acolytes.

That brought us to the secret loans case, which is analytically interesting in its excesses: if the goal was to enrich the Mozambican politically exposed people, they may end up personally ruined. If the goal was to secure political power for the ruling party, or a faction of it, the debacle may well have severely undermined its legitimacy and threatened its hold on political power.

We also find that the secret loans affair is difficult to explain by greed alone. Political ambition and the need to secure large funding for patronage to 'buy' clients and political power is a likely motive. The sheer scale of the conspiratorial operation suggests that the very political top had knowledge of the scam. It is therefore tempting to hypothesise that it was President Guebuza's ambition to secure a third term in power that best explains the drive to secure the secret loans.

None of it would have been possible, however, without the specific historical trajectory laid out above, which has made political corruption a central tenet of the political economy of the Mozambican party-state. The question now is if the forces within Frelimo, and the pressures from civil society and external actors, will be enough to ensure accountability for the perpetrators of the giant corruption of the secret loans affair – and yet ensure Frelimo's cohesion and electoral victories in the future. No members of the Mozambican justice system are accused, or suspected, of taking bribes. It is yet to be known if that signals that accountability is in the pipeline, or the contrary. Frelimo's factions may eventually ensure unity and status quo, or one faction may ensure that another is held accountable for grand corruption. Achieving both may prove very hard, but hitherto a major systemic schism has been avoided – or delayed.

REFERENCES

Abrahamsson, H. and A. Nilsson (1995), *Mozambique The Troubled Transition: From Socialist Construction to Free Market Capitalism*, London: Zed Books.

Bertelsen, B.E. (2016), *Violent Becomings. State Formation, Sociality, and Power in Mozambique*, New York and Oxford: Berghahn.

Brito, L. (2016), 'Intituições políticas e unidade nacional', in IESE (eds), *Desafios para Moçambique 2016*, Maputo: IESE.

Buur, L. and L. Whitfield (2014), 'The politics of industrial policy: ruling elites and their alliances', *Third World Quarterly*, 35(1): 126–44.

Castel-Branco, C.N. (2015), 'Capitalizando' o capitalismo doméstico. Porosidade e acumulação primtiva de capital em Moçambique', *Desafios para Moçambique 2015*, Maputo: IESE.

Castel-Branco, C.N. and F. Massarongo (2016a), 'Chronic of a crisis foretold in advance: public debt in the context of the extractive economy', in *IDeIAS*, 89, Maputo: IESE.

Castel-Branco, C.N. and F. Massarongo (2016b), 'Introduction to the public debt problematic: context and immediate questions', in *IDeIAS*, 85, Maputo: IESE.

Castel-Branco, C.N. and F. Massarongo (2016c), 'Mozambique's secret debt: the impact on the structure of the debt and the economic consequences', in *IDeIAS*, 86, Maputo: IESE.

Chingono, M.F. (1996), *The State, Violence and Development: The Political Economy of War in Mozambique*, Aldershot: Avebury.

CIP (2007), 'Procurement público e transparência em Moçambique: O caso dos scanners de inspecção não intrusiva', in Centre for Public Integrity newsletter, 2, Maputo: CIP.

CIP&CMI (2016), *The Costs of Corruption to the Mozambican Economy. Why it is Important to Fight Corruption in a Climate of Fiscal Fragility*, CMI report 6, Bergen: CMI.

Comissão Parlamentar de Inquérito (2016), *Relatório da Comissão Parlamentar de Inquérito para Averiguar a Situação da Dívida Pública*, 30 November 2016, Maputo: Assembleia Nacional de Moçambique.

Cortês, E. (2018), 'Velhos amigos, novos adversários. As disputas, alianças e reconfigurações empresariais na elite política Moçambicana', PhD, Faculty of Social Sciences, Lisboa: Universidade de Lisboa.

Cotterill, J. (2017), 'State loans at heart of Mozambique debt scandal', Financial Times, 25 June 2019, https://www.ft.com/content/805d2b58-59a2-11e7-b553-e2df1b0c3220 (accessed 25 April 2019).Gastrow, P. and

M. Mosse (2002), Mozambique: threats posed by the penetration of criminal networks, paper presented for the ISS regional seminar, 18 and 19 April, Pretoria.

GoM (2019), Mozambique Mining Cadastre Portal, Maputo: Government of Mozambique, http://portals.flexicadastre.com/mozambique/pt/ (accessed 8 July 2013).

Hall, M. and T. Young (1997), *Confronting Leviathan: Mozambique Since Independence*, London: Hurst.

Hanlon, J. (1990), *Mozambique: The Revolution Under Fire*, London: Zed Press.

Hanlon, J. (1996), *Peace without Profit: How the IMF Blocks Rebuilding in Mozambique*, Oxford: James Currey.

Hanlon, J. (2002), 'Bank corruption becomes site of struggle in Mozambique', *Review of African Political Economy*, 29(91): 53.

Hanlon, J. (2004), 'Do donors promote corruption? The case of Mozambique', *Third World Quarterly*, 25(4).

Hanlon, J. (2017), 'Following the donor-designed path to Mozambique's US$2.2 billion secret debt deal', *Third World Quarterly*, 38(3).

Hanlon, J. and M. Mosse (2009), Is Mozambique's elite moving from corruption to development?, paper presented at UNU-WIDER Conference 12–13 June, Helsinki: UNU-WIDER.

Kroll (2017), Independent audit related to the loans contracted by ProIndicus S.A., EMATUM S.A and Mozambique Asset Management S.A., report prepared for the Office of the Public Prosecutor of the Republic of Mozambique (Private and confidential, leaked report).

Mosse, M. (2005). 'Can Mozambique's new president lead the fight against corruption?', *Review of African Political Economy*, 32(104/105).

Mosse, M. (2006), Siba Siba Macuacua – Cinco anos de injustiça. Maputo: Centro de Integridade Pública.

MPPB (2000), 'Chissano and Frelimo win; Supreme Court rejects Renamo protest', *Mozambique Peace Process Bulletin*, 24.

Newitt, M. (2017), *A Short History of Mozambique*, London: Hurst & Company.

Nuvunga, A. (2014), From the two-party to the dominant party system in Mozambique, 1994–2012. Framing Frelimo Party dominance in context', PhD ', Rotterdam: Erasmus University.

Orre, A. (2010), 'Entrenching the party-state in the multiparty era: opposition parties, traditional authorities and new councils of local representatives in Angola and Mozambique', PhD thesis, Faculty of Social Sciences, University of Bergen.

Orre, A. and S.C. Forquilha (2012), '"Uma iniciativa condenada ao sucesso". O fundo distrital dos 7 milhões e suas consequências para governação em Moçambique', in B. Weimer (ed), *Moçambique: Descentralizar o centralismo. Economia politica, recursos, resultados*, Maputo: IESE.

Orre, A. and H. Rønning (2017), *Mozambique: A Political Economy Analysis*, Report commissioned by the Norwegian Ministry of Foreign Affairs, Oslo: NUPI/CMI.

PGR (2019), *Acusação registada sob nº 33/2019* (Attorney General's indictment against 20 actors in the secret loans affair), 25 March 2019, Tribunal Judicial da Cidade de Maputo.

Pitcher, M.A. (2002), *Transforming Mozambique: The Politics of Privatization, 1975–2000*. New York: Cambridge University Press.

S&P (2019), 'Standard and Poor's Sovereign Risk Indicators', https://www.spratings.com/sri/ (accessed 3 April 2019).

Savana (2019), 'A malta que levou o país à desgraça: Turma dos gangsters', *Savana* (Maputo), 29 March.

Sumich, J. (2008), 'Politics after the time of hunger in Mozambique: a critique of neo-patrimonial interpretation of African elites', *Journal of Southern African Studies*, 34(1).

Sumich, J. (2018), *The Middle Class in Mozambique: The State and the Politics of Transformation in Southern Africa*, New York, NY; Cambridge University Press.

Telegeography (2011), 'Viettel launches Mozambique network', 10 October 2011, https://www.telegeography.com/products/commsupdate/articles/2011/10/10/viettel-launches-mozambique-network/ (accessed 25 April 2019).

Tvedten, I. (2016), *Reality Checks in Mozambique. Final Report 2011–15*, Royal Embassy of Sweden, Bergen & Maputo: CMI & COWI.

UNDP (2018), *Latest Human Development Index (HDI) Ranking*, Statistical Update 2018, http://hdr.undp.org/en/2018-update (accessed 26 April 2019).

US Indictment (2018), *Indictment against Jean Boustani, Manuel Chang, Andrew Pearse, Surjan Singh and Detelina Subeva*, United States District Court, Eastern District of New York, 19 December 2019.

US Treasury (2010), 'Treasury sanctions entities owned by drug kingpin Mohamed Bachir Suleman', U.S. Department of the Treasury, Washington, DC, https://www.treasury.gov/press-center/press-releases/Pages/tg729.aspx (accessed 25 April 2019).

van Dokkum, A. (2017), *Probabilistic Presidency in Mozambique: Anatomy of a Scrambled Election*, Macau: Ukama Academic.

Weimer, B. and J. Carrilho (2017), *Political Economy of Decentralisation in Mozambique – Dynamics, Outcomes, Challenges*, Maputo: IESE.

Weimer, B., J.J. Macuane and L. Buur (2012), 'A economia do political settlement em Moçambique: contexto e implicações da descentralização', in B. Weimer (ed.), *Moçambique: Descentralizar o centralismo. Economia política, recursos e resultados*, Maputo: IESE.

World Bank (2019), World bank data, https://data.worldbank.org (accessed 3 April 2019).

7. Political parties, campaign financing and political corruption in Malawi

Boniface Dulani

REGULATING POLITICAL PARTIES

In the absence of a comprehensive law regulating political parties, the Malawian political parties effectively operated in an unregulated environment from 1994 to 2018. This institutional vacuum made it possible for the parties to operate with very minimal transparency and accountability, especially regarding how they raised and spent funds. This led to numerous cases of political corruption.

This argument, that a weak legal framework governing political parties in Malawi contributed to high levels of political corruption, has, however, largely been based on anecdotal and selective evidence of episodic cases that have not been systematically assessed. The claim cannot be adequately proven without the counterfactual case: whether the enactment of new legislation would lead to greater transparency and accountability in the operation of political parties, and lead to a reduction of political corruption.

The enactment in 2018 of a new, comprehensive law to regulate the activities of political parties in Malawi has made it possible to adopt a comparative analytical framework to assess the state of political corruption before and after 2018. This chapter seeks to answer two main questions. The first is how, and to what extent, a weak regulatory framework governing political parties between 1993 and 2018 contributed to political corruption in Malawi. The second is what provisions were included in the Political Parties Act (2018) aimed at curbing political corruption, and to what effect.

This chapter draws from an extensive literature review, supplemented by interviews with key informants, to trace the linkage in Malawi between the laws regulating political parties and the extent of political corruption. The literature review examined legal texts, media reports and academic literature, and key informant interviews were conducted in March 2019 with individuals drawn from the worlds of academia, civil society and political leaders.

The evidence adduced in this chapter is consistent with the literature that suggests that corruption is likely to increase in a weak legal environment. In particular, when Malawi had no effective regulation on the activities of political parties, there were several high-profile cases of political corruption involving political parties and political leaders. This includes cases where political parties failed to account for public funds that sometimes ended up in the pockets of party leaders; cases of abuse of public resources to advance partisan goals through 'handouts'; as well as cases where political parties from both the opposition and ruling sides solicited funding from private donors seeking to gain government business and contracts.

However, the lengthy delay in effecting the Act, which only came into force in December 2018, means that the new law's ability to reduce political corruption is yet to be truly tested. Although the new legislation has introduced several clauses that increase the prospects of curbing political corruption in Malawi, the extent to which the new law has served as a panacea for eliminating political corruption in Malawi remains anecdotal, but it is, unfortunately, not very promising.

INSTITUTIONS AND DETERRENCE OF POLITICAL CORRUPTION

It is generally agreed that strong institutions are an important deterrent in preventing corruption in any society (Alence 2004, Gerring and Thacker 2005, World Bank 1997). Conversely, weak institutions, while they do not in themselves cause corruption, serve as less of a deterrent and can therefore lead to the proliferation of corruption. The World Bank (1997: 12) sums up this linkage when contending that 'corruption tends to flourish when institutions are weak'.

While agreeing that institutional weakness can, and does, lead to corruption, most analyses fail to recognise that political leaders might create and deliberately maintain weak institutions as a strategy to allow themselves access to the proceeds of corruption. This is especially the case in societies where political access thrives on rent-seeking behaviour. The weakness of institutions and the resultant corruption, therefore, might be a manifestation of the way political power is organised, contested and exercised. In such cases, corruption might be viewed as a tool for political management.

After a brief experiment with democratic politics between 1964 and 1966, Malawi adopted a new constitution in 1966 that declared the country as a one-party state, which lasted for the next 28 years. During the one-party era, corruption was controlled, with laws imposing stiff penalties for individuals convicted of indulging in corrupt behaviour (Mkamanga 2018). The view that the authoritarian regime suppressed corruption is further echoed by Anders (2002: 4) when he contends that 'between 1964 and 1994, crime and corruption were rare exceptions [...] people got their jobs in the government on grounds of their qualifications and not because of their connections to senior civil servants and politicians'.

However, a combination of poor economic performance from the mid-1970s through the 1980s resulted in the weakening of the economic foundations of the one-party state, and ultimately led to domestic protests and calls for political reform. The combination of domestic and global forces eventually compelled the government of then president-for-life Hastings Kamuzu Banda to call for a referendum to decide whether to maintain one-party rule or adopt multiparty democratic politics. The results of the referendum, which was held in June 1993, saw just slightly under two-thirds of voters (63 per cent) expressing preference for adopting multiparty democracy (Dzimbiri 1998: 91).

In the aftermath of the 1993 referendum, the 1966 Constitution was repealed to allow for competitive multiparty politics. Additionally, new governance institutions were established, and new laws enacted, including laws that sought to regulate political parties and stymie corruption. Among these new rules was the Political Parties (Registration and Regulation) Act of 1993, the aim of which was to govern the registration and regulation of political parties, and the Corrupt Practices Act (1995), which established the Anti-Corruption Bureau as a body mandated to lead the fight against corruption in the country. Following the passage of the Corrupt Practices Act, several new pieces of legislation have been enacted with the goal of closing off opportunities for corrupt behaviour. These include the Public Procurement Act (2003); Public Audit Act (2003); Money Laundering, Proceeds of Serious Crime and Terrorism Act (2006); Declaration of Assets, Liabilities and Business Act (2013); Access to Information Act (2017), and the Political Parties Act (2018), just to mention a few. The Public Procurement Act set out to promote transparency in public procurement of goods and services while the Declaration of Assets Act seeks to promote accountability among senior public officials, including senior politicians, by requiring them to declare their assets and liabilities upon assuming their positions and at regular intervals.

REGULATION OF POLITICAL PARTIES IN MALAWI

In November 2017, after nearly a quarter century of procrastinating, Malawi passed the Political Parties Act to better govern the registration and regulation of political parties. The new law replaced the one that had been passed on the eve of the reintroduction of democratic politics in 1993. The old Political Parties (Registration and Regulation) Act was based on the understanding that substantive legislation on political parties would be enacted by the new democratic parliament after the 1994 elections. However, no such new legislation was ever debated until 2017 when parliament passed the new comprehensive bill. The new law provided detailed guidelines for the registration and regulation of political parties.

Although the 1993 Act was praised for laying the foundations for multiparty politics in Malawi, it was criticised for not including provisions that would have promoted a culture of transparency and accountability among political parties (Chunga 2014, Gloppen et al. 2004, Nyondo 2016, Patel 2005, Svasand 2014). The absence of an effective regulation of political parties stemmed from the law's silence on party finances: there was no regulation to require the parties to disclose the sources of their funding, or publicly account for the use of their assets (Patel 2005: 40). Contributing to the muddling of the situation was the fact that the new constitution adopted in 1994 included a provision for public funding to political parties that won at least 10 per cent of the national vote in parliamentary elections.[1] However, unlike other recipients of public funds, the law did not oblige the political parties to present audited reports to parliament (Chirwa et al. 2013: 68).

The combined absence of legal rules requiring political parties to declare their sources of funding (public and private) and to account for their spending created an environment that festered corruption in Malawi. In the words of one key informant:

> By omitting all requirements for transparency in how parties acquire funds and how they are utilized, the Political Parties (Registration and Regulation) Act of 1993, inadvertently perhaps, created an environment where political parties act corruptly and without accountability. This has led to the entrenchment of a political culture where business people and companies seeking government contracts have to grease the palms of political leaders of all types in return for government business and contracts.[2]

OPACITY IN PARTY FINANCES

As stated earlier, between 1994 and 2018 Malawi law did not require political parties to declare their sources of funding, and in this absence the Malawian political parties have not been very open in disclosing who their main donors are. In a study of five major political parties (Patel 2005), it was even found that none had any records on the sources and amounts of funds they had raised.

According to the constitutions of Malawi's five largest political parties – Democratic Progressive Party (DPP), Malawi Congress Party (MCP), People's Party (PP), United Democratic Front (UDF) and the new United Transformation Movement (UTM) – there are no limitations to either the sources of funds nor the amounts that can be donated. The UDF Constitution, for example, simply states that the party will raise funds 'through the acceptance of donations, gifts of money or other property [...] from any source' and the constitution of the newest political party in Malawi, UTM, states

1 See: Section 40(2) of the Malawi Constitution.
2 Interview with a Zomba University academic, Zomba, 21 March 2019.

that 'any person or group of persons [...] may make donations to the party'.[3]

The absence of legal requirements meant that political parties have had to rely on their own internal rules to guide them on whether or not to declare their key donors, and to what audience. This reliance on internal party rules opened up opportunities where party leaders solicit funding from within and outside the country without declaring them.

The political parties, and especially when in power, solicit funds from the business sector and wealthy individuals in return for promises for awarding government business and contracts (Chirwa et al. 2013: 90). At the same time, business leaders rush to make financial and material donations to political parties, especially during election campaign periods, in anticipation of being offered government contracts and businesses. Chikoko (2015) for example, quotes a politician from the governing DPP who acknowledged that the major source of funding for political parties in Malawi, including his own DPP, is 'people who have either interest to have access to government business or have motives that have to be promoted by government'.

Relying on internal party rules has also proved problematic since the constitutions of the major political parties do not oblige their leadership to inform anyone about the sources of their funding. A review of the constitutions of the major political parties in Malawi shows that they are nominally required to present audited financial reports to their rank and file members during party conventions. However, these conferences are rarely held according to schedule, and when they are held they are usually held prior to national elections with a main agenda of filling party leadership positions and selecting the party's presidential candidates for national elections, which pushes the financial controls off the agenda and denies party members information on the financial status of their parties.[4]

In other words, party leaders can use party financial resources as they please. This liberty is used both to serve the interests of the party, and to buttress the power of the party leaders. The latter point was illustrated in mid-2018 when the Secretary General of DPP

---

[3] See UDF Constitution (2012) article 6c, and UTM Constitution article 5(2).

[4] Interview with Executive Director of *Youth and Society*, Mzuzu, 26 November 2018.

denied knowledge of the party's bank account, whose sole signatory was President Peter Mutharika (The Nation 2018). Chikoko (2015) describes the treasurers of Malawi's political parties as 'mere figure heads who hold the titles without actually executing responsibilities expected of their office. Instead, it is party presidents that keep the money, and only the presidents know sources of the funds.' As noted by Svasand (2014: 285), this has contributed to 'the centralization of power in the parties' especially since 'the funding is paid out to the bank account managed by the party leader'.

The lack of accountability extends beyond the management of externally sourced funds, and into the public funds that the Malawian political parties receive from parliament. Although the Constitution mandates the government to provide funding to political parties that secure at least 10 per cent of the national parliamentary vote, both the Political Parties Act of 1993 and the Constitution were silent on the terms of accountability and reporting of these funds.

Therefore, the general practice between 1994 and 2018 was that political parties did not have to explain how the government funds were spent (Chirwa et al. 2013: 68). Matoga (2016) pointed out that 'Malawian political parties that get funding from Parliament are not audited for the millions of taxpayers' money they receive', and Chirwa et al (2013: 36) pointed out that the Malawian political parties even had legal cover for not providing any financial reports on how funds received from state coffers were being spent, as they were not considered state institutions (Chirwa et al. 2013: 36).

Several cases can illustrate the extent to which opaque party financing rules have led to the proliferation of a culture of political corruption in Malawi.

Sugar, Aid and UDF Funding

In 1994, when Malawi ushered in a new democratic government, led by President Bakili Muluzi and his UDF party, Muluzi is said to have used the office of president to gain personal control of 60 per cent of Malawi's lucrative sugar distribution trade. Muluzi was using the profits from his sugar distribution business to build his 'political empire' and to promote the activities of the UDF without being pressured to account for the sources of his funds (Tangri 1999: 107).

Furthermore, a year after stepping down as president in 2004, Muluzi was arrested by the Anti-Corruption Bureau on accusations of pocketing aid funds meant for the Malawi government amounting to 1.7 billion Malawian kwacha (about 12 million US dollars at the time). These aid funds from Taiwan, Libya and other donors were used by Muluzi to finance the UDF's 2004 election campaign (IOL News 2005, Mkandawire 2016). Muluzi's defence in the case (which remains unresolved at the time of writing in 2019) has been that the funds were meant for his UDF party, and not the government of Malawi. It is telling that the funds were deposited into Muluzi's personal bank account instead of the party's, highlighting the weakness of the legal framework on party financing and the extent to which party leaders could use it to accumulate personal wealth and power.

Cashgate and PP Funding

The absence of rules and regulations on the funding of the political parties in Malawi also contributed to one of the country's greatest corruption scandals, dubbed 'Cashgate'. The scandal, which came to light in August 2013, involved the misappropriation by civil servants of nearly US$32 million of public funds from various ministries. They were exploiting the government financial accounting system to syphon funds under the guise of paying for non-existent supplies (Baker Tilly 2014). Although the Cashgate scandal mostly involved civil servants, it later transpired that some of the main culprits were connected to the then ruling People's Party (PP) of President Joyce Banda. For example, among the individuals central to the scandal was Osward Lutepo, who was later convicted and sentenced to serve 11 years for conniving with public officials to defraud the Malawi government of the sum of 4.7 billion Malawian kwacha (about 14 million US dollars at the time). Lutepo was a member of the PP's National Governing Council, and he had donated 22 vehicles to the party. These were reported to have been financed partly by the proceeds from Cashgate (Pasungwi 2018, Zodiak 2014). During his sentencing, Lutepo suggested that his business was used as a means to channel money out from the government and into the People's Party account to finance its political activities (Phiri 2015).

The Lutepo case and other Cashgate-related cases demonstrate how public funds in Malawi are embezzled by politicians and public officials through dubious transactions and contract awards (Kainja 2015). Furthermore, the fact that Cashgate took place over a long period illustrates how public officials are comfortable with corruption as long as it benefits them. Had the Cashgate scandal not been exposed, the Malawi public might never have known that some of its proceeds had gone towards funding the activities of the ruling party at the time.

Pioneer Investments and DPP Funding

A 2018 case involving a Malawian company, Pioneer Investments, and the ruling DPP, offers another example of how the lack of legal guidelines leads to massive corruption going all the way up to the presidency. According to an Anti-Corruption Bureau dossier, Pioneer Investments was awarded a tender to supply food rations to the Malawi Police Services (MPS) in the early part of 2018 (BBC 2018). It transpired, however, that several months before the contract was formally awarded, officials from Pioneer Investments had persuaded MPS officials to issue them with a letter of guarantee to enable them to obtain a bank loan to finance the food rations contract, worth US$3.9 million.

After Pioneer Investments emerged as the 'winning' bidder with the lowest bid, they immediately wrote to the police authorities to increase the price for each food ration unit. MPS yet again agreed to this fresh request and went ahead to request the Treasury to pay the additional fee. Upon being paid, the owner of Pioneer Investments deposited a sum of 145 million Malawian kwacha (about 200,000 US dollars) into a bank account belonging to the ruling Democratic Progressive Party (DPP), of which president Peter Mutharika was the sole signatory (BBC 2018, Mauka 2018).

The DPP initially denied having received the said sums, and the party's Treasurer General claimed ignorance on the existence of the bank account that had been used to deposit the funds. However, confronted with evidence by the media and civil society that included copies of forms indicating that President Mutharika had withdrawn some of the funds from the said bank account, the DPP acknowledged the donation from Pioneer Investments, and agreed to refund the money. However, in the absence of party finance records, there is no proof that the DPP refunded the money as promised (Chitete 2018, Sangala 2018).

A few months after the 145 million Malawian kwacha scandal had been exposed, investigative media reports revealed a new funding scandal involving Pioneer Investments and the DPP. Pioneer Investments was reported to have made yet another donation, this time involving five new vehicles to the DPP (Kasakura and Chikoko 2018). These vehicles, the combined price of which was reported to be 85 million kwacha (about 118,000 US dollars), were all registered in the name of President Peter Mutharika (ibid).

The two Pioneer Investments cases again underline the effects of the absence of a regulatory framework for political parties. The fact that the DPP Treasurer General was unaware of the existence of the bank account that Pioneer Investments used to deposit its funds highlights the extent to which funds are tightly controlled by the party president and the limits of relying on party rules to achieve accountability in the use of party funds.

In a subsequent television interview, Mutharika defended the fact that he was the sole signatory to the DPP bank account, pointing out that this was a common occurrence among organisations (Mandowa 2018, Njalam'mano 2018a). This raises questions not only about transparency and accountability, but also the possibility that the DPP might be operating similar accounts elsewhere that are unknown to the party officials who are supposed to be custodians of the finances of the party.

ABUSE OF PUBLIC RESOURCES

The public funding that Malawian political parties receive, as well as the funding from private sources, have been used in fraudulent ways for party purposes. One of the mechanisms is 'handouts' to buy votes at elections, another is the use of resources of government departments and ministries for party (election) purposes.

Handouts and Vote-Buying

One area where the weaknesses in the legal framework have been exploited is the abuse of funds for 'handouts'. Handouts and vote-buying have become ubiquitous features in Malawian elections. In their discussion on the 2014 elections, Dulani and Dionne (2014b: 220) attribute the prevalence of campaign handouts to the absence of clear ideological distinction between political parties in Africa's new democracies, like Malawi. This, they contend, forces politicians to resort to buy votes through handouts in local government, parliamentary and presidential elections.

Election contestants are distributing private goods, such as cash and gifts, in exchange for electoral support or higher turnout during elections (Cook and Chisoni 2014, Dulani and Dionne 2014a, MESN 2004). In their report on the 2004 elections, for example, it was noted that the then ruling party UDF, and its allies, abused public resources that were given as handouts. 'Supporters were [...] given financial and maize handouts at rallies. These handouts were intended to influence the voting choices of the electorate' (MESN 2004: 4). Dulani and Dionne (2014b: 219) made a similar observation during the 2014 elections, noting that then President Joyce Banda gave out an assortment of handouts during her 'Development Rallies': bags of maize, livestock, houses for the poor and elderly, and even motorbikes to the youth.

The centrality of handouts in Malawi's electoral politics was arguably summed up in the words of former Director of Women in the DPP, Patricia Kaliati, when she observed that politicians cannot do without handouts:

> Giving handouts is part of our political career. You can do your research on how many politicians have survived without giving handouts [...] Without handouts, your people in the constituency can take you as a useless parliamentarian. Whenever I am at home, I spend almost K100 000 (US$239) in handouts every day. (MNA 2014)

Although handouts and vote-buying practices are not necessarily corrupt in a strict legal sense, it is part of a power-preserving mechanism, and it is widely acknowledged that handouts distort elections in favour of wealthy candidates and well-funded political parties (Patel 2005: 59). Ultimately, political campaigns have become very expensive and biased in favour of the incumbent parties, and it can be argued that handouts fuel abuse of public resources when parties use the public money they have received to finance these 'elections gifts'.

Abuse of Public Resources for Campaigning

Another mechanism is the use of public resources for election purposes. Not only have the ruling political parties in Malawi indirectly obtained public funds through parastatal agencies and local government councils, they have also been using public resources for instance to monopolise media coverage on the state-funded broadcaster, the Malawi Broadcasting Corporation (MBC). For example, Gloppen et al. (2004: 11) note that despite the rules that all should have equal campaign coverage on MBC during the election campaign periods, the national broadcaster has been very biased in favour of the ruling parties. During the 1999 elections, MBC is reported to have given 92.9 per cent of positive election news in main news bulletins to the governing UDF party, leaving 7.1 per cent to be shared between all opposition parties and candidates (ibid.).

In addition to government monopoly of the public media, there have been numerous reports of ruling parties using government resources in other ways to support party activities and election campaigns (Gloppen et al. 2004: 11, MESN 2004: 4). Citing election observation reports, Gloppen et al. (2004: 11), for example, point out that during the 1999 elections, the ruling 'UDF and the State President used state resources, including government vehicles, to ferry supporters to their campaign events'.

Another example is that during the 2014 election campaign President Joyce Banda travelled across the country using government resources to preside over events that were described as 'Developmental Rallies'. In fact, these were aimed at campaigning for her party (Dulani and Dionne 2014b: 219, MESN 2014: 30).

More recent examples have been reported in the local media. In 2016, the Blantyre and Mzuzu City Councils each contributed more than US$10,000 towards the DPP's fundraising campaign, while the Lilongwe Water Board contributed nearly US$12,000 towards the same campaign (Daily Times 2017). The expropriation of public funds through 'donations' from government agencies have subverted these agencies and given an unfair advantage to ruling parties, and the practice has been repeated by nearly all Malawian ruling parties.

THE NEW REGULATIONS

The preceding discussion demonstrates the need for reforms in political party regulations in Malawi, a need emphasised by a number of political observers and commentators (Chirwa et al. 2013, Mkamanga 2018, Nyondo 2016). At the same time, and in some respects, the weakness of the laws governing political party affairs can be said to have been deliberate since the political parties were benefitting from the status quo. As Buntaine et al. (2017: 472) note, many developing countries create anti-corruption commissions and pass legislation that is ostensibly aimed at eradicating corruption but is instead used specifically to curb opposition members and intra-party rivals. In the case of Malawi, although the Anti-Corruption Bureau (ACB) has been active in arresting and undertaking efforts to prosecute public officials, trials are infrequent and tend to befall lower-level officials (Freedom House 2012:11). More recently, the ACB decided to exonerate President Peter Mutharika from the Pioneer Investments scam (see above), as 'the president did not personally benefit from the money' (Njalam'mano 2018b).

If the political parties (and their leaders) in Malawi were benefitting from the weak regulatory framework, why did they agree to a new and compressive law that regulates their activities? It has been argued that in a largely aid-dependent country like Malawi, the adoption of anti-corruption legislation was made at the behest of donors (Kolstad et al. 2008: 39). But some domestic actors might also be motivated to adopt rules that might promote party regulations and reduce corruption. For the ruling party, there was the possibility of being lauded for enacting legislation for accountability and democracy, and for the opposition parties there was an opportunity to narrow the funding gap between themselves and the ruling party.

Financial Transparency

The tabling of the Political Parties Bill followed a nation-wide consultative process. The bill was first tabled in parliament in June 2017, and eventually passed in November 2017. President Peter Mutharika assented to the bill two months later, in January 2018, giving it the force of law. However, it was not until 1 November

2018 when the Minister of Justice published an official statement setting 1 December 2018 as the commencement date of the new Act.

The introductory words of the Act state that the law is meant to 'make provision for regulating the registration, financing and functioning of political parties' (GoM 2018), and the new law included several provisions aimed at increasing transparency and accountability in the management and usage of party funds. Among the new innovations was the creation of the office of the Registrar of Political Parties, whose responsibilities include the registration and deregistration of political parties and ensuring the publication of audited annual accounts of political parties.

The 2018 Act introduces several mechanisms that are meant to govern the financing of political parties by the state and by private sources. For instance, the law outlines specific clauses on what activities the public funds given to political parties can pay for, such as parliamentary representation, election expenses and party administration. At the same time, the law explicitly prohibits the use of the public funds for 'personal gain' (GoM 2018: Article 21 (1) (2)). In the event of abuse of these resources, the law empowers the Registrar of Political Parties to recommend the suspension of funds.

The Act further sets out a comprehensive process for accounting, which forms a benchmark to continue to receive public funds. This includes keeping the funds received from the government in a separate bank account, producing statements of final accounts within six months after the end of each financial year, and submitting these to the Registrar of Political Parties, who in turn is required to forward copies to the Auditor General and the Clerk of the National Assembly (Article 23 (1)).

Another innovation in the 2018 Act is a clause that empowers the Auditor General to audit the use of the state funds received. If the Auditor General finds evidence of misuse, he can recommend to the Treasury to impose a variety of punitive measures. In the ultimate case, the Secretary to the Treasury may suspend the allocation of funds to the party (Article 23 (2) (5) and 24 (1)).

The Act also provides details on how private funding and donations are to be handled and processed. While the new law still allows political parties to receive private funding from 'any individual or organization, within or outside Malawi' (Article 27), it nonetheless requires that parties should declare, within 90 days, donations exceeding 1 million Malawian kwacha from individuals and 2 million kwacha from organisations (approximately 1,400 and 2,800 US dollars, respectively) (Article 27 (2)). Furthermore, under Article 27 (3), political parties are prohibited from receiving donations from state-owned corporations, closing off a loophole that had previously been exploited by ruling parties to access public funds to finance their activities.

In addition to promoting greater transparency in the sourcing of party funding, the 2018 law further introduces a number of clauses aimed at promoting accountability in the management of funds that are privately donated to political parties. This includes a requirement for political parties to open dedicated bank accounts in the name of the party for funds donated by private individuals and business (Article 28). Additionally, parties are required by law to have the financial records of privately donated funds audited by a certified public accountant, and to make all financial records available to its members at least once every year (Articles 30 and 31).

Prohibition of Handouts

Another important innovation under the new Political Parties Act is the prohibition of handouts during election campaigns. Article 41 (1) (2) of the 2018 law makes it a crime for candidates and political parties that are contesting or intending to contest in an election to issue handouts. Furthermore, it is also a crime for a person to solicit or procure another person to issue handouts. Any person who contravenes the ban can be prosecuted and is, if convicted, liable to a fine of 10 million Malawian kwacha (14,000 US dollars) and to imprisonment for five years (Article 41 (3)). In addition, the law empowers the line minister to work together with the Electoral Commission, political parties represented in the National Assembly, and other electoral stakeholders to make additional regulations to govern the prohibition of handouts.

A NEW BEGINNING?

In the words of one leading civil society actor, 'the new law offers Malawi a new beginning as it seeks to end the culture of political corruption and impunity'.[5] However, as the Legal Affairs Committee of Parliament chairperson Maxwell Thyolera expressed optimism about the new law, he added that it is 'one thing to have a law, and another thing to abide by it' (Namangale 2018).

Several studies have in the past alluded to the fact that Malawi has always had a tradition of enacting very good laws and developing impressive policies that are not sufficiently applied or implemented. Dulani and Kayuni (2014: viii), for example, argue that Malawi can be considered a star performer when it comes to enacting progressive laws and committing to international protocols, but it is weak when it comes to implementation. Record et al. (2018: 56) note that one of Malawi's major challenges is 'lack of implementation', which results in 'large gaps between the de jure legal and institutional framework and the de facto situation in practice'.

There is thus a real danger that the new Political Parties Law might not be fully implemented. At the time of this writing (early 2019), the Political Parties Act has only been in place for a few months, and it is too early to properly assess the extent to which the new law is transforming the operations of the political parties and contributing towards a reduction in political corruption.

However, some anecdotal evidence points at a rather slow shift in how political parties are operating under the new legal context. First, the fact that the government took a full ten months (February to November 2018) to promulgate the law demonstrates the government's lukewarm commitment to it. Then, the government's failure to initiate the process of appointing a Registrar of Political Parties means that, several months after the 2018 law came into effect, the key office to oversee the law remains unfilled.

Further, as Malawi is gearing up for elections in May 2019, the Centre for Multiparty Democracy (CMD) has bemoaned the fact that, four months after the Political Parties Act became effective,

---

[5] Interview with a youth civil society activist, Mzuzu, 26 November 2018.

there is limited adherence to several provisions of the Act, including the requirement for political parties to declare donations and to end the culture of handouts. There are still some undisclosed 'well-wishers' and some parties are trying to beat the law by putting their party symbols on handouts like sugar bags to make it look like a campaign material (Chirambo 2019).

Thus, although the new legal environment is promising, there is still need for caution, as Malawi has been in similarly promising situations before, but failed to reap the desired benefits. The existence of the law alone might, therefore, not be sufficient to change the political culture of limited transparency and accountability in the operations of political parties and especially how they handle the issue of money. Also, more than a quarter century of campaign politics that largely depend on giving handouts to prospective voters requires a mindset change on the part of the parties, the candidates and the voters to find new ways of campaigning that rely more on issue politics.

REFERENCES

Alence, R. (2004), 'Political institutions and developmental governance in Sub-Saharan Africa', *The Journal of Modern African Studies*, 42(2): 163–87.

Anders, G. (2002), 'Like chameleons. Civil servants and corruption in Malawi', *Bulletin de l'APAD*, 23–24: 1–21.

Baker Tilly (2014), *Report on Fraud and Mismanagement of Malawi Government Finances*, report provided for the Auditor General of the Government of Malawi, 21 February 2014, London: Baker Tilly Business Services Limited.

BBC (2018), 'Malawi's President Mutharika and the police food scandal', BBC News (UK), 4 July 2018, https://www.bbc.com/news/world-africa-44714224 (accessed 18 September 2018).

Buntaine M., B.C. Parks and B.P. Buch (2017), 'Aiming at the wrong targets: the domestic consequences of international efforts to build institutions', *International Studies Quarterly*, 61(2): 471–88.

Chikoko, R. (2015), 'Parties mum on funding', The Nation (Malawi), 11 October 2015, https://mwnation.com/parties-mum-on-funding/ (accessed 22 March 2019).

Chirambo, M. (2019), 'Parties dared on funding', The Nation (Malawi), 1 April 2019, https://mwnation.com/parties-dared-on-funding (accessed 12 April 2019).

Chirwa, W., N. Patel and E. Kanyongolo (2013), *Democracy Report for Malawi*, Stockholm: International IDEA.

Chitete, S. (2018), 'DPP plans to return K145m to Pioneer Investments', *The Nation* (Malawi), 4 August 2018, https://mwnation.com/dpp-plans-to-return-k145m-to-pioneer-investments/ (accessed 4 April 2019).

Chunga, J. (2014), 'Examining the relevance of political parties in Malawi', Afrobarometer Briefing Paper no. 125, East Lansing: Afrobarometer.

Cook, T.D. and C. Chisoni (2014), *Preparing for Elections: Citizens Share their Views on Key Issues & the 2014 Vote*, Lilongwe: Catholic Commission for Justice and Peace (CCJP).

Daily Times (2017), 'DPP must return money to parastatals', Daily Times (Malawi), 18 August 2018, https://www.times.mw/dpp-must-return-money-to-parastatals/ (accessed 8 January 2019).

Dulani, B. and K.Y. Dionne (2014a), 'Incumbency and handouts don't guarantee winning an African election', *Al Jazeera*, 31 May 2014, http://america.aljazeera.com/opinions/2014/5/malawi-electionsjoycebandapeter mutharikaafrica.html (accessed 6 February 2019).

Dulani, B. and K.Y. Dionne (2014b), 'Presidential, parliamentary, and local government elections in Malawi, May 2014', *Electoral Studies*, 36 (December 2014): 218–25.

Dulani, B. and H. Kayuni (2014), *State of the Union: Malawi Country Report*, Lilongwe: SOTU.

Dzimbiri, L. (1998), 'Democratic politics and chameleon like leaders', in K.M. Phiri and K.R. Ross (eds), *Democratisation in Malawi: A Stocktaking*, Blantyre: CLAIM.

Freedom House (2012), *Countries at the Crossroads 2012: Malawi*, Freedom in the World Report, Washington: Freedom House.

Gerring, J. and C. Thacker (2005), 'Do neoliberal policies deter political corruption?', *International Organization*, 59(1): 233–54.

Gloppen, S., E. Kanyongolo, N. Khembo, N. Patel, L. Rakner, L. Svasand, A. Tostensen and M. Bakken (2004), *The Institutional Context of the 2004 General Elections in Malawi*, CMI Report R 2006:21, Bergen: Christian Michelsen Institute.

GoM (2018), *Political Parties Act 2018*, Government of Malawi. Lilongwe: Government Printer.

IOL News (2005), 'Malawi court spares Muluzi from graft bureau', IOL News (South Africa), 25 October 2005, https://www.iol.co.za/news/africa/malawi-court-spares-muluzi-from-graft-bureau-256920 (accessed 5 January 2019).

Kainja, J. (2015), 'What drives corruption in Malawi and why it won', The Conversation, 30 September 2015, http://theconversation.com/what-drives-corruption-in-malawi-and-why-it-wont-disappear-soon-48183 (accessed 6 January 2019).

Kasakura, A. and R. Chikoko (2018), 'Karim still haunts APM', The Nation (Malawi), 20 October 2018, https://mwnation.com/karim-still-haunts-apm/ (accessed 12 February 2019).

Kolstad, I., V. Fritz and T. O'Neil (2008), *Corruption, Anti-Corruption Efforts and Aid: Do Donors Have the Right Approach?*, Working Paper 3, London: ODI (Overseas Development Institute).

Mandowa, P. (2018), 'Malawi President Mutharika defends DPP MK145 million scam', Maravipost (Malawi), 9 August 2018, http://www.maravipost.com/malawi-president-muthalika-defends-dpp-mk145-million-scam/ (accessed 5 January 2019).

Matoga, G. (2016), 'Parties fail to account for public money', The Nation (Malawi), 8 May 2016, https://mwnation.com/parties-fail-to-account-for-public-money/ (accessed 21 January 2019).

Mauka, P. (2018), 'Corruption denying Malawi President Mutharika the legacy he desperately needs', Maravipost (Malawi), 7 December 2018, http://www.maravipost.com/corruption-denying-malawi-president-mutharika-the-legacy-he-desperately-needs/ (accessed 12 January 2019).

MESN (2004), *Republic of Malawi 2004 Parliamentary and Presidential Elections 20 May: Interim Statement*, Blantyre: MESN (Malawi Electoral Support Network).

MESN (2014), *Elections Report: 20th May 2014 Tripartite Elections in Malawi*, Blantyre: MESN (Malawi Electoral Support Network).

Mkamanga, E. (2018), 'Our turn to eat fuelling corruption', The Nation (Malawi), 21 January 2018, https://mwnation.com/turn-eat-fuelling-corruption/ (accessed 21 February 2019).

Mkandawire, L. (2016), 'State fails to prove K1.1 billion corruption', The Nation (Malawi), 7 September 2016, https://mwnation.com/state-fails-to-prove-k1-1bn-corruption/ (accessed 5 January 2019).

MNA (2014), 'Kaliati defends handouts', Malawi News Agency, 12 January 2014, http://mwnation.com/kaliati-defends-handouts/ (accessed 12 October 2018).

Namangale, F. (2018), 'Political Parties Act operational Dec 1', The Nation (Malawi), 4 November 2018, https://mwnation.com/political-parties-act-operational-dec-1/ (accessed 7 April 2019).

Njalam'mano, H. (2018a), 'APM admits receipt of K145 million', Zodiak Online (Malawi), 10 August 2018, https://zodiakmalawi.com/top-stories/apm-admits-receipt-of-k145-million (accessed 5 January 2018).

Njalam'mano, H. (2018b), 'Mutharika cleared in K145 million scam', Zodiak Online (Malawi), 13 August 2018, https://zodiakmalawi.com/top-stories/mutharika-cleared-in-k145-million-scam (accessed 25 April 2018).

Nyondo, E. (2016), 'New law will strengthen political party regulation', *The Nation* (Malawi), 2 September 2016, https://mwnation.com/new-law-will-strengthen-political-party-regulation/ (accessed 11 November 2018).

Pasungwi, J. (2018), 'Lutepo pleads for pardon', The Nation (Malawi), 22 June 2018, https://mwnation.com/lutepo-pleads-for-pardon/ (accessed 5 January 2019).

Patel, N. (2005), *Political Parties: Development and Change in Malawi*, EISA Research Report No 21, Johannesburg/SA: EISA.

Phiri, A. (2015), 'Lutepo jailed 11 years, his illness raises suspicion', The Times (Malawi), 4 September 2015, https://www.times.mw/lutepo-sentenced-to-11-years-as-his-illness-raises-suspicion/ (accessed 7 April 2019).

Record, R., P. Kumar and P. Kondoole (2018), *From Falling Behind to Catching Up. A Country Economic Memorandum for Malawi*, World Bank: Washington DC.

Sangala, T. (2018), 'Mutharika responds to graft claims', The Times (Malawi), 1 July 2018, http://www.times.mw/mutharika-responds-to-graft-claims/ (accessed 14 March 2019).

Svasand, L. (2014), 'Regulating political parties and party functions in Malawi: incentives structures and selective application of the rules', *International Political Science Review*, 35(3): 275–90.

Tangri, R. (1999), *The Politics of Patronage in Africa: Parastatals, Privatization & Private Enterprise*, Oxford: James Currey.

The Nation (2018), 'Police mess snares DPP', The Nation (Malawi), 30 June 2018, https://mwnation.com/police-mess-snares-dpp/ (accessed 22 March 2019).

World Bank (1997), *Helping Countries Combat Corruption*, Washington DC: The World Bank.

Zodiak (2014), 'Lutepo implicates JB in Cashgate', Zodiak Online (Malawi), 21 November 2014, https://www.zodiakmalawi.com/component/k2/lutepo-implicates-jb-in-cashgate (accessed 6 February 2019).

8. Political corruption and state capture in South Africa

Trevor Budhram

FROM COLONIAL RENT-SEEKING TO MODERN STATE CAPTURE

In South Africa the notion of corruption (in the modern sense of the word) can be traced as far back as the colonial occupation and the Paul Kruger era. Hyslop (2005: 779) points out that all interested parties 'advocating a British takeover of the territory made administrative corruption one of their major themes', and that Kruger ensured that his supporters benefitted from the new wealth by developing 'economic policies that might bring new rent-seeking opportunities to those within his patronage networks' (ibid.).

Similarly, the apartheid era re-enforced acts of corruption. In a report entitled *Apartheid Grand Corruption* (van Vuuren 2006), startling incidences of corrupt activity between 1976 and 1994 are described. For example, the Information Scandal of the late 1970s, the cloak-and-dagger operations of the Broederbond, stories of mysterious Swiss bank accounts and illicit ivory trading by the South African Defence Force (ibid.).

Former president F.W. de Klerk, however, claimed in 1997 that crime and corruption have deteriorated seriously since the African National Congress (ANC) took over from the National Party (ibid.: 5). In this, de Klerk fails to acknowledge that in closed and militarised societies under dictatorial rule the truth is hidden from the public view by design, as was the case under his National Party government.

Nevertheless, the advent of democracy in 1994 has seen a relentless upward spiral of corrupt practices in South Africa. There are reports of cabinet ministers and civil servants at all levels being accused, and some found guilty, of perpetrating acts of corruption.

In the post-apartheid era, the procurement of arms by the South African government in the mid- to late 1990s under the Strategic Defence Procurement Package (SDPP) is widely seen as the starting point of large-scale government corruption (Hogg 2016, Sekhotho 2014). Then, in 2005 and 2006, 330 members and former members of parliament (MPs) were implicated in the so-called Travelgate case, where a forensic report described abuse of official travel vouchers in fraudulent and corrupt ways (Jordaan 2005, Mail and Guardian 2008).

Recently, reports and evidence of 'state capture' in South Africa, involving improper and corrupt relationships between high-ranking policymakers and government officials, senior managers of parastatals, corporates, business people and their family members, have been surfacing and continue to surface at regular intervals. Several of these reports have been written or commissioned by different state agencies for oversight and control.

For instance, the Commission of Inquiry into Allegations of State Capture (the so-called Zondo commission) exposed the relationship between a private company, politicians and state functionaries, and placed former President Jacob Zuma and his allies at the centre of the web of corruption (Business Day 2018).

In a report called 'State of Capture' released in October 2016, the Public Protector investigated:

> Alleged improper and unethical conduct by the President and other state functionaries relating to alleged improper relationships and involvement of the Gupta family in the removal and appointment of Ministers and Directors of State-Owned Enterprises resulting in improper and possibly corrupt award of state contracts and benefits to the Gupta family's businesses. (Public Protector 2016/17: frontpage)

Following this, the Public Protector instructed the appointment of a judicial commission of inquiry to investigate, with a view of reporting any crimes to the National Prosecuting Authority (NPA) and the Directorate for Priority Crime Investigation (DPCI). A group of academics also followed up, under the auspices of the State Capacity Research Project (SCRP) and released a report that in broad terms echoed the findings of the Public Protector. They reported that a 'shadow state' and system of patronage had developed at the highest levels under the presidency of Jacob Zuma (Bhorat et al. 2017: 3).

From the above outline of the trajectory from colonial rent-seeking and modern-day state capture, we will look at the context and different manifestations of political corruption in South Africa. The discussion that follows looks at 'power' and its ability to corrupt; it outlines some examples of political corruption and summarises how 'the shadow state' almost ended up with complete state capture and a failed state in South Africa.

POWER CORRUPTS

The phenomena of globalisation and trade liberalisation have brought corruption to public attention, worldwide, and given rise to demands for transparency in both domestic and global politics and markets. Camerer (2009: 3) argues that it is the 'global impetus towards democratization [that] has uncovered large scale abuses of power in previously authoritarian regimes, and citizens everywhere are demanding a greater probity and accountability from their elected representatives'.

It is important to note that Camerer's point leans towards state corruption, which is often associated with self-enrichment opportunities, and the general abuse of entrusted power for personal gain. Similarly, Mbaku (2010: 19) points out that the use of 'public office for private gain' binds it closely to politicians and civil servants. The forms of corruption perpetrated in the public sector vary, but include bribery, extortion, cronyism, nepotism, patronage, graft and embezzlement. While corruption may facilitate criminal enterprise such as drug trafficking, money laundering and human trafficking, it is not restricted to these activities (UN 2004: 3). Corruption is a feature of all societies to varying degrees, and most members of the public understand the word corruption much more broadly to include the abuse of resources, maladministration, theft and fraud.

Corruption has become an issue of major political and economic significance in recent years. The perception in an African context that democratisation and economic liberalisation offer potential routes in dealing with the scourge presents many challenges, in that the secrecy of the crime allows for the elite such as government and large corporate companies to maintain monopolies, prevent entry and discourage innovation if expanding the ranks of the elite would expose existing corruption practices (Johnston 1997, Shleifer and Vishny 1993). The authors argue that democratisation and economic liberalisation improve access to political and economic markets for a few previously disadvantaged but now powerful elites, such as politicians, to illegally amass wealth for themselves and to allow politically influential businesses to protect their businesses and stay in operation indefinitely by securing state contracts.

Mbaku (2010: 18) explains that most people in developing countries see corruption in very practical terms: as theft of public resources by politicians and civil servants; as illegal taxation; as nepotism and favouring relatives, friends and acquaintances in the distribution of public goods and services and in public sector employment; as embezzlement of public funds; as the misuse of one's public office to extract extra-legal income and other benefits; as capricious and selective law enforcement; and as differential treatment of business owners in expectation of bribes for preferential treatment.

According to the law, for instance, the general offence of corruption is in South Africa defined in Section 3 of the Prevention and Combating of Corrupt Activities (PCCA) Act 12 of 2004. This Act states that corruption is where a person (A) gives (or offers to give) someone in a position of power (B) something (called 'gratification' in the Act) to use that power, illegally and unfairly, to the advantage of A or a third person. B will also be guilty of the same crime if he/she accepts (or offers to accept) the gratification to wrongly use his/her position (Moran 2004).

Taken together, these descriptions and definitions all have a certain commonality. They all refer to a form of dereliction of duty that is caused by some form of gratification, whether in the form of wealth or power, and that is considered detrimental to the society in question. Considering the summation of dereliction and power, detriment acts of corruption by persons in the public sector continue unabated, amidst the plethora of legislation and anti-corruption initiatives.

The development of these phenomena in South Africa under the Zuma regime was real, despite the existence of anti-corruption legislation, institutions, initiatives and campaigns. The problem is, as stated in Lord Acton's now famous dictum, that 'all power tends to corrupt and absolute power corrupts absolutely' (cited in Friedrich 1990: 16).

EXTRACTION AND POWER PRESERVATION

Political power is occupied by politicians and their administrative appointees, and position of power is the ultimate enabler for corrupt practices. In South Africa, there is evidence of political corruption where power is used for private gain and getting access to self-enrichment opportunities, and to maintain political power. The political parties have demonstrated an interest in preserving their power positions by dubious means and, in the process, they have compromised their political will to curb corruption.

One example of 'extraction' is described by 'Zondo commission' of inquiry into state capture, which outlined how a powerful politician, then Minister of Environmental Affairs Nomvula Mokonyane, solicited cash, property maintenance and food, using the huge power she wielded in the ANC. Evidence presented suggested that Mokonyane may have been given these benefits to make key environmental decisions in favour of a bidding company (Legalbrief Today 2019: 1). An example of 'power preservation' is the ruling ANC government, which has, during election time, used the resources of the Social Security Agency (SASSA) to give food parcels to 'buy' the votes of the most vulnerable and needy (Public Protector 2016).

The ultimate example of 'extraction' and 'power preservation' in South Africa is described in a 2017 report by the State Capacity Research Project (Bhorat et al 2017). This report shows how the Zuma-centred power elite repurposed and realigned public institutions to build, consolidate and support a 'shadow state'. This 'shadow state' was described as a well-organised clientelistic and patronage network that facilitated corruption and enrichment of a small power elite at the highest levels of government, ensuring a 'ballooning of the public service to create a compliant politically-dependent, bureaucratic class' (ibid.: 2).

This has, of course, the consequence that the implicated political leaders have no political will to address corruption in any serious way. The Kenyan Professor Patrick Lumumba said that a 'lack of willingness among political leaders to fight corruption is fuelling the vice in many African countries' (cited in Malenga 2017). Although South Africa has the legal framework to tackle corruption, it is the lack of political will to prosecute that let the perpetrators off without any repercussions for a long while.

Political leaders in the ANC during the Zuma presidency became complicit, and therefore went into a state of paralysis regarding corruption perpetrated by their colleagues, and Zuma in particular himself. The ANC government opted to back Zuma and took collective responsibility for his corrupt behaviour, in a system of patronage at work with Zuma as the puppet master. No less than a series of nine 'no confidence' motions were brought in parliament to oust Zuma as president by opposition parties, but the ANC closed ranks and backed Zuma.

Most notable, in April 2016, Zuma survived a motion of no confidence following his 'violation of the constitution' and the Nkandla scandal. He later addressed the nation on television and apologised for breaching the country's constitution and using public funds to upgrade his personal homestead in Nkandla in the KwaZulu-Natal province. What is most disturbing of the ANC's response in terms of collective responsibility is its strong tendency to place organisational loyalty above probity. In the process the ANC compromised their political will to fight corruption.

EXAMPLES OF CORRUPTION IN SOUTH AFRICA

Since the advent of democracy in 1994, corruption has allegedly permeated all spheres of government. According to Helen Zille, the Premier of Western Cape and former leader of the country's official opposition party Democratic Alliance, the phenomenon started under former president Nelson Mandela's term in office. She points out that the 'cadre deployment' in government paved the way for cronyism, corruption and the criminal capture of the state (Deklerk 2019).

The following examples outline and trace incidents of large-scale government corruption from the mid-1990s to most recent examples that culminated with the inquiry into state capture.

Extractive: Defence Contract Corruption

Transparency International postulates that defence procurement has produced some of the biggest international corruption scandals (TI 2016: 7). Gili (2013) suggests that 'corruption in defence is dangerous, divisive and wasteful, and the cost is paid by citizens, soldiers, companies and governments. Yet the majority of governments do too little to prevent it, leaving numerous opportunities to hide corruption away from public scrutiny and waste money that could be better spent.' According to the first-ever index measuring how governments prevent and counter corruption in defence, it was found that 70 per cent of countries leave the door open to waste and security threats as they lack the tools to prevent corruption (TI 2015). Countries are scored in bands from very low risk (A) to critical risk (F), and the index places South Africa in Band D, which represents high risk.

The procurement of arms by the South African government in the mid- to late 1990s under the Strategic Defence Procurement Package (SDPP) is widely seen as the starting point of large-scale government corruption in the country (Corruption Watch 2014). Mr Tony Yengeni, at the time chairperson of the parliament's Joint Standing Committee on Defence, admitted to having received an improper benefit in the form of a 47 per cent discount on a luxury vehicle (a Mercedes Benz ML320), arranged by Daimler-Benz Aerospace (Pty) Ltd and Daimler-Benz Aerospace AG, potential suppliers of armaments to the South African government. Yengeni pleaded guilty on a count of fraud, and was sentenced to imprisonment in 2006 (SAFLII 2005).

However, he was not the only one implicated in corrupt dealings related to the SDPP. Patricia de Lille, a former member of parliament for the Pan-Africanist Congress and later the Independent Democrats and former executive mayor of Cape Town, was the first politician to expose corruption in the arms deal, with her De Lille Dossier, a document that showed evidence of bribery within the procurement processes (De Lille 1999).

Her evidence showed that several high-ranking officials, consultants, businesspeople and their families benefitted in one way or another from contracts related to the SDPP, including former minister Joe Modise and Stella Sigcau, his adviser at the time, the adviser and businessman Fana Hlongwane, and the businessmen brothers Shamin, Chippy and Schabir Shaik (SAFLII 2005). The latter was sentenced to imprisonment in 2005, after having been convicted of making a series of corrupt payments to a member of the Executive Council of the Economic Affairs and Tourism in KwaZulu-Natal, Jacob Zuma (later president of South Africa) between 1995 and 1999 (ibid.). Shaik bought Zuma by bribing him with 500,000 South African rand a year (30,000 US dollars), in return for Zuma using his power to lobby in favour of Thompson CSF, a French arms company (Head 2018). During the trial the judge was convinced that Thompson CSF was corrupt and stated that 'we have no doubt that an agreement was reached by Shaik and Thetard that Thompson would pay Zuma R500,000 a year to secure benefits' (Business Report 2005).

Extractive: Travel Vouchers, Kickbacks and More

Corruption by government officials is often designed as an extraction from resources intended for infrastructure development, poverty alleviation programmes, healthcare and a myriad of services that government is constitutionally obligated to provide. Such extraction for private gain from government resources during the Zuma era was endemic and saw the political elite and politically connected individuals systematically benefit, partly because they were not effectively constrained by the law.

For instance, in 2005 and 2006, 330 MPs and former MPs were implicated in abusing official travel vouchers in fraudulent and corrupt ways (Mail and Guardian 2008). At least 25 MPs were convicted of fraud, one of whom was the former Minister of Social Development and now Minister of Women in the Presidency, Bathabile Dlamini.

Later, the Constitutional Court held that Dlamini, who was also the acting CEO of the South African Social Security Agency (SASSA), should be liable for costs relating to a fraudulent contract extension with a distributor of social grants (the Cash Paymaster Services, CPS). The court ordered Dlamini, in her personal capacity, to pay 20 per cent of the costs of the applicants' legal fees, including the cost of two counsel (ENCA 2018). Justice Johan Froneman was very critical of Dlamini's behaviour and said that 'she misled the court to protect herself and so, to prevent the same situation from happening again, Dlamini must be accountable for her part in the sorry saga' (ibid.: 1).

Another graft case is when in December 2016 the former Northern Cape ANC provincial chairman, John Block, and the CEO of the Trifecta group of companies, Christo Scholtz, were each sentenced to 15 years' imprisonment after having been found guilty of corruption and fraud by the Northern Cape High Court (Hoo 2016). The conviction stems from government leases in excess of 100 million rand (6.5 million US dollars), which were arranged with Trifecta in exchange for kickbacks paid to Block. The lease agreements from May 2006 to August 2008 between various state entities and departments in the Northern Cape were a business model that identified rundown buildings that could be renovated into offices and then leased to state entities. Block, a senior politician in the province, had corruptly used his influence to ensure that Scholtz and his companies obtained some of the leases. They were concluded with the state without the necessary statutory protocols and procedures being followed. Block, in return, was paid substantial gratifications (SAFLII 2013).

Brink (2015) provides more examples of political corruption in South Africa, including corruption in local government, widespread 'tenderpreneurship' (a portmanteau of 'tendering' and 'entrepreneur'), the Tshwane Prepaid Meters contract, corruption in the South African Police Service (SAPS), the improper extending of contracts by the Passenger Rail Agency of South Africa (PRASA), and upgrades of a private nature at President Zuma's private home at Nkandla, KwaZulu-Natal. In addition to these, other irregular, unauthorised, fruitless and wasteful expenditures by government in 2015/16 amounted to 79.13 billion rand (5 billion US dollars) (Public Protector 2015/16: 22–45). Amidst the plethora of corruption scandals in South Africa a discussion of every corrupt activity is too many, therefore, the most notable and most illustrative examples of corruption will be discussed.

The Nkandla Scandal

One of the most notable and most illustrative examples of corruption in South Africa is the Nkandla scandal.

The presidency of Jacob Zuma has been plagued with a constant stream of proven misconduct, maladministration, and questionable and corrupt dealings with non-state actors, and most South Africans will agree that Zuma was the chief enabler. At the heart of the scandals is the Nkandla saga, arguably one of the most controversial cases faced by the democratically elected government in South Africa. It can be regarded as the epitome of political corruption in South Africa, which reached the highest levels of government and implicated the president of South Africa himself. In so doing, this corruption scandal became an obstacle to addressing corruption in South Africa (Bruce 2014: 48).

Nkandla, a rural village in the province of KwaZulu-Natal, was the birthplace of Jacob Zuma. His ascendency to the presidency resulted in some major construction and renovation works to his homestead, which comprised of seven relatively small buildings, commonly referred to as 'rondavels' and a 'kraal' for farm animals. Authorised by the Ministry of Public Works, in order to better secure the complex to protect the president and his immediate family, these upgrades were called 'security upgrades' and included fences, alarms and other security items.

However, the upgrades also came to include a chicken coop, a cattle kraal, an amphitheatre and a visitors' centre. These features, which had nothing to do with security, became the centre of the scandal that was to follow (Public Protector 2014). After several complaints by different political parties, the Public Protector initiated an investigation and in 2014 released a report titled 'Secure in Comfort'. However, during this period the Department of Public Works initiated its own investigation and its findings exonerated the president of all wrongdoings, whilst the executive moved to interdict the release of the Public Protector's report (news24 2017).

The report by the Public Protector found that the president had unduly benefitted from the Nkandla upgrades and recommended that he pay back a portion of the cost spent on the non-security upgrades. The Public Protector concluded that none of the government's arguments, such as declaring the president's home a 'national key point', could be advanced, and instead found that the government had created a situation where there was a 'license to loot' (Public Protector 2014). The government's response to the findings of the report was to ignore the recommendations and form an ad hoc committee, chaired by the Minister of Police, who later reported to parliament that the president was exonerated of all wrongdoing on the multimillion rand overspend, and was not required to pay back any money (news24 2017).

Inadvertently, several legal battles ensued. Most notable of the cases is the *Economic Freedom Fighters v. the Speaker of the National Assembly* court case (SAFLII 2016). This was not about the substance of the Nkandla report, but it clarified the role of the Public Protector in the constitutional framework and held that the recommendations of the Public Protector are binding unless overturned by a court of law.

Jacob Zuma was thus made liable for payment of all non-security upgrades. As outlined in the Public Protector report (2014) the president, with the assistance of the South African Police Service and National Treasury, was to determine the costs for non-security upgrades and repay a reasonable portion thereof (news24 2016). In September 2016, the National Treasury released a statement confirming that President Jacob Zuma had paid 7.8 million rand (approximately 500,000 US dollars) for the non-security upgrades to his private Nkandla home, in line with a court order issued in March 2016.

According to the presidency, the president raised the amount through a home loan obtained from VBS Mutual Bank. Many South Africans were sceptical: how did Zuma qualify for such a large sum, and how could he afford to pay back the money? The answers were soon revealed when the VBS Mutual Bank was placed under curatorship in March 2018. The explosive findings of a damning report on the failure of VBS Mutual Bank, named 'The Great Bank Heist' (Motau 2018), reveal how the heist's architects and accomplices stole a bank. Zuma's association with the scandal-ridden bank is not surprising, and it was later learnt that the bank had granted an 8.5 million rand (600,000 US dollar) mortgage to Zuma, which he could not possibly afford, at least nine months before any documents were signed to give the bank security over the loan (news24 2018).

STATE CAPTURE AND THE 'SHADOW STATE'

In an article by Hellman et al. (2003), amply titled 'Seize the State, Seize the Day', the authors postulate that captured economies have emerged in many transition countries, where rent-generating advantages are sold by public officials and politicians to private firms. Pesic (2007: 1) agrees and explains that state capture is carried out by any group or social strata external to the state that exercise decisive influence over state institutions and policies for their own interest, against the public good.

These arguments have found abundant resonance in South Africa, where the term 'state capture' has come to be associated with the Zuma presidency. Bhorat et al. (2017: 4), in their report entitled 'Betrayal of the Promise: How South Africa Is Being Stolen', argues that state capture is a vast, systemic threat akin to a silent coup, and must, therefore, be understood as 'a political project that is given a cover of legitimacy by the vision of radical economic transformation' (ibid.: 4). They argue that unlike political corruption – which can be understood as an individual action that occurs in exceptional cases, facilitated by a loose network of corrupt players, fragmented and opportunistic – state capture is:

> systemic and well-organised by people with established relations. It involves repeated transactions, often on an increasing scale. The focus is not on small-scale looting, but on accessing and redirecting rents away from their intended targets into private hands. To succeed, this needs high-level political protection, including from law enforcement agencies, intense loyalty and a climate of fear; and competitors need to be eliminated (ibid.: 5).

The Bhorat report argues further that 'Jacob Zuma's presidency is aimed at repurposing state institutions to consolidate the Zuma-centred power elite' (ibid.: 4). Its purpose was the maintenance of systemic illegal and/or unethical rent-seeking action, consisting of premeditated and coordinated activities designed to enrich a core group of beneficiaries, to consolidate political power and to ensure the long-term survival of what the report called a 'rent-seeking system' (ibid.: 43).

The Gupta-Zuma Relationship

In this system, the Gupta-Zuma relationship was pivotal. It was in the wake of the Nkandla saga, in which the national executive was perceived to be possibly tainted by corruption, that there arose questions regarding the impartiality and ethics of those in cabinet.

Of particular note was the seemingly close relationship of Jacob Zuma and the influential Gupta family, business 'moguls' who controlled a large conglomerate known as Oakbay Investments (Hogg 2015).

Whilst there were concerns over Jacob Zuma's increasingly erratic behaviour, increasingly the close relationship he seemed to have with the Gupta family came into critique. One of the earliest instances of this was the 'Waterkloof' scandal of 2013, which saw a South African air-force base being used for landing a private jet with guests for a wedding of the Gupta family (Quintal 2018). This resulted is public outcry as the base should only be used by the military or government.

The close relationship between the Guptas and Jacob Zuma came to the fore again in 2015, when President Zuma took an executive decision to dismiss the then finance minister, Nhlanhla Nene. In the aftermath of this decision the deputy finance minister, Mcebisi Jonas, revealed to the nation via television that he had been approached by the Gupta family, taken to their private home in Johannesburg and offered the post of finance minister by them in order to secure their business interests in the country (Bhorat et al. 2017: 38). As the president is the only person in South Africa who can select and appoint cabinet ministers – and the fact that a private, unelected family was now alleged to have infiltrated the president's office to such an extent – was a serious cause of concern to the public.

Similarly, various state bodies were revealed to have potentially unethical connections with the Gupta's company, Oakbay Investments, and/or their various holding companies. State-owned enterprises such as Denel, PRASA, Transnet and Eskom were not immune from the clutches of the Guptas. Evidence shows that the Minister of Public Enterprises at the time made various appointments to the boards of state-owned enterprises (SOEs) that were favourable to the Guptas (ibid.: 39). Findings by the Public Protector (2016) showed that the board of the public power utility, Eskom, was appointed irregularly and in contravention of the King Code of Governance.

Furthermore, Eskom had colluded with a Gupta-owned subsidiary, Tegata, to benefit the private enterprise through the purchasing of shares of Eskom subsidiaries, thereby contravening the Public Finance Management Act of 1999. Investigations also revealed that the Gupta family was aware of Jacob Zuma's plans to remove minister Nene from the position of finance minister at least six weeks prior to announcing it. Of concern was his replacement, Minister Des van Rooyen, who was placed via mobile-phone triangulation at the Gupta's private residence at least seven times in the weeks prior to his appointment (ibid.: 343).

The Bhorat report concludes that a symbiotic relationship between the constitutional state and a 'shadow state' had been built, at the heart of which 12 companies and 15 individuals were connected in one way or another to the Gupta-Zuma family network (Bhorat et al. 2017: 61).

The Bhorat report provided evidence of improper and corrupt relationships between government, parastatals, corporates and individuals, involving vast amounts of money, and these findings were strengthened by the *Sunday Times* in May 2017. The newspaper revealed a series of emails implicating senior employees of the Gupta-owned companies Sahara Holdings and TNA Media, several government ministers and high-ranking officials (Jika 2017). These emails ostensibly showed evidence of improper influence and relationships between the Gupta brothers, their employees and members of the South African government. The strategic composition of this network constitutes the 'shadow state'.

The 'shadow state' also turned to unconstitutional means to protect this business–politics network. For example, the author and outspoken critic of corrupt state employees Paul O'Sullivan firmly believes that the police and National Prosecuting Authority (NPA) had been captured. He outlines a deliberate and effective capture of the criminal justice system by Zuma by removing honest personalities such as Mxolisi Nxasana (head of the NPA), Anwar Dramat (head of the Directorate for Priority Crime Investigation, DPCI) and replacing them with individuals who were willing and able to abandon their constitutional oath of office, and do the bidding for the political corrupt elite (O'Sullivan 2017: 2).

The sacking of the 'good cops' from the police and intelligence services and their replacement with loyalists prepared the ground for the cover-up of illegal rent-seeking and for the redirection of the procurement-spend of the state-owned enterprises. Furthermore, companies and individuals who were prepared to deal with the Gupta-Zuma network were favoured, and those who were not were disfavoured (for instance by not getting contracts, even if they had better Black Employment Equity (BEE) credentials and offered lower prices (Bhorat et al: 2017: 2).

Importantly, the subversion of 'executive authority' has resulted in the hollowing out of the cabinet as South Africa's pre-eminent decision-making body and in its place the establishment of a set of 'kitchen cabinets' of informally constituted elites who compete for favour with Zuma in an unstable crisis-prone complex network – the consolidation of the 'Premier League' as a network of party bosses, to ensure that the National Executive Committee of the ANC remained loyal (ibid.: 3).

After the revelations of state capture, the new president, Cyril Ramaphosa, instituted a commission of inquiry into state capture, corruption and fraud in the public sector. Chaired by the deputy chief justice, Raymond Zondo, the astonishing revelations of testimony, piled on top of the still-unravelling saga of the Gupta state capture – and a growing list of other embarrassing, costly financial shenanigans in South Africa – merely highlight the slippery slope of corruption and how it undermines a nation (du Toit 2018).

For instance, Angelo Agrizzi, the former director of the facilities management company Bosasa, turned whistle-blower and delivered an explosive testimony before the State Capture Commission of Inquiry by revealing how the company had secured multimillion-rand government contracts during Jacob Zuma's presidency. His evidence unpacked corruption, fraud and money laundering as well as collaboration between corrupt managers at Bosasa and government officials in securing massive government contracts and tenders (Legalbrief Today 2019). Agrizzi worked for Bosasa between 1999 and 2017 and had intimate knowledge of how the company improperly secured security, fencing, catering and other contracts from the Departments of Home Affairs, Correctional Services, as well as Justice and Constitutional Development. The total value of these contracts soared to more than 1 billion rand (around 100 million US dollars at the time).

Agrizzi further stated that the NPA officials were bribed to impede the prosecution of Bosasa employees implicated in a Special Investigating Unit (SIU) probe (ibid.). In 2009, the SIU finalised a report that detailed how Bosasa had bribed former prisons boss Linda Mti as well as former correctional services chief financial officer (CFO) Patrick Gillingham with cash, cars and gifts in exchange for major catering and fencing tenders at prisons around the country. The report was referred to the NPA in February 2010, but here the case has been delayed and gathered dust amid allegations of 'political interference' and incompetence (Umraw 2019).

CONCLUSION

This brief foray into some instances of political corruption in South Africa highlights abuse of political power as a contributor to corrupt practices. Corruption in its many forms has penetrated insidiously into the South African government despite existing legislation, the introduction of various statutory bodies to investigate corruption, the government's anti-corruption campaigns and appeals to moral standards in public service, and despite the integrity of many individuals.

Our main concern is the fact that the perpetrators have been willing to compromise their oath of office and, in the process, they are undermining the key pillars of democracy that are responsible for holding those in power to account. South Africa's experience of state capture is an example of how corruption is undermining democracy and rule of law.

South Africa needs some bold steps to combat corruption. The state capture inquiry is one of these necessary bold and remarkable political as well as legal events. The fact that the various commissions of enquiry into corruption have been set up by President Ramaphosa, amidst the fact that it implicates and damages the ruling party ANC, as it implicates some of its most senior members, is a true testament to the strength of South Africa's democracy, its Constitution and rule of law. As the various commissions continue to unpack the extent of the problem, hopefully it will help restore the constitutional state, assert the principle of accountability of the government duly elected to serve all the people of South Africa, and help rebuild the key institutions of the state.

REFERENCES

Bhorat, H., M. Buthelezi, I. Chipkin, S. Duma, L. Mondi, C. Peter, M. Qobo, M. Swilling and H. Friedenstein (2017), 'Betrayal of the promise: how

South Africa is being stolen', *State Capacity Research Project*, May 2017, http://pari.org.za/wp-content/uploads/2017/05/Betrayal-of-the-Promise-2505 2017.pdf (accessed 11 January 2019).

Brink, E. (2015), 'Corruption bigger than Nkandla', Centurion: Solidarity Research Institute, September, https://solidariteit.co.za/wp-content/uploads/2015/09/Solidarity-Corruption-Report-September-2015.pdf (accessed 16 January 2018).

Bruce, D. (2014), 'Control, discipline and punish? Addressing corruption in South Africa', *South African Crime Quarterly*,. 48: 49–62.

Business Day (2018), 'Judge invites Zuma to tell his side of the state capture story', Business Day (South Africa), 14 September 2018, https://www.businesslive.co.za/bd/national/2018-09-13-ranjeni-munusamy-raymond-zondo-wants-jacob-zuma-to-testify-at-state-capture-inquiry/ (accessed 16 March 2019).

Business Report (2005), 'Thomson-CSF is as guilty as Shaik', Business Report (South Africa), 6 June 2005, https://www.iol.co.za/business-report/opinion/thomson-csf-is-as-guilty-as-shaik-752275 (accessed 2 April 2019).

Camerer, M.I. (2009), 'Corruption and reform in democratic South Africa', PhD thesis, Faculty of Political Studies, Johannesburg: University of Witwatersrand.

Corruption Watch (2014), 'The arms deal, what you need to know', http://www.corruptionwatch.org.za/sa-sees-saps-as-most-corrupt-within-the-state-survey/ (accessed 19 December 2019).

Deklerk, A. (2019), 'State capture started under Mandela: Helen Zille', Times Live, 5 April 2019, https://www.timeslive.co.za/politics/2019-04-05-state-capture-started-under-mandela-helen-zille/ (accessed 5 April 2019).

De Lille, P, (1999), 'The Delille dossier', The Arms Deal Virtual Press Office (online resources), http://www.armsdeal-vpo.co.za/special_items/reports/deLilleDossier-01.pdf (accessed 1 April 2019).

du Toit, P. (2018), 'The state capture inquiry: what you need to know', News24, 20 August 2018, https://www.news24.com/Analysis/the-state-capture-inquiry-what-you-need-to-know-20180819 (accessed 12 January 2019).

ENCA, (2018), Dlamini slapped with costs for social grants case, ENCA, 27 September 2018, https://www.enca.com/news/dlamini-slapped-costs-social-grants-case (accessed 12 April 2019).

Friedrich, C.J. (1990), 'Corruption concepts in historical perspective', in A.J. Heidenheimer, M. Johnston and V.T. LeVine (eds), *Political Corruption: A Handbook*, New Brunswick, NJ: Transaction Publishers.

Gili, M. (2013), '70% of governments fail to protect against corruption in the defence sector', Transparency International, Defence and Security press release, 29 January 2013, https://www.transparency.org/news/pressrelease/70_of_governments_fail_to_protect_against_corruption_in_the_defence_sector (accessed 4 April 2019).

Head, T. (2018), 'Who is Schabir Shaik, and what are his links to Jacob Zuma?', The South African, 16 March 2018, https://www.thesouthafrican.com/who-is-schabir-shaik/ (accessed 8 April 2019).

Hellman, J.S., G. Jones and D. Kaufmann (2003), 'Seize the state, seize the day: state capture and influence in transition economies', *Journal of Comparative Economics*, 31(4): 751–73.

Hogg, A. (2015), 'Meet the Gupta family, Zuma's close pals, SA's "chieftains of patronage"', BizNews (South Africa), 17 December 2015, https://www.biznews.com/leadership/2015/12/17/meet-the-gupta-family-zumas-best-pals-sas-chieftains-of-patronage (accessed 3 April 2019).

Hogg, A. (2016), 'Zuma probe clears everyone, himself and ANC included, of arms deal bribery', Biz News, 21 April 2016, https://www.biznews.com/undictated/2016/04/21/zuma-probe-clears-everyone-himself-and-anc-included-of-arms-deal-bribery (accessed 11 January 2019).

Hoo, S.K. (2016), 'ANC's John Block jailed for 15 years', IOL News (South Africa), 6 December 2016, http://www.iol.co.za/news/crime-courts/ancs-john-block-jailed-for-15-years-7111550 (accessed 10 February 2019).

Hyslop, J. (2005), 'Political corruption in South Africa: before and after apartheid', *Journal of Southern African Studies*, 31(4): 773–89.

Jika, T. (2017), 'Exposed: explosive Gupta e-mails at the heart of state capture', Sunday Times, 28 May 2017, http://www.timeslive.co.za/sundaytimes/stnews/2017/05/28/Exposed-Explosive-Gupta-e-mails-at-the-heart-of-state-capture (accessed 11 February 2019).

Johnston, M. (1997), 'Public officials, private interests, and sustainable democracy: when politics and corruption meet', in K. Elliot (ed.), *Corruption and the Global Economy* (Washington, D.C: Institute for international Economics, 1997).

Jordaan, W. (2005), 'Travel scam: NNP man sentenced', News24, 1 April 2005, https://www.news24.com/SouthAfrica/News/Travel-scam-NNP-man-sentenced-20050401 (accessed 17 February 2019).

Legalbrief Today (2019), 'Magistrates' Commission to consider Nair's response', *Legalbrief Today*, 4645, 22 February.

Mail & Guardian (2008), 'Parliament "cover-up" in court', *Mail & Guardian*, 23 May 2008, https://mg.co.za/article/2008-05-23-parliament-cover-up-in-court (accessed on 17 June 2017).

Malenga, B. (2017), 'Lack of political will fueling corruption in Africa', Malawi24, 28 April 2017, https://malawi24.com/2017/04/28/lack-political-will-fueling-corruption-africa-lumumba/ (accessed 1 April 2019).

Mbaku, J.M. (2010), *Corruption in Africa. Causes, Consequences, and Clean-ups*, Lanham/UK: Rowan and Littlefield Publishing Group Inc.

Moran, G. (2004), *Guide to the Prevention and Combating of Corrupt Activities Act*, National Anti-Corruption Forum Report 12 of 2004, Pretoria: National Anti-Corruption Forum.

Motau, T. (2018), *The Great Bank Heist. Investigator's Report to the Prudential Authority*, Johannesburg: VBS Mutual Bank and Werksmann Attorneys, https://www.resbank.co.za/Lists/News%20and%20Publications/Attachments/8830/VBS%20Mutual%20Bank%20-%20The%20Great%20Bank%20Heist.pdf (accessed 9 April 2019).

news24 (2016), 'Full judgment: Constitutional Court rules on Nkandla', news24 (South Africa), 31 March 2016, https://www.news24.com/South

Africa/News/full-text-constitutional-court-rules-on-nkandla-public-protector-20160331 (accessed 2 April 2019).

news24 (2017), 'Officials implicated in Nkandla scandal paid millions', news24 (South Africa), 8 May 2017, https://www.news24.com/SouthAfrica/News/officials-implicated-in-nkandla-scandal-paid-millions-20170508 (accessed 8 April 2019).

news24 (2018), 'VBS, Jacob Zuma and the "sham" Nkandla bond he couldn't afford', news24 (South Africa), 14 October 2018, https://www.news24.com/SouthAfrica/News/vbs-jacob-zuma-and-the-sham-nkandla-bond-he-couldnt-afford-20181014 (accessed 3 April 2019).

O'Sullivan, P. (2017), 'Joining the dots: capture of the criminal justice system', Forensics for Justice, public report, https://www.forensicsforjustice.org/wp-content/uploads/2017/07/00-Joining-the-dots-Capture-of-the-Criminal-Justice-System-2017-06-30.pdf (accessed 2 April 2019).

Pesic, V. (2007), *State Capture and Widespread Corruption in Serbia*, Centre for European Policy Studies (CEPS), Working Document No. 262/March 2007, Brussels: CEPS.

Public Protector (2014), 'Secure in comfort', Public Protector, South Africa, Investigation Report No. 25 of 2014, http://www.pprotect.org/sites/default/files/Legislation_report/Final%20Report%2019%20March%202014%20.pdf (accessed 7 April 2019).

Public Protector (2015), 'Derailed', Public Protector, South Africa, Investigation Report No. 3 of 2015/16, http://www.pprotect.org/sites/default/files/Legislation_report/PRASA_FINAL_28_August_2015.pdf (accessed 22 May 2017).

Public Protector (2016), 'State and party, blurred lines', Public Protector, South Africa, Investigation Report No.12 of 2016, http://www.publicprotector.org/sites/default/files/legislation_report/SASSA_Report.pdf (accessed 3 January 2019).

Public Protector (2016/17), 'State of capture', Public Protector, South Africa, Investigation Report No. 6 of 2016/17, http://www.pprotect.org/sites/default/files/legislation_report/State_Capture_14October2016.pdf (accessed 22 May 2017).

Quintal, G. (2018), 'Jacob Zuma had hand in Guptas' Waterkloof landing', Business Day, 28 November 2018, https://www.businesslive.co.za/bd/national/2018-11-28-jacob-zuma-had-hand-in-guptas-waterkloof-landing-ngoako-ramatlhodi-testifies/ (accessed 18 January 2019).

SAFLII (2005), 'S v Yengeni 2005', Southern African Legal Information Institute (SAFLII), ZAGPHC 117, 11 November 2005, http://www.saflii.org/za/cases/ZAGPHC/2005/117.html (accessed 1 April 2019).

SAFLII (2013), 'National Director of Public Prosecutions v Scholtz and Others', Southern African Legal Information Institute (SAFLII), ZANCHC 48 (2027/2012), 13 December 2013, http://www.saflii.org/za/cases/ZANCHC/2013/48.html (accessed 8 April 2019).

SAFLII (2016), 'Economic Freedom Fighters v Speaker of the National Assembly and Others', Southern African Legal Information Institute

(SAFLII), SA 580 (CC), 31 March 2016, http://www.saflii.org/za/cases/ZACC/2016/11.html (accessed 8 April 2019).

Sekhotho, K. (2014), 'Right2Know, corruption watch to challenge Seriti Commission findings in court', Eyewitness News, 10 November 2018, https://ewn.co.za/2018/10/11/right2know-corruption-watch-to-challenge-seriti-commission-findings-in-court (accessed 13 January 2019).

Shleifer, A. and R. Vishny (1993), 'Corruption', *Quarterly Journal of Economics*, 108(3): 599–617.

TI (2015), 'Government Defence Anti-Corruption Index 2015', Transparency International (TI), http://government.defenceindex.org (accessed 3 April 2019).

TI (2016), *Licence to Bribe? Reducing Corruption Risks Around the Use of Agents in Defence Procurement*, Berlin: Transparency International.

Umraw, A. (2019), 'State capture: Bosasa furnished prison boss Linda Mti's house', Times Live, 22 January 2019, https://www.timeslive.co.za/politics/2019-01-22-state-capture-bosasa-furnished-prison-boss-linda-mtis-house/ (accessed 3 April 2019).

UN (2004), *United Nations Convention against Corruption*, Office on Drugs and Crime, New York: United Nations Publication.

van Vuuren, H. (2006), *Apartheid Grand Corruption. Assessing the Scale of Crimes of Profit in South Africa from 1976 to 1994*, Report, Pretoria, South Africa: Institute for Security Studies (ISS).

9. Stuck in transition: political corruption as power abuse

Inge Amundsen

DEMOCRACY IN RETREAT

Democracy in the world is in retreat, according to several global indexes. According to the 'Freedom in the World' index by Freedom House (2019: 1), freedom in the world has declined over the last 13 consecutive years, and although the overall losses are still shallow compared with the gains of the late twentieth century, the pattern is consistent and ominous. Specifically, many of the countries that democratised between 1988 and 2005 have backslided, 'demonstrating the particular vulnerability of countries whose democratic institutions have shallow roots' (ibid.: 4).

According to the World Bank Institute's Worldwide Governance Indicators, Sub-Sahara Africa has declined on all six indicators since 2006 from a globally low level (WBI 2018). This is confirmed by the V-Dem data-measuring democracy; Africa south of the Sahara has seen little if any progress on liberal democracy over the last decade (V-Dem 2018: 17). Furthermore, as the data on control of corruption in Sub-Sahara Africa also demonstrates a decline over the last decade (V-Dem 2018, WBI 2018), these are good indications that the governance institutions in these countries have been unable to withstand the corruption pressures. This indicates a region stuck in transition; the further democratic progress has stalled.

HELD BACK BY POLITICAL CORRUPTION

Throughout this book, we have highlighted the mechanisms of extraction, how ruling elites are getting the money in; we have highlighted the mechanisms of corrupt power preservation, how ruling elites are spending money to preserve their grip on power. Political corruption leads to entrenched political elites, and the power-preserving mechanisms have been effective in preserving many Sub-Saharan African regimes and their democratic deficiencies. We believe political corruption is contributing significantly in holding back Sub-Sahara Africa's democratic developments.

This is, however, only one out of two basic perspectives on political corruption: the demand-oriented perspective, which in its pure and extreme form can be called kleptocracy – a 'rule by thieves'. This perspective of ours does not rule out the alternative perception on corruption, the supply-oriented perspective that put the bribers in the role as the main corruption drivers. Businesses and economic interests in general, national and international, are indeed central to the corruption problem, and sometimes the key party and main driver. In its pure and extreme form, the bribers can succeed in buying up the entire state apparatus, and when private interests significantly influence a state's decision-making processes to their own advantage, we have a situation of state capture.

In Budhram's chapter on South Africa (Chapter 8 in this volume), he argues that the collusion between the Zuma regime and private interests represented by the Gupta family created a 'shadow state' that almost ended up with state capture and a failed state. In Ojo, Prusa and Amundsen's chapter on Nigeria (Chapter 4 in this volume), it is explained how 'godfatherism' serves the same purpose; a godfather is a billionaire sponsoring anointed candidates for elections at all levels in return for political favours and advantages. The 'godson' will then protect the interests of the godfather in many ways; he will provide government services, appointments, policy decisions and (in particular) grant contracts for the godfather's companies. The initial support given by the godfather is an investment with substantial returns.

Still, the perspective on the extractive and power-preserving practices of the ruling elite is important, and particularly so when the two mechanisms of political corruption feed into each other. An evil circle of extraction and reinvestment in power occurs when these two forms of political corruption are mutually reinforcing; when ruling elites engage in extractive corruption to preserve their power, and this power is abused to extract further. When the two are in play, when the ruling elite is extracting to hold on to power and holds on to power to extract, the distribution of political and economic resources becomes very unfair and uneven, and democracy is held back.

This seems to be the case in most of the country examples outlined in this book. We can deduct from the analyses given in the previous chapters that the riches extracted through political corruption to a large extent are providing the means to retain control of the state. We have numerous examples of situations in which the proceeds of extraction are reinvested in power, which go way beyond the usual understanding of extractive corruption as driven by greed.

One notable exception is the Nkandla scandal in South Africa, as described by Budhram. This was the epitome of political corruption in South Africa, implicating the president of South Africa himself. The construction and renovation work to his homestead, Nkandla in KwaZulu-Natal, and the money and favours he was granted by banks and the Gupta family businesses, seem not to have been spent on preserving his or the ruling party's power position. On the contrary, President Zuma lost his presidency (his investments in power-preservations were insufficient, after all).

In Mozambique, in contrast, the political elite have found ways of accumulating public wealth for personal benefit, indeed. But, as argued by Nuvunga and Orre (Chapter 6 in this volume), as 'no economic elite has developed outside of the Frelimo-connected elite network' and 'access to economic opportunity is monopolised by the Frelimo party-state system', 'personal enrichment is the way to secure political power, and political power is the way to secure personal enrichment'. The authors add a little qualification here by stating that 'the Guebuza's presidency was marked by a turn toward making use of corruption to secure political power for the elite – and then, in the end, to secure political power for Guebuza himself and his acolytes'.

In the case of Uganda, as described by Khisa (Chapter 5 in this volume), money from grand corruption of donor-funded projects in the Ministry of Health were 'used to pay presidential pledges in different parts of the country', and 'used in political activities including the 2004–5 referendum campaigns'. Likewise, the NRM government is buying parliamentary support by spending public money lavishly on the MPs. '[President] Museveni has become increasingly reliant on using financial inducements to mollify MPs and assure cohesion within the NRM. In particular, when there is a controversial legislation before parliament, MPs are paid money under the guise of "consultation", even when there is no necessity for consultations and when the MPs do not carry out any consultations.'

In Nigeria, the 'legislators often monetize their constitutional roles, enriching themselves and building up their campaign war chests', according to Ojo, Prusa and Amundsen. These 'war chests' are spent on legitimate campaigning (on rallies, security, posters, ads, and so on), 'but also on buying supporters to win primaries, buying votes, buying "militants", and buying election officials and public control bodies'. One of the most brazen cases of spending on campaigning in Nigeria involved the national security adviser Dasuki who has been investigated since 2015 for allegedly diverting around US$2 billion to political campaigning for the ruling party, as well as for his private use.

GETTING THE MONEY IN

Corruption is a form of power abuse, and the abusive methods of extractive political corruption described in the previous country chapters range from the petty and mundane to the grand schemes rocking the country's economic and political foundations.

The 'Anane case' in Ghana, as described by Asante and Khisa (Chapter 2 in this volume), was about spending public money on private trips abroad, a mistress and a baby. Seemingly a trivial case involving small funds, it nevertheless had political significance as Mr Anane managed to maintain the support of the presidency, he got his own youth support group, and he managed to fend off criminal charges and to be renominated to a ministerial post, despite public outcry. The case demonstrates what a political insider can get away with.

In the case of the misuse of travel vouchers in South Africa, described by Budhram, the sums were again small, but the case implicated 330 MPs and former MPs, of whom 25 were convicted of fraud, including one government minister. The political significance of this case was that it showed an attitude of self-service that permeated the ruling class and laid the foundation for even bigger cases to come.

Asante and Khisa make a suitable distinction between what they term 'individual-level' versus 'institutional-level' corruption. They distinguish between one or a few individuals versus an entire (state) organisation or several in concert. They further argue that individual-level corruption tends to be more extractive and institutional corruption more regime-preserving. In Ghana, the 'Anane scandal' was a case at the individual level, involving the perpetrator only, and benefitting basically himself and his mistress. However, the 'kickback saga' involved a network that included the presidency, the ruling party and private economic actors acting in concert, according to Asante and Khisa.

Another 'institutional-level' case was military procurement fraud in Nigeria, as described by Ojo, Prusa and Amundsen. It was about 'phantom contracts' in defence worth billions of dollars and involved the various hardware suppliers, national security advisers, current and retired military officers, and numbers of influential politicians. At this high level of involvement, corruption is best described as systemic. Much corrupt extraction also stems from non-military public procurement, especially large infrastructure projects. In Nigeria it is estimated that between 60 and 75 per cent of the graft and corruption cases are procurement related, necessarily involving several state agencies.

Likewise, the South African 'defence contract corruption' described by Budhram was a large-scale corruption scandal that involved people in the parliament and several high-ranking officials, consultants, government advisers and one government minister (and Jacob Zuma, at the time in a position in a province government). As it implicated a number of individuals in several state agencies, in addition to the private business interest that corrupted them, the case can be seen as one at the institutional level.

According to Nuvunga and Orre, there are reports that in Mozambique, even in socialist 'Samoraist' times, that some agents of the state received generous offers or deals from foreign intermediaries on public purchases in the 1980s. The large-scale extractive political corruption took off only with the policies of structural adjustment and privatisation in the late 1980s and 1990s, however.

In the case of Mozambique, it even seemed to be a deliberate political strategy to establish a domestic capitalist class from the foundations of a (former) 'vanguard' socialist party, as argued by Nuvunga and Orre. They argue that extractive political corruption can establish an elite, a national bourgeoisie or entrepreneurial capitalist class, and that corruption-for-enrichment can be an intentional and beneficial policy objective to do this, and that in the case of Mozambique an 'amalgamated political and economic elite consolidated itself under Frelimo's party-state system'. There was again a cultural-attitudinal aspect to this, expressed by one of the old guard Frelimo men who said, 'we fought for freedom, now we have the right to be rich'.

More or less all country chapters in this volume give examples of extractive corruption that has been carried out for the purpose not of individual gain, but 'institutional' advantage; money is extracted by corrupt means by ruling elites for reinvesting in power. The parochial interests go far beyond the personal interest (for personal gain, for consumption and meeting the needs of their extended families); it goes into preserving the power of the ruling party and safeguarding the regime.

One of the best examples is the building up of 'war chests', as described in both Kenya (D'Arcy, Chapter 3 in this volume) and Nigeria (Ojo, Prusa and Amundsen). Where vote-buying is expected and the norm, and considerable sums are needed, prospective candidates need to build a 'war chest' to fight elections. This increases the incentives for politicians to engage in extractive corruption, and crony capitalism is one favoured avenue as reported from both Kenya and Nigeria: the support of rich patrons/businesspeople (in Nigeria called 'godfathers' and 'king-makers'). Political influence is sold for the benefit of gaining it.

A not-so-much used strategy to get the money into the ruling party's coffers is the strategy of Frelimo, as described by Nuvunga and Orre: to create a party-owned and controlled business and holding company. In Mozambique the party-owned company Gestão e Investimentos Lda. obtained state property, government contracts and joint ventures (without tender or without being the best bidder), and numerous other government favours.

SPENDING ON POWER PRESERVATION

The abusive methods of power-preserving political corruption described in the previous country chapters range from petty 'handouts' to buying votes in elections to the buying off of entire state institutions of checks and balances. In between is the buying of popular support between elections and the support of strategic social groups, the buying off of rivals and opposition, the buying of civil society and the media, and the purchase of government institutions of oversight and control. These methods range from the protection and impunity of individual perpetrators within the regime, to a situation where there are no institutions of effective checks and balances left and no real counter-power to the ruling elite.

Vote-Buying and Electoral Manipulation

Vote-buying or 'handouts' have been described as prevalent in most of the country cases in this volume, but vote-buying in Kenya, Nigeria and Malawi seems to have taken different paths lately. Nigeria made a ban on vote-buying prior to the last elections in early 2019 (Ojo, Prusa and Amundsen, Chapter 4). Likewise, Malawi introduced legislation under the new Political Parties Act of 2018, which explicitly prohibits handouts or vote-buying, and made it a crime also for a person to solicit or procure another person to issue handouts (Dulani, Chapter 7 in this volume).

However, the effect of this ban is not yet known, but there are indications that handouts have continued, at least in some parts of Nigeria and Malawi, also in the latest elections. The chapter on Kenya can explain this persistence. D'Arcy argues that handouts are expected by the voters, and a necessary aspect not only of winning elections but also of being a 'Big Man' who can provide for his electorate. 'Voters expect that their politicians conform to the prevailing cultural norms and the rational incentives within the system, demanding a certain kind of politician: one who actively engages in power-preserving corruption.'

In addition to vote-buying, the buying of election commissions and officers has had its ups and downs in several of our sample countries. In Kenya, officials of the Independent Elections and Boundary Commission (IEBC) have reportedly been bought, according to D'Arcy. In Nigeria, election rigging used to be commonplace to 'reproducing regimes in power' at least up to the 2015 election, according to Ojo, Prusa and Amundsen. The political parties in Nigeria even budgeted for bribes to be paid to the Independent National Electoral Commission (INEC), and the 2007 elections were so blatantly rigged that the European Union (EU) observers described them as the worst they had ever seen anywhere in the world.

After that, the outright and 'blatant' buying of elections seems to have halted, at least in some of our sample countries. Other, more subtle – but still corrupt – practices are prevailing, though. In Kenya, bribing the media is a form of power-preserving corruption employed in elections, bribing the media to 'sing your praises twenty-four hours a day', as described by D'Arcy. Besides, candidates must ensure (by financial inducements) that their 'militants' are not bought up by their opponents and that they are monitoring the voting and tallying at the polling stations correctly.

Candidates also have to pay up for security on the campaign trail and pay for their 'militants' to chant the candidate's name and slogans louder than the other candidates' and – as in the case of Kenya in the 2013 gubernatorial election and in Nigeria at least until the 2015 elections – to pay them to commit acts of thuggery, intimidation and violence. In Ghana, Asante and Khisa argue that during the voter registration exercise in 2004 the ruling party chairman received around US$1 million from the presidency to help the party mobilise its base, that is, 'to pay for party militants deployed to counter threats from its main rival'.

Anti-Corruption Corruption

Other institutions are also 'bought' to intimidate the power-holders' opponents and rivals. The use of the anti-corruption agencies (ACAs) as a political weapon is reported from Nigeria by Ojo, Prusa and Amundsen, where the president in some cases has been using the Independent Corrupt Practices and Other Related Offences Commission (ICPC), the Economic and Financial Crimes

Commission (EFCC), and the Code of Conduct Bureau and Tribunal (CCB) for this purpose.

Likewise, in Malawi, both the Anti-Corruption Bureau (ACB) and anti-corruption legislation have been used specifically to curb opposition members and intra-party rivals, as reported by Dulani.

Pardon and Impunity

That certain regime insiders enjoy protection and impunity from their corrupt and other power-abusing activities is seen from several of the country examples in this volume. Presidential pardon was for instance given to Mr Alamieyeseigha in 2013 by the Nigerian president, his 'political benefactor' or 'godfather', and powerful politicians who faced corruption investigations in 2018 were 'forgiven' as they defected and joined the ruling party, as described by Ojo, Prusa and Amundsen.

In a large number of cases described in the country chapters above, the courts 'cannot find evidence' or they find some (trumped-up) technical reasons to dismiss the corruption cases against the politically connected and powerful, suggesting the courts are under political influence. In many cases where the politically connected are sentenced to pay fines, there is no proof they are actually paid.

In the case of Muhwezi in Uganda as described by Khisa, and in a number of other cases, we have seen that politically connected people censured by the parliament or sentenced in court will have their comeback. It is a form of impunity when they are (re)nominated to ministerial positions or other high-office positions after a while.

Also in Uganda, as reported by Khisa, the Auditor General, the Inspectorate of Government (IG) and the Criminal Investigations Department and various ad hoc committees set up in the president's office have for the most part been inefficient when it comes to the big cases involving the powerful people at the top. All these bodies and institutions were effectively undermined by the top political leadership whenever they threaten to expose the corrupt ways of Uganda's state elite.

Favouritism and Kleptocracy

Sometimes, incumbent regimes will have to buy the support of various forces in society in order to maintain their power position. Military and business elites of strategic importance, influential 'families', clans and social groups sometimes 'need' to be 'bought' through favours. This is the 'political settlement thesis', where favouritism and patronage are seen as the 'glue' that holds regimes together when state institutions are weak.

This has not been the case in our sample countries, at least not as reported in our country chapters. In Mozambique, there has been no systematic and strategic use of co-optation of the ruling party's main contender, even in a situation of civil war and in clear contrast to the Angolan case where the ruling party MPLA finally bought off its main civil-war contender UNITA (Amundsen 2014: 181).

The closest we get is Nigeria, where vast resources are required to hold the country together and to secure loyalty from a majority of the 36 states. In addition to the constitutional and legal transfer of federal funds to the states (more than half of all federal government spending, with a high level of autonomy for the states' spending), some additional methods have been used to secure the loyalty (and delivery of votes) to the federal government. One of these are the so-called Security Votes. According to Ojo, Prusa and Amundsen, the Security Vote funds are monthly allowances allocated for the purpose of security, but funds are disbursed at the discretion of certain officials without any legislative oversight or independent audit. Given this lack of transparency of these funds, it is impossible to know how much is privately embezzled, how much is used for advancing political agendas, and how much is used for legitimate security expenditures.

Nepotism, on the other hand, is reported from some of our country cases as a power-preserving tool. In Kenya, the Kenyattas have held the presidency twice (as the country's first and current president) (D'Arcy). In Mozambique, former president Guebuza's two sons and daughter were among the children of the ruling elite enriched through government contracts and selective public procurement, according to Nuvunga and Orre. In Uganda, the Museveni regime is infamous for the high level of nepotism; numerous individuals within the extended presidential family hold high political office (and run large businesses, often at the same time). Khisa found that in many of the political corruption cases the main actors were inner-circle political and military cronies and first-family members.

The latter point is important. In most of our case studies, the political elite is using its political power to enter into business – it is not so much the other way around. Private companies are indeed using their pecuniary influence to gain access to state resources, as noted in the 'supply-oriented' perspective outlined above where the bribers of the private business side are understood as the main corruption drivers, and as noted for instance from the South Africa example of an 'almost' state capture.

However, in most of our cases we see a clear tendency of politicians using (abusing) their political power to establish their own private businesses, to gain access to preferential government treatment of these, and to establish themselves and their families and cronies as 'successful businessmen'. The ensuing crony capitalism seems to be one-sided: what we see is 'kleptocracy', not 'state capture'.

WHAT WORKS?

So, what works to curb political corruption? Our seven country chapters do not present any hard evidence on that (and were not asked to), but they offer a few clues. As always, there is a mix of deep structural (economic, social) factors at play, some important international actors, and a particular constellation of domestic forces and actors that can have a positive bearing in certain situations.

One structural factor is economic crisis or hardship that weakens the government and its ability to extract resources and thus to spend it on regime survival. In the Nigeria chapter (Chapter 4), it is hinted to the fact of oil revenue going down and the government's ability to buy support going down with it. In the case of Malawi, the huge 'Cashgate' scandal made the international donors pull out, forcing the government to accept stricter regulations on party financing as a conditionality. In South Africa, the Zuma maladministration took the local currency, the rand, on a slide, and made the ruling ANC party lose a lot in terms of popular support and legitimacy. In the case of Mozambique and the secret loans affair, the economy as well as the ruling party are severely weakened. This demonstrates that political corruption can cause much damage to the economy.

In the case of South Africa, the institutions of oversight and control, and of checks and balances, fought back. They seemed to be able to encounter and halt the excesses at the political top level. There is also reason to believe that the kind of South African political corruption was more about personal enrichment and greed and less about reinvestment in power. Therefore, it led to fewer incursions into the system of control and balance, and was easier to withstand by the existing institutions. Furthermore, the ruling party saw its legitimacy wane and had to take action to safeguard itself.

The particular constellation of factors that led to some of the 'victories' in Ghana, as described by Asante and Khisa in the Smarttys bus-branding case, was a lead civil society organisation with lawyers and other professionals on their side, being able to mobilise the Attorney General, parliament and other state agencies in prosecuting the officials involved and in retrieving the money lost. Likewise, skilled activism resulted in modest anti-corruption victories in the audacious GYEEDA scandal.

On the other hand, civil society activism could not match the impunity enjoyed by a regime insider (Anane), and it could not curb the political corruption of the 'kickback saga', as it involved an institutionalised corrupt network comprised of the presidency, the ruling party and their business cronies. The 'kickback saga' was also a case of money being reinvested in power; there was a vast patronage network behind it and the proceeds were supposed to boost the party, mobilise its base and win elections.

In both Nigeria and in Malawi, the ruling elite has banned one of its preferred methods of corrupt power-preservation: handouts. Although the ban is yet to be proven effective, this is an important step that is difficult to explain. Why would the regimes want to do this?

Dulani offer a few hints in his chapter on Malawi: the country is largely aid-dependent, and the adoption of anti-corruption legislation and the new Political Parties Act of 2018 were partly made at the behest of donors. But there were also some domestic actors motivated by idealism, and the ruling party sought legitimacy and the opposition parties found it an opportunity to level the field. In the Nigeria case, it was, as mentioned, hinted to the fact that oil revenues were going down and the government's ability to buy support going down with it.

In conclusion, political corruption in the form of greed and personal enrichment is not too difficult to curb. Ruling parties have effectively done that when their legitimacy, party cohesion or survival is at stake. But to restrict the regime-enhancing forms of political corruption seems to take an economic crisis and sustained and politically skilled external and internal pressure.

REFERENCES

Amundsen, I. (2014), 'Drowning in oil: Angola's institutions and the "resource curse"', *Comparative Politics*, 46(2): 169–89.

Freedom House (2019), 'Freedom in the World 2019', Washington: Freedom House, https://freedomhouse.org/sites/default/files/Feb2019_FH_FITW_2019_Report_ForWeb-compressed.pdf (accessed 27 April 2019).

V-Dem (2018), *Democracy for All? V-Dem Annual Democracy Report 2018*, Gothenburg: Varieties of Democracy Institute.

WBI (2018), 'Worldwide governance indicators', World Bank Institute, https://info.worldbank.org/governance/wgi/#home (accessed 26 April 2019).

Index